PORNOGRAPHY

PORNOGRAPHY

A Philosophical Introduction

Mari Mikkola

OXFORD
UNIVERSITY PRESS

OXFORD
UNIVERSITY PRESS

Oxford University Press is a department of the University of Oxford. It furthers
the University's objective of excellence in research, scholarship, and education
by publishing worldwide. Oxford is a registered trade mark of Oxford University
Press in the UK and certain other countries.

Published in the United States of America by Oxford University Press
198 Madison Avenue, New York, NY 10016, United States of America.

Library of Congress Cataloging-in-Publication Data
Names: Mikkola, Mari, author.
Title: Pornography : a philosophical introduction / Mari Mikkola.
Description: New York : Oxford University Press, [2019] |
Includes bibliographical references and index.
Identifiers: LCCN 2018018520 | ISBN 9780190640071 (pbk. : alk. paper) |
ISBN 9780190640064 (cloth : alk. paper) | ISBN 9780190640101 (online content) |
ISBN 9780190640088 (updf) | ISBN 9780190640095 (epub)
Subjects: LCSH: Pornography.
Classification: LCC HQ471 .M635 2018 | DDC 306.77/1—dc23
LC record available at https://lccn.loc.gov/2018018520

1 3 5 7 9 8 6 4 2

Paperback printed by WebCom, Inc., Canada
Hardback printed by Bridgeport National Bindery, Inc., United States of America

CONTENTS

ACKNOWLEDGMENTS

In response to hearing that I was writing this book, someone once remarked to me: Is there really *that* much to say about pornography philosophically? After a talk that I recently gave on philosophical treatments of pornography, someone else remarked that since the topic is so profoundly disgusting and vulgar, I cannot call my work philosophical in any genuine sense at all. From the pages of this book, I hope readers will come to agree with me that there is still much to say about pornography philosophically and that my treatment of the topic is genuinely philosophical.

Thankfully, many have not viewed this project with suspicion or apprehension. As I have presented materials from this book over the past couple of years, I have found lots of academic philosophers who consider the topic not only of importance to the discipline but also (and rightly so) crucial for understanding our contemporary social and cultural lives. I hope to advance our knowledge in philosophy and beyond with this work, and I am indebted to the many helpful and challenging discussions that have taken place. I have presented draft versions of this book's materials at numerous conferences, workshops, and reading groups over the past few years. These events took place (to the best of my recollection) in Amsterdam; Ann Arbor; Barcelona; Berlin; Cambridge, Massachusetts; Chicago; Frankfurt; Groningen; Hamburg; Helsinki; Kent; Lancaster; London; Oxford; and Rotterdam. I am very grateful to audiences for their comments, critiques, and conversations on the topics of this book. Specific thanks go to (with apologies for anyone I may have missed): Louise Antony, Nancy Bauer, Lisa Baurmann, Bridget Brasher, Francesca Bunkenborg, Esa Díaz-León, Catarina Dutilh Novaes, Anne Eaton, Stephanie Elsen, Irina Florea, Yasmin Granfar, Sally Haslanger, Frank Hindriks, Felicia Hoeer, Miguel Hoeltje, Jules Holroyd, Hilkje Hänel, Cathrin Höfs, Antti Kauppinen, Nora Kreft, Patsy l'Amour laLove, Rae Langton, Maria Lasonen-Aarnio, Dan López de Sa, Resa-Philip Lunau, Hans Maes, Ishani Maitra, Laura Méritt, Johanna Müller, Lina Papadaki, Jon Robson, Gonzalo Rodriguez-Pereyra, Komarine Romdenh-Romluc, Jennifer Saul, Grant Tavinor, Alex Thinius, Cain Todd, Michel Vargas Vargas, Pekka Väyrynen, Garrath Williams, Charlotte Witt, Lou Witte, Richard Woodward, Julia Zakkou, and Valeria Zaitseva. I am also grateful to the participants of a graduate class based on this book that took place at the Humboldt-Universität zu Berlin for having read the entire manuscript. A huge debt of gratitude goes to Oxford University Press's fantastic editorial team: Lucy Randall, and Hannah Doyle. Two anonymous referees provided further significant challenges that greatly improved my thinking along the way.

Some parts of the book have previously been published in: "Illocution, Silencing and the Act of Refusal," *Pacific Philosophical Quarterly* 92 (2011): 415–437; "Pornography, Art and Porno-Art," in *Pornographic Art and the Aesthetics of Pornography*, ed. H. Maes, 27–42 (Basingstoke: Palgrave-Macmillan, 2013); "Pornographic Artifacts: Maker's Intentions Model," in *Beyond Speech: Pornography and Analytic Feminist Philosophy*, ed. M. Mikkola, 113–134 (New York: Oxford University Press,

2017); and "Pornographic Videogames: A Feminist Examination," in *The Aesthetics of Video Games*, ed. Jon Robson and Grant Tavinor (New York: Routledge, 2018). I express my thanks and acknowledge permission to use these works in revised and abridged form. Additionally, I acknowledge my gratitude to the Humboldt-Universität zu Berlin Excellence cluster "Freiräume" for having provided me with a personal research grant that allowed me to write the first half of this book.

Finally, I am grateful to my "Dutch team" for providing much needed R&R over the past few years and while conducting this research: as always, an immense thanks to my partner Bas. *Dank je* is also due to my good friend Robbie for having helped me with some of the more empirical parts of this book.

Chapter 1

Introduction

What Is Pornography?

I know it, when I see it.

Justice Potter Stewart

The explicit description or exhibition of sexual subjects or activity in literature, painting, films, etc., in a manner intended to stimulate erotic rather than aesthetic feelings.

Oxford English Dictionary

Playboy is art, not pornography.

Cooper Hefner

Pornography is the undiluted essence of anti-female propaganda.

Susan Brownmiller

If it exists, there is porn on it.

Rule 34, *The Urban Dictionary*

1.1. TASK OF THE BOOK

This book offers an opinionated introduction to and an analysis of philosophical treatments of pornography. It is a work in analytic philosophy; hence, one might expect my first move to be to define the concept of *pornography* and to offer some necessary and sufficient conditions for some film, image, or text to count as pornography.[1] Perhaps surprisingly, I won't start with such a definitional task. Perhaps even more surprisingly, this is because such a definitional undertaking has turned out to be far from straightforward. As US Supreme Court Justice Potter Stewart in 1964 famously claimed, although he cannot provide a clear definition of *pornography*, he knows what counts as pornography when he encounters it. Justice Stewart was relying on his intuitive conception of *pornography*; unfortunately, other people rely on theirs. For instance, many Americans (at least of a certain generation) would say that magazines like *Hustler* and *Playboy* are paradigm instances of pornography. The heir of *Playboy*, Cooper Hefner, disagrees: as cited in the epigraph, he stated in a more recent newspaper article that the magazine is not pornography and that it empowers women.[2] The *OED*'s definition of *pornography* is rather innocuous and tame sounding. Then again, Susan Brownmiller takes pornography to be the "undiluted essence of anti-female propaganda" (1975, 394). And even the most innocent sounding Internet searches can yield a wealth of pornography hits.

Many philosophers disagree with all of the above conceptions irrespective of their stance on the morality of pornography. Pretheoretically, pornography involves the following: sexually explicit content, materials without social value, intention to sexually arouse consumers, and/or being used in certain ways (e.g., as "masturbation materials"). How to understand any of these in detail and how to conceptualize their importance when examining pornography are live questions though. As things stand, there is no agreed

1. Throughout I will use the italicized expression *pornography* to denote the concept, while 'pornography' denotes the term. When I speak of pornography without italic or single-quotes, I am talking about the real-world phenomenon.
2. Bignell, "Playboy Is Art, Not Porn, Says Hefner Heir," *The Independent*, January 6, 2013, https://www.independent.co.uk/news/people/news/playboy-is-art-not-porn-says-hefner-heir-8439849.html. Accessed August 7, 2018.

upon definition of *pornography* either in philosophy or in society at large. Yet, pornography seems to play a huge role in contemporary lives: pornography-related inquiries figure as some of the most frequent Internet searches. "Our" inability to say precisely what pornography amounts to is puzzling given how commonplace pornography has become.

One hindrance to defining and understanding pornography is its highly emotive and deeply divisive nature not only in the wider society but also in philosophy. Over the past few decades, entrenched and seemingly straightforward anti- and pro-pornography positions have emerged. In the popular press, those opposing pornography are often portrayed as prudish, sex-negative feminists, who advocate censorship; pornography's defenders are characterized as sex-positive liberals, who fight for free speech and expression. Lively philosophical debates about pornography have emerged since the 1980s, and there is by now a rich literature on the topic. Nonetheless, these debates are still fraught with many difficult questions, and precious little agreement exists on basic questions: What is pornography? What (if anything) does pornography do? Is the consumption of pornography a harmless private matter, or does it harm its users in some ways? Does pornography harm nonusers, like women generally, by increasing the prevalence of sexualized violence? What, if anything, should legally be done about pornography? Is feminist pornography possible, and if so, what would make pornography feminist? Not having a clear idea about what we are talking about when we talk about pornography has hindered philosophical attempts to answer these questions. There is still much confusion over the conceptual and political commitments of different anti- and pro-pornography positions, while different sides tend to portray a simplistic picture of their opponents. Participants in the debates end up easily talking past one another. Furthermore, given the emotive nature of the topic, interlocutors can miss the fact that existing positions are much more nuanced and far more complex than they might at first seem. Indeed, different sides on the debate might not even disagree with one another, *contra* appearances.

In light of these difficulties and (apparent) disagreements, this book examines philosophical pornography debates with the aim to steady and clarify the waters. It does not put forward one overarching argument throughout but rather evaluates relevant arguments thematically. In so doing, the book has three broad goals. First, to conduct a comprehensive and careful investigation of different philosophical positions for and against pornography, which will provide much needed clarity on how *pornography* and other key notions are (and should be) understood. The book hence also clarifies what different views are theoretically and politically committed to. Second, to investigate important methodological issues by considering how empirically adequate existing philosophical positions are relative to the sizeable pornography industry. This will involve also considering alternative pornographies that are said to be feminist, "female-friendly," and nonheteronormative. Third, to enrich extant philosophical debates by examining how discussions in different subareas (like feminist philosophy and aesthetics) intersect with and profit from one another—something surprisingly absent in contemporary philosophizing over pornography. Although my investigation in this book advances unapologetically from an analytic feminist philosophical perspective, it will be neutral about pornography's moral status at the outset.[3] One of the big lessons to emerge from this work is that given how complex a phenomenon pornography is, it is far

---

3. To clarify: analytic feminism combines the practical focus of feminism as a political movement to end sex- and/or gender-related injustices with common analytical methods (e.g., conceptual analysis and systematic argumentation). Feminist philosophy aims both to critique patriarchal social structures by utilizing mainstream philosophical tools and to shape mainstream philosophy with the help of feminist political insights. It offers a way to do politically informed philosophical investigation without being restricted just to political philosophy.

from easy (if not impossible) to say that all pornography is harmful in some sense or that pornography does no harm at all. Our evaluative judgments about pornography must be made in a piecemeal fashion, and the prospects of making general normative claims about pornography are poor. However, as I will argue, this does not preclude meaningful philosophical work on pornography. There is still much to be done, as will become clear from the pages of this book. Nevertheless, before we can see what work still needs to be done, let us briefly look at what work has already been undertaken by way of background and in preparation for the discussions to come.

1.2. FROM OBSCENITY TO DEGRADATION

At the time of Justice Stewart's comment in the epigraph, pornography in the United States and the United Kingdom was understood on the model of obscenity. Although the precise formulation of the US obscenity laws underwent a number of changes, the most relevant for philosophical interjections into pornography debates dates to the 1973 case of *Miller v. California*. Following this case, a work is obscene if an average, reasonable, person applying community standards would find the work as a whole to lack any serious literary, artistic, political, or scientific value, and the work describes or depicts in an obvious way offensive sexual conduct (Dwyer 1995, 242). Key aspects of this understanding are that the work is sexually explicit, primarily intended to produce sexual arousal in viewers and, in some sense, bad—it has a morally corrupting influence, and it is indecent or causes indecency. This understanding makes pornography a matter of public morality, and it pits conservative opponents of pornography against "sexual radicals." According to the former, pornography removes sex from its proper setting of monogamous, heterosexual marriage, which in turn debases humanity and regresses human progress (for an overview of such views, see Berger 1977). Pornography is morally corrupting, and to prevent this, the state is permitted to prohibit access to pornography even to consenting adults (Baird and Rosenbaum 1991, pt. 4).

Feminist philosophers and theorists, however, commonly renounce the obscenity standard, regardless of whether they oppose pornography. In opposing patriarchy, feminist theorists and activists welcome ruptures to community standards. They have also found the talk of "reasonable persons" to be about "reasonable *men*" in disguise Furthermore, feminists do not typically oppose pornography for its sexual content or putative offensiveness, and so they vehemently disagree with pornography's conservative opponents. Rather, they argue, pornography *harms* women. One cluster of such arguments has been framed around the idea that pornography involves the degradation of women. These arguments advance content-based moral objections to pornography too, albeit in a very different form to those advanced by conservative critics. In short: although pornography is not morally objectionable due to its sexual content, in treating women as mere sex objects, it degrades women (for a discussion of this argument, see Garry 1978). On this view, what is morally objectionable about pornography's content is that it de-grades [*sic*] women by assigning them lower value and lower moral status (Hill 1987). Typically, though, the mere depiction of lower value does not suffice. Rather, pornography is about verbal and pictorial materials that represent and describe "sexual behavior that is degrading or abusive to one or more of participants in *such a way as to endorse the degradation*" (Longino 1980, 43). For pornography to endorse degradation is for it to communicate its approval and recommendation of sexual behavior that devalues women. More specifically, this means that the degradation is represented as pleasurable for both the male and female performers, and there is "no suggestion that this sort of treatment of others is inappropriate to their status as human beings" (Longino 1980, 43–44). In a slightly different vein, Rosemarie Tong (1982) argues that pornography celebrates and encourages inequality: the sexual exchanges are degrading in that the desires and experiences of one party (usually, female) are not regarded by other participants as having validity or equal importance. Either way, pornography supposedly tells deep and vicious lies about women that both Longino and Tong consider defamatory.

1.3. FROM DEGRADATION TO SEX DISCRIMINATION

Although sharing many aspects with the above positions, in championing their antipornography stance, Catharine MacKinnon and Andrea Dworkin put forward a subtly different feminist analysis of pornography's harm. For them, pornography is not a 'moral issue'. That is, a feminist argument against pornography should not be based on pornography being morally objectionable. Instead, they advanced a well-known view of pornography as a practice of sex discrimination: it is harmful in violating women's civil rights (A. Dworkin 1981; MacKinnon 1987, 1989b, 1993). This view is less about what pornography represents (its morally problematic content), and more about what pornography *does*. In short, pornography celebrates, promotes, and legitimizes sexualized violence against women. It eroticizes male dominance and female submissiveness and puts this forward as the apparent truth about sex (MacKinnon 1987, 171). Pornography purports to mirror reality, but it, according to this view, constructs one. This is what pornography does and not merely what it depicts: "It institutionalizes the sexuality of male supremacy, fusing the erotization of dominance and submission with the social construction of [gender]" (MacKinnon 1987, 172). With this in mind, and against the obscenity standard, MacKinnon and Dworkin famously defined *pornography* as

> the graphic sexually explicit subordination of women through pictures and words that also includes women dehumanized as sexual objects, things, or commodities; enjoying pain or humiliation or rape; being tied up, cut up, mutilated, bruised, or physically hurt; in postures of sexual submission or servility or display; reduced to body parts, penetrated by objects or animals, or presented in scenarios of degradation, injury, torture; shown as filthy or inferior; bleeding, bruised, or hurt in a context that makes these conditions sexual. (MacKinnon 1987, 176)

Pornography is said to be about power with sex used as a weapon of women's subjugation. This is supposedly apparent from the root of 'pornography' being 'porno', which means *prostitute* or *female captive* (Steinem 1995). In pornography, then, free choice is absent and replaced by violence and dominance. Sexually explicit materials that are premised on equality and positive free choice count as erotica, which is about passionate love and mutual pleasure (MacKinnon 1987; see also Steinem 1995).[4] If men, trans* people, or children are used in the place of and treated as if they were women, the work also counts as pornography.[5] The Dworkin-MacKinnon view renders *pornography* by definition a gendered notion in that the manufacture

---

4. Andrea Dworkin (1981) rejects the distinction between inegalitarian pornography and egalitarian erotica. For Dworkin, the latter is simply a high-class variant of the former.
5. Quick note about terminology. In this book I will use 'trans*' as an inclusive umbrella term to capture a multitude of gender nonconforming identities. The term 'transsexual' is typically used to refer to individuals who use medical means and technologies to alter their bodies, so that their bodily presentation conforms to their gendered sense of self (Bettcher 2009). By contrast, 'transgender' refers to

> people who "do not conform to prevailing expectations about gender" by presenting and living genders that were not assigned to them at birth or by presenting and living

and consumption of pornography constitute women's subordination (albeit only partially; more on this later). However, subordination is not the only thing that pornography does: it also silences women. In making violence the apparent truth about sex, pornography prevents women from saying otherwise. Pornography "strips and devastates women of credibility" in their attempts to articulate experiences of sexual assault, which are seen as part of ordinary sexual realities due to pornography—women are thus "stripped of authority and reduced and devalidated and silenced" (MacKinnon 1987, 193). In subordinating and silencing women, pornography is a practice of sex discrimination.

This Dworkin-MacKinnon account has been immensely influential both philosophically and legally, but (perhaps unsurprisingly) it has not convinced everyone. The view has been challenged by activists and theorists alike, and from both feminist and nonfeminist perspectives. I will consider a number of issues with the Dworkin-MacKinnon definition in the pages to come. But by way of background, consider some initial concerns. First, some object that feminist antipornography positions seemingly single out pornography as central to women's oppression, which is problematic. It turns feminism into a single-issue movement organized around opposing pornography (for the history of US antipornography feminism, see Bronstein 2011). This, however, leaves other sites of oppression—such as the nuclear family, education, and politics—conspicuously undertheorized from a feminist perspective (Califia 1994; Loots 2000; Valverde 1995; Willis 1995). Second, antipornography

genders in ways that may not be readily intelligible in terms of more traditional conceptions of gender. (Bettcher 2009)

Trans* is contrasted with 'cis' that denotes (roughly) women-born-female and men-born-male, who have typical gender identities and presentations. 'Trans*' is also considered to be more inclusive than 'trans' by including a wider range of gender nonconforming individuals, who may or may not consider themselves to be transgender.

feminism reprimands women who might genuinely enjoy pornography or takes these women to be somehow disingenuous or brainwashed. The view that pornography constructs sex as the eroticization of dominance and submission suggests that all sex under patriarchy is violence. Consensual heterosexual sex becomes impossible, and this problematically turns women who engage in heterosexual sex into collaborators in their own oppression (Valverde 1995; Willis 1995). Third, whether pornography is centrally responsible for a damaging view of women is not obvious. After all, advertisements, television, other media outlets, and romantic novels portray women in highly stereotyped and sexualized ways (R. Dworkin 1991; Vance 1992). At least prior to the onset of the Internet era, these were much more prevalent than pornography, which raises questions about how influential pornography is in causally shaping men's attitudes about women. (We will return to this issue with the Internet in mind later on.) Fourth, some have claimed that positions advanced by white US antipornography feminists fail to grasp the intersectionality of oppression in pornography. For instance, Patricia Hill Collins holds that pornography must be "reconceptualized as an example of the interlocking nature of race, gender, and class oppression" (1993, 100). Pornography is not primarily a "white phenomenon," where race makes up an additional problematic layer as an afterthought. Rather, the history of black women's sexual exploitation shows that pornography is grounded in *both* racism and sexism. Still others have argued that in failing to theorize and recognize queer, nonheterosexual pornography, antipornography feminism actually represses already-repressed sexualities. (For a view that racialized pornography may at times be liberating, see Zheng 2017. I will discuss this and queer pornography further in chapter 7.)

Some of the most devastating critiques, however, have come from challenges to the philosophical cogency of the Dworkin-MacKinnon position. First, although the move away from the obscenity standard of public morality has been welcomed, whether it is helpful to conceive of pornography as being *by definition* women's subordination and silencing is not uncontroversial. One set of issues pertains to whether it is helpful to understand *pornography* as a moralized and gendered notion, or whether it would be more fruitful to define it first and foremost in a neutral manner (Feinberg 1985; Russell 1993a). If we define pornography as MacKinnon and Dworkin do, there simply cannot be egalitarian pornography. Perhaps, then, we should endorse a nonevaluative definition of *pornography* that is applied to all sexually explicit materials, of which some endorse the abuse and degradation of women. In this way, we could distinguish inegalitarian and egalitarian pornography as well as erotica, where erotica would be understood as sexually suggestive and titillating (but not explicit) materials. Although not solely arguing against the Dworkin-MacKinnon understanding, Michael Rea holds that a nonstipulative "real" definition of *pornography* is methodologically preferable. Such a real definition "respects commonly held views and widely shared intuitions [about pornography] and attempts to capture these in a set of necessary and sufficient conditions" (Rea 2000, 119). The reason to think that this is methodologically better boils down to our ability to forge public policies about pornography. This is because stipulative accounts can only be interpreted and assessed relative to "a working knowledge of our ordinary concept of pornography" (Rea 2000, 119). So if we are to judge whether some image (say) reduces a woman to her body parts, we won't be able to do so unless we already have a clear understanding of the ordinary concept of *pornography*. If we do not have such a prior pretheoretical conception, a stipulative definition like the Dworkin-MacKinnon one apparently cannot do meaningful work for us. Subsequently, a real definition that fits our intuitions would be "of great use" (Rea 2000, 119). Furthermore, a real definition would enable us better to conduct meaningful moral debates about the topic in bringing clarity to those debates. Finally, a real definition does not steer the debate off course, but elucidates pornography *itself*. This is apparently what the participants in the debate are after, due to which Rea takes any definition of *pornography* that seeks to revise it to be impoverished.

A different line of attack comes from prominent liberal philosophers. Even while denying that pornography is somehow valuable, these philosophers intensely critiqued the Dworkin-MacKinnon view during the late-1980s and early-1990s. Ronald Dworkin (1991) famously claimed that the Dworkin-MacKinnon position was based on a "dangerous confusion" between negative and positive liberty. This is the well-known distinction between enjoying freedom *from* some interference and having the liberty *to* do something. Our negative liberty may be restricted in a manner that is consistent with free speech protections. However, the view that pornography silences women seeks to argue against pornography by appealing to women's positive liberty to be heard and to make speech acts. Such guarantees are not within the remit of the law though, and the law need not protect the freedom to make certain claims, such as those of cranks and flat-earthers. R. Dworkin further rejects the view that pornography causes women's subordination and silencing in general by appealing to the lack of available empirical evidence that supports such a causal story. (We will return to this point in chapter 2.) Then again, William Parent holds that the Dworkin-MacKinnon definition of *pornography* is philosophically indefensible because subordination is "an action or a practice engaged in by human beings and directed against other beings . . . the logic of 'subordinates' requires that it have some human action or actions as a subject" (Parent 1990, 208). As books, magazines, and images are not human beings, antipornography feminism commits a category mistake: pornographic materials simply are not the sorts of things that can subordinate. Joel Feinberg (1985) in turn argues that feminist arguments against pornography made in terms of a "harm principle"— pornography harms women by either defaming them or by inciting male violence against women—are unsuccessful. The former argument fails due to difficulties with defamation and libel laws: the legal burden of proof to demonstrate the relevant group-wide harm to women's interest in reputation looks insurmountable. The latter case allegedly fails because empirical evidence does not demonstrate that pornography incites violence against women.[6] (I will discuss these points in more detail in chapters 4 and 2, respectively.)

1.4. FROM SEX DISCRIMINATION TO SUBORDINATING AND SILENCING SPEECH

With the above liberal critiques in mind, Rae Langton (1993) defends the philosophical cogency of the Dworkin-MacKinnon position in her by-now classic article "Speech Acts and Unspeakable Acts." She articulates further defenses together with Jennifer Hornsby (see Hornsby and Langton 1998). Langton's defense marks another watershed moment in philosophical discussions about pornography. She draws on J. L. Austin's (1962) speech act theory to make good the idea that pornography does something— that it is a practice of sex discrimination.[7] Austin argued that our statements can do (and do) more than simply make true or false claims about the world—sometimes we perform actions other than just speaking with our utterances. With this in mind, Austin divides

6. For more on these liberal critiques and an introduction to the relevant free speech debates, see Watson (2010) and West (2013).
7. Not everyone holds that this is necessary. Lorna Finlayson (2014) has more recently argued that MacKinnon's claims are coherent and contentful even without an appeal to Austin's speech act theory.

speech acts into locutions, perlocutions, and illocutions: the speaker's locution (the words uttered) can perform some illocutionary action (*in* uttering something, the speaker's locution can *count as* øing), and the locution can have some perlocutionary effects (*by* uttering something, the speaker's locution can *cause* further extra-linguistic effects). Now, US legislation takes pornography to be a form of speech insofar as free speech legislation protects its manufacture and distribution; subsequently, Langton argues that pornographic speech illocutionarily subordinates and silences women. *In saying* something about women, pornographic speech does something other than make mere utterances. It functions like the speech of a priest who in declaring, "I pronounce you a married couple" performs the action of marrying. Pornographic speech, however, performs harmful actions. It subordinates and silences women in ranking them as inferior, in legitimating discrimination against them, and in depriving women of important free speech rights (Langton 1993, 305–313). This allows us to see that the Dworkin-MacKinnon position is not philosophically indefensible and that it does not rest on a category mistake: pornographic content, in being a form of speech, can perform subordinating actions.

The speech act theoretic defense of the Dworkin-MacKinnon position has dominated much of Anglo-American philosophizing about pornography over the past thirty years. Many of the subsequent debates draw on this approach, and a number of theorists from various backgrounds have either critiqued or defended Langton's original position. In the chapters to come, I will examine the philosophical legacy of the speech act defense in detail and consider how philosophical debates on pornography might take novel new turns. But prior to doing so, let me briefly say something about the methodology and structure of this book.

1.5. METHODOLOGICAL CONSIDERATIONS

As noted, the book has three main goals.

1. To conduct a comprehensive and careful investigation of different philosophical positions in order to provide much needed clarity on how *pornography* and other key notions are understood.
2. To investigate methodological issues by considering how empirically adequate existing philosophical positions are and by considering alternative pornographies.
3. To enrich extant philosophical debates by examining how discussions in different subareas intersect with and profit from one another.

With these in mind, let me spell out some preliminary methodological commitments. First, the book aims to be sensitive to the empirical realities of the pornography industry. This not only means that I employ real-world examples; it also points to something more. The aim is to conduct an empirically informed philosophical analysis of pornography—something I think is missing from much of philosophical work on pornography. This does not mean that current philosophical work ignores examples. However, there is a difference between doing empirically informed philosophical work and citing empirical examples in one's work. Part of this book's methodological point is to argue that mentioning examples not particularly representative of the current pornography industry does not suffice for empirically informed philosophical investigation of the topic. One of this book's methodological lessons, then, is that our philosophical accounts must do justice to a sizeable industry and complex phenomenon—citing a few examples that fit one's philosophical view while ignoring examples that go against it is not empirically informed in the right kind of way.

My above points may suggest that the forthcoming analysis will be descriptive in looking at what pornography currently is about. One might, however, wonder whether this is the right method as we are engaged in a philosophical (rather than a sociological) examination of pornography. Let me clarify this point at the outset. The book aims to provide clarity on how *pornography* and other key notions are to be understood, while considering methodological issues by taking into account how empirically adequate existing philosophical analyses are. This aim (I contend) falls under the banner of doing what Burgess and Plunkett (2013) call "conceptual ethics" and what Sally Haslanger (2000) terms "amelioration." Instead of looking at our linguistic intuitions when trying to elucidate something—the concept of *pornography* here being the case in point—we should rather engage in normative and evaluative inquiry. This is because our intuitions about the concept at issue are too muddled and unclear, and our uses of the term expressing that concept too idiosyncratic. We should not then ask how we do understand x, but how we should understand x in order to bring about conceptual clarity and advance other practical goals that we may have. Subsequently, my aim in the book is to clarify what pornography is and ought to be in a manner that does justice to pornography as an industry and a complex empirical phenomenon. In so doing, we can meaningfully revise what we mean by *pornography*, but in a manner that is empirically informed. Hence, in the pages to come, I aspire to strike a balance between normative and descriptive analyses.

This departs significantly from the above-outlined methodology advanced by Rea (2000). Rea holds that a nonstipulative "real" definition of *pornography* that "respects commonly held views and widely shared intuitions [about pornography] and attempts to capture these in a set of necessary and sufficient conditions" (2000, 119) is preferable. I agree with Rea that we need to clarify the definition of *pornography* for public and moral debates. But I am unconvinced that an appeal to a real definition that fits "our" ordinary conception of *pornography* is the most helpful way to proceed. For one thing, it is not obvious to me that there is *an* intuitive ordinary conception. This is precisely one of the major stumbling blocks with articulating a definition of *pornography*. Sexual explicitness is often taken to be a hallmark of pornography. But clearly not all visual depictions that are sexually explicit count intuitively as pornography (just think of the oft-cited example of anatomy books). Sexual arousal is commonly said to be another distinguishing feature of pornography. But sexual arousal is highly subjective, and many pornographic works fail to sexually arouse individual viewers. Furthermore, many nonpornographic films are clearly intended to sexually arouse—and they do. This may make them pornographic, but something's being pornographic is not equivalent to it being a piece of pornography. (Compare a painting that is iconic in the sense of resembling an icon stylistically to an actual icon.) And as noted, some take pornography to be by definition morally repugnant, while others disagree. Taking this into account, I am not convinced that a real nonstipulative definition of *pornography* that fits "our" intuitions would be particularly helpful or that we can articulate such a definition to begin with. Furthermore, Rea's intention to elucidate pornography *itself*, rather than revise what we take pornography to amount to, is not unproblematic. Is there such a thing as pornography itself? I think not. The content and nature of pornography has changed significantly over time, and (I suspect) contemporary viewers would not see much of past pornography as pornography anymore. Given that pornography evolves, there seems to be no trans-historical conception of *pornography* for our intuitions to track. In light of this, revising "our" conception of *pornography* on the basis of changes to the genre seems rather more appropriate.[8]

My approach departs from Rea's in another important respect too. Rea classifies live sex shows as pornography (he is not alone in doing so). This is, in my view, a mistake. Performing in pornography is one type of sex work; lap dancing and live sex shows are different types of sex work. In what follows, then, my discussion does not extend to live sex shows, lap dancing, or prostitution. I will also avoid extending my discussion to "camming": live, interactive, and often more relationship-like webcam performance. Although many pornography performers also do camming to earn more, I contend, it is a mistake to collapse the distinction. For instance, there is a perfectly ordinary and straightforward distinction between cinema and theater even though they both involve acting. So, even though the separation of pornography from live performance is somewhat unhappy and highly pretheoretical, I do not see huge obstacles in drawing this distinction. (For more on feminist perspectives on sex work, see Shrage 2015.)

Finally, let me return to the point about starting from a morally neutral position. One might immediately object to such a starting point by citing some glaring counterexamples: What about child pornography and the so-called revenge porn?[9] The morally objectionable character of child pornography is clear-cut, while "revenge

---

8. Actually, *contra* Rea, the Dworkin-MacKinnon definition of *pornography* was not intended to be stipulative and revisionary. Rather, they took their definition to be descriptive of actual pornographic materials. At the time even critics appreciated this point in accepting that examples of violent and degrading pornography that fit the Dworkin-MacKinnon definition are "abundant and depressing" (Feinberg 1985, 147). What such critics nevertheless objected to was the generalization that all pornography is of this kind. So, MacKinnon and Dworkin are not to be reproached for offering a definition that stipulatively revises the notion of *pornography*; their mistake was to offer an overly generalized account of pornography.

9. The latter refers to the relatively recent phenomenon of ex-partners (usually, male) distributing sexually explicit or suggestive images of their ex-partners (usually, female) on the Internet without the latter's consent and in an effort to humiliate them.

porn" is morally condemnable in being nonconsensual and involving serious privacy violations. So how can I start from a morally neutral perspective when presented with such examples? I think that these examples nicely illustrate the need for this book and the need for conceptual amelioration when thinking about what pornography is and should be—but amelioration that is informed by empirical issues. As I see it, it is a mistake to classify images of children's sexual abuse as pornography to begin with; rather, such images are documentations of abuse and their harmfulness is unequivocal. However, what we should philosophically say about sexually explicit materials that involve at least *prima facie* consenting adults is not so clear-cut. Of course, this raises other issues that I will return to in later chapters. For instance: Which images count as children's sexual abuse? Does this include virtual and cartoon images of children in sexualized depictions? What should we say about pornography involving supposedly adult performers who are portrayed as underage or child-like? Answers to these questions are far less equivocal and require serious philosophical reflection. However, as I will argue later on, sexual arousal and sexual explicitness are neither necessary nor sufficient for some imagery counting as pornography. Therefore, even if documentations of children's sexual abuse are currently classified as pornography, there is no reason to do so based on "the sexual nature" of the imagery. The fact that someone documented the abuse does not render the documentation a piece of pornography, just as the documentation of an art performance is not *eo ipso* a piece of art. (It might be, but this depends on other factors to which I will return later.) By the same token, I think it is also a mistake to describe the phenomenon of revenge porn as a kind of pornography. What is intuitively doing the work is that the images are sexually explicit and/or suggestive, and pretheoretically pornography is about sexual explicitness. But imagine that I had written a very sexually explicit letter to a former partner who then publishes it online without my consent.

I think that many would be hard-pressed to say that this is an instance of pornography, albeit being an intimacy violation for sure. Once we see that pornography is about something other than surface sexual explicitness, we can see that some phenomena currently subsumed under 'pornography' in the popular press and media should not be so subsumed. This subsequently enables us to formulate a unified notion of pornography to overcome conceptual and terminological difficulties. Moreover, all of this demonstrates the methodological need for amelioration that is empirically informed in order to avoid talking at cross-purposes when we talk about pornography.

1.6. STRUCTURE OF THE BOOK

This book has seven forthcoming chapters, in which I will consider philosophical pornography debates along the following themes. Chapter 2 ("Subordination: Causal and Constitutive") outlines and discusses Langton's famous subordination claim: pornography both causes and is the subordination of women. Next in chapter 3 ("Does Pornography Silence Women?"), I turn to Langton's other key view: pornography causes and is the silencing of women— the silencing claim. Chapter 4 ("Free, Regulated, or Prohibited Speech?") carefully detangles various politico-legal stances on pornography's permissibility. The chapter discusses liberal pro- and feminist antipornography positions, showing that these positions are far more complex than usually characterized and that they are actually in agreement on many central issues pertaining to pornography. The following chapter 5 ("Pornographic Knowledge and Sexual Objectification") examines a more recent claim that pornography generates harmful knowledge about women with the objectification of women being pornography's mechanism for doing so. Chapter 6 ("The Aesthetics of Pornography") connects debates in aesthetics and feminist philosophy when analyzing the ethics and aesthetics of pornography. In chapter 7 ("Pornography as Liberation"), I discuss the idea that some pornography may liberate, rather than subordinate. This involves considering racialized, queer, feminist, and trans* pornography as well as claims made by disability advocates that pornographic portrayals of "disabled bodies" are sexually enriching. The book closes with chapter 8 ("What Is Pornography Revisited"), which considers social ontological analyses of pornography as potentially fruitful alternatives to prevalent speech act theoretic approaches.

Chapter 2

Subordination

Causal and Constitutive

2.1. INTRODUCTION

At the request of the Minneapolis City Council in 1983, Catharine MacKinnon and Andrea Dworkin drafted antipornography ordinances that were premised on women's civil rights violations rather than on the moral condemnation, obscenity, or indecency of pornography. The ordinances make use of the definition of *pornography* cited in the previous chapter: pornography is "the graphic sexually explicit subordination of women through pictures and words" (MacKinnon 1987, 176). In challenging the prevalent obscenity-based antipornography legislation, the ordinances did not advocate censoring or criminalizing the production, distribution, or consumption of pornographic materials. Rather, they intended to give women legal recourse to seek remedies for harms and injuries caused to them by pornography (A. Dworkin 2000; Itzin 1992b; MacKinnon and A. Dworkin 1997). In particular, these harms pertain to being trafficked into or coerced to perform in pornography, forcing pornography onto someone, and/or experiencing assaults caused by pornography consumption. The ordinance would have given performers and women in general the opportunity to sue the makers and consumers of pornography who harmed them. The Indianapolis City Council passed similar ordinances in 1984, although they were soon overturned as unconstitutional.

Not all feminists welcomed the ordinances. The US Feminist Anti-Censorship Taskforce argued in a well-known amicus brief (a letter written by an individual or individuals not party to a case, but who offer information that bears on the case to assist the court in decision-making) that the ordinances were flawed in conflating images and fictional texts with discriminatory conduct (Hunter and Law 1997). However, against this and other arguments, Rae Langton famously defends the Dworkin-MacKinnon idea that pornography is a practice of sex discrimination. She advances the view that pornography is and causes women's subordination by drawing on J. L. Austin's (1962) speech act theory. In short, pornography is the illocutionary subordination of women: in saying something about women, pornographic speech subordinates them. As MacKinnon puts it, pornographic speech is not "only words"; rather, it is a kind of discriminatory conduct performed with words.

This chapter examines the subordination claim: pornography causes and is women's subordination. I will first spell out Langton's view in detail. The chapter will then consider how plausible the claim is. The general argumentative gist of the chapter is as follows. *Contra* critics of the causal subordination claim, I will argue that the claim is not so implausible after all. Or, at the very least, prevalent critiques do not "conclusively refute" the subordination claim, as one author claims (Strossen 1995, 254). Nonetheless, the chapter will also show that the constitutive formulation of the subordination claim is much harder to sustain.

2.2. THE SUBORDINATION CLAIM

The basic premise of Langton's argument, supported by US courts, is that pornography is speech. Or more accurately, pornography is a form of expression that includes spoken words and utterances, public recordings, written word, nonverbal images, and other means of expression. As speech or expression, pornography *depicts* the subordination of women. However, pornography does more according to MacKinnon and Dworkin: it *causes* women's subordination. This much was accepted even by Judge Easterbrook who presided over the case of *American Booksellers v. Hudnut*, which struck down MacKinnon and Dworkin's antipornography ordinance as unconstitutional because it aimed to regulate speech in a content-specific manner:[1]

> We accept the premises of this legislation. Depictions of subordination tend to perpetuate subordination. The subordinate status of women in turn leads to affront and lower pay at work, insult and injury at home, battery and rape on the streets. (Easterbrook, quoted in Gruen and Pachinas 1997, 169)

Although accepted by some, the causal claim has faced many objections (discussed shortly). However, critics have found the constitutive claim that pornography *is* a form of subordination to be philosophically untenable, highly indefensible, and deeply incoherent. These critiques were briefly outlined in the previous chapter. By contrast, Langton argues with the help of Austin's speech act theory that the constitutive subordination claim is perfectly coherent and philosophically cogent. Note that she does not aim to argue that

---

1. The First Amendment of the US Constitution prohibits content-specific regulation of speech. I will say more about this in chapter 4.

the constitutive claim is true, only that it is philosophically defensible. However, Langton also takes the claim to be true if we grant "some not entirely implausible empirical assumptions" (1993, 300).[2] We perform a whole range of actions with our words (e.g., warning, promising, refusing). This demonstrates that our statements can do (and do) more than simply make true or false claims about the world. Thus, Austin identifies *performatives* as a type of speech act, and he divides such speech acts into locutions, perlocutions, and illocutions. When we utter a sentence that has a particular traditionally conceived meaning, we have performed a locutionary act. But with our words, we can do more: *by* uttering something, our words can *cause* extra-linguistic perlocutionary effects. And *in* uttering something, our words (or locutions) can *count as* actions of some sort—we have performed some illocutionary action, where our action is constituted by the words intentionally uttered in their usual meaning.

For instance, take the example of warning. Imagine that I notice a fire break out in a bakery I am passing by. I utter the right words intending to warn the customers ("Danger, fire!"), who understand my words and my intention to warn them. Warning the customers was my intended action that I performed with my words. This was my intended illocutionary action, which my locution successfully pulled off. Now, I also intend to bring about some extra-linguistic effects: that the customers leave the shop for safety. Provided that they do, I will also have succeeded in bringing about my intended perlocutionary effects. Furthermore, speech in the strict sense is not necessary for performing such actions. Imagine that due to an illness I have lost my voice. Instead of shouting "Danger, fire!" I write those words on a sign and run into the shop. This act of expression

2. Langton's work on pornography and objectification has more recently been published in her 2009 book *Sexual Solipsism*. By and large, I will refer to the original versions of her papers to clarify the historical trajectory of various debates and views put forward.

(if successful) will have performed the same action as uttering the words.[3]

According to Langton, although some critics of MacKinnon and Dworkin have appreciated pornography's locutionary actions (depicting subordination) and its perlocutionary effects (causing subordination), they have failed to grasp pornography's illocutionary force. This is what the constitutive subordination claim homes in on. With the help of Austin, we can see that the claim is perfectly sensible, coherent, and not committing a category mistake (as Parent [1990] claims). Illocutionary force hinges on satisfying certain felicity conditions. First, whether the speaker's *intentions* are satisfied; after all, illocutionary speech acts are not just idle noises but intentionally performed actions. Second, whether the speaker achieves *uptake*: the hearer recognizes the particular intended illocution being performed. Third, whether the speaker is *authoritative* relative to the intended illocution's domain. (Not all successful illocutions require satisfaction of these conditions, but the ones relevant to pornography do.) Consider again the earlier example of warning. In order for my illocutionary act to succeed, I must intend to warn (rather than merely exercise my vocal cords for no apparent reason), the audience must recognize my intention to warn (rather than think I am joking), and I need to be somehow authoritative to do so (something about me must not prevent me from being taken seriously). Now entertain the oft-cited example where I am an actor on stage and see a fire break out behind the audience. I shout "Danger, fire!" intending to warn, but the audience takes this to be part of the play. In this case, there

---

3. Note that speech acts are not equivalent to action by speech: for instance, in uttering "Danger, fire!" I made my vocal cords vibrate. But clearly this is not sufficient to have performed the intended illocution of warning. This difference is further demonstrated by the example of using a sign to perform the same illocutionary action: my vocal cord vibrations are absent (there is no action by speech), but I can still perform the same intended illocutionary speech act.

is a failure of uptake since the audience does not recognize my intended illocution to warn, and I lack the right kind of authority—the audience does not take my utterance seriously since they think my utterance is part of the play (i.e., they think I am merely acting). In this case, I have not successfully performed the illocutionary act of warning; I have merely attempted to warn.

So much for the nature of illocutionary speech acts; how can such acts subordinate? Langton considers a legislator in Pretoria during Apartheid who utters "blacks are not permitted to vote" in the context of enacting a piece of legislation. This utterance does not merely report some prior state of affairs. Nor does it merely have the result that black South Africans won't show up at polling stations on election days. Rather, the utterance enacts a piece of legislation that is subordinating in making it the case that black South Africans are deprived of voting rights (Langton 1993, 302). The speech act subordinates in virtue of (1) unfairly *ranking* black people as inferior; (2) *legitimating* unjust racial discrimination; and (3) illegitimately *depriving* black South Africans important powers and rights (Langton 1993, 303). Some of these subordinating illocutionary speech acts—like ranking and valuing—are, as Austin put it, *verdictive* in giving a verdict about something. Others—for example, ordering, permitting, prohibiting, authorizing, and enacting laws—are *exercitive* speech acts: they confer or deprive powers and rights (Langton 1993, 304).

In virtue of what, then, might pornographic speech subordinate in a parallel manner? The mere depiction of subordination does not suffice; plenty of films and news reports can depict women's subordination without counting as such. Rather, Langton holds that pornography is (1) verdictive speech that *ranks* women as inferior sex objects whose purpose is to "service" men's sexual needs; and (2) it is exercitive speech that *legitimates* sexualized violence against women in depicting women's degradation in a manner that endorses, celebrates, and authorizes such degradation (Langton 1993, 307–308). Following

Dworkin and MacKinnon, this is what pornography does and not just what it says. How plausible is this view though? Langton herself readily admits that pornographic speech falls short of paradigm illocutionary subordination. Nevertheless, there are ways to see the plausibility of the constitutive subordination claim. First, we can appeal to an inference to the best explanation. What explains best the perlocutionary effects of pornography that even the critics of MacKinnon and Dworkin accept? In short, its illocutionary force: this explains how pornography can affect attitudes and behavior, make consumers more ready to accept rape myths, and desensitize consumers to sexualized violence (Langton 1993, 310). Second, we can look at audience interpretation of pornography: if its audiences take pornography to be women's subordination, this supports the view that pornography does illocutionarily subordinate women—if you like, pornography achieves uptake. Third, we might look at whether some other important felicity conditions for illocutionary force have been satisfied. Specifically, since verdictive and exercitive speech are authoritative acts, we should examine whether pornography can authoritatively rank women as inferior and legitimate sexualized violence against them. If it does, pornography has the authority to illocutionarily subordinate women. Langton holds that pornography plausibly has such authority, which provides the strongest case for pornography counting as the illocutionary subordination of women. *Contra* liberal critics, pornographers are not a "powerless minority, a fringe group especially vulnerable to moralistic persecution" (Langton 1993, 311). Instead, they are the ruling power when it comes to the domain of sex. Thus, pornography subordinates not due to its content, but due to its authoritativeness about sex.

In sum, Langton claims that pornography harms women in a particular manner in causing and being their subordination. To assess this view, let's consider the two central aspects—causation and constitution—separately starting with the former.

2.3. EMPIRICAL EVIDENCE FOR THE CAUSAL SUBORDINATION CLAIM

To begin assessing whether pornography causes women's subordination, we need to first ask: Which women are or might be harmed in this manner? One immediate answer is that pornography harms female performers. At its most extreme formulation, pornography is literally taken to be the documentation of rape. Alternatively, pornography has postproduction harms suffered by individual women who are nonperformers. It is commonly used to groom vulnerable and young individuals for abuse and, together with sexual assaults, to "season" women for different types of sex work (like prostitution). Then again, other nonperforming women have been sexually attacked by perpetrators, who aimed to re-enact scenes from violent, inegalitarian pornography.[4] Plenty of women self-report disliking their male partners' pornography consumption. It is not difficult to find stories of women being pressured into re-enacting sexual scenarios from pornography (such as being pressured to engage in BDSM or anal sex), and how this causes emotional and psychological distress to these women.

A wealth of evidence shows that pornography is at least incidentally linked to such production and postproduction harms to women. MacKinnon and Dworkin (1997) provide an impressive catalogue of first-person stories of how pornography has harmed individual women in the above ways. The stories were collected in hearings that

4. To clarify: not all pornography that depicts violence is inegalitarian nor does inegalitarian pornography necessarily involve violent depictions. For instance, BDSM (bondage-discipline, dominance-submission, sadism-masochism) pornography may depict violence but, for reasons discussed later on, it is not *eo ipso* inegalitarian (though of course on other grounds it might be). For now, I will use 'violent pornography' as shorthand for 'violent inegalitarian pornography'. This denotes pornographic depictions that are violent and sexually explicit in a way that "as a whole eroticize relations (acts, scenarios, or postures) characterized by gender inequity" (Eaton 2007, 676).

took place as part of the effort to institute the Dworkin-MacKinnon antipornography ordinances. These personal accounts are certainly not alone in suggesting that pornography has causally contributed to serious harms suffered by girls and individual women (both performers and nonperformers) (Itzin 1992c; Itzin and Sweet 1992; Russell 1993b; Wyre 1992). It is fairly uncontroversial that pornography is causally linked to some sexualized assaults, and this is something that even Judge Easterbrook accepted.[5]

However, antipornography feminism has advanced a stronger and more controversial thesis: pornography harms women as *a group*. This is a claim about pornography contributing causally to a culture of *systematic* sexual violence against women by sexualizing inequality; as Robin Morgan (1980) put it in provocative terms, pornography is the theory and rape is the practice. The causal effects of pornography do not just reach some "bad apples" who are adversely influenced by its message. Rather, pornography consumption changes attitudes more broadly and can negatively influence even ordinary "good guys." Thus, it plays an important role in the epidemic of sexualized violence against women. An important presumption is made in such arguments: pornography disseminates deep and vicious lies about women and their sexuality (Langton 1993; Longino 1980; MacKinnon 1987; Tong 1982). It plays a key role in shaping attitudes about women's sexuality in educating men and women alike about sex in insidious ways (Dines 2011; Paul 2005; Russell 2000). This sort of problematic sex education—or what some call "antifemale propaganda" (Brownmiller 1975)—extends to other areas of life and causally contributes to women's oppression more generally.

---

5. Of course, there are many positive stories from female performers in pornography too. These will be discussed in chapter 7. Nevertheless, it is important to bear in mind that positive stories do not cancel negative ones or render the pornography industry beyond moral and legal critique. It simply demonstrates that the issue of harm is highly complex and that the industry is multifaceted.

Pornography distorts both men and women's views about gender relations, about what supposedly women want in sexual and non-sexual contexts, and about women's "nature" that fixes their supposed proper societal place. Generally speaking, pornography supports sexist attitudes, which reinforces the oppression and exploitation of women (Tirrell 1999).

Whether the systematic causal connection holds has been vigorously debated. Although critics accept that pornography has lead to individual attacks against women, some take issue with the subordination claim by pointing out that a systematic causal link between pornography and sexualized violence remains to be conclusively established (R. Dworkin 1991; Feinberg 1985). There is significant disagreement among social scientists, policymakers, and philosophers about this connection (Segal 1990). Furthermore, countries like Denmark and Japan are often cited as counterevidence to the subordination claims: Japan has low reported sexual assault figures but extremely high pornography consumption figures, whereas the liberalization of pornography in Denmark apparently did not increase the incidence of rape and seemingly led to a decrease of sex crimes (see Kutchinsky 1970; Pally 1994; Posner 1994; Strossen 1995).

It is far from easy to tell whether pornography is causally responsible for the fact that some men sexually attack women: some suggest that these men have a predisposition to such violence, which simply correlates with their consumption of pornography. Perpetrators consume pornography because they are predisposed to commit sexualized violence, not vice versa. Joel Feinberg (1985) puts forward this line of argument.[6] He does not dispute the existence of male violence against women but offers an alternative explanation for such violence. Feinberg points out that works of literature and

---

6. See also Stark (1997) for a more recent variant of the view that pornography caters to men who have a predisposition to find its message compelling.

crime reporting can prompt copycat offenses; but if we take this to be sufficient for prohibiting such works, we will have to prohibit much literature and film, along with works we do not want to prohibit (like *The Brothers Karamazov*). He further accepts that a violent episode in a pornographic work may be "causally necessary" for perpetrating some specific crime: were it not for that episode, the perpetrator might not have done what they did. But since this depends so heavily on individual psychologies, Feinberg holds, it may well be that some other nonpornographic work would have had the same causal influence. This suggests that nonperpetrators are not converted into perpetrators simply by consuming pornography. Instead:

> If pornography has a serious causal bearing on the occurrence of rape (as opposed to the trivial copy-cat effect) it must be in virtue of its role (still to be established) in implanting the appropriate cruel dispositions in the first place. (Feinberg 1985, 151)

On this view, pornography may incidentally act as a catalyst, but the underlying cruel dispositions come from somewhere else. Since there are many possible ways in which these dispositions can be activated, we cannot single out pornography as *the* cause of sexualized violence.

By way of an alternative explanation, Feinberg suggests that such "cruel" dispositions stem from men being socialized into a macho culture, where masculinity is tied to being a tough, reckless, unsentimental, hard-boiled, disrespectful, sexual athlete (1985, 151). Violent pornography then appeals to men who are in "the grip of the macho cult," and it functions to express and reinforce "the macho ideology" (Feinberg 1985, 152). And so, pornography does not cause "normal decent chaps" to become perpetrators after a singular exposure to pornography; rather, it is the pornography-consuming machos who commit sexualized violence against women because of their prior macho values. Feinberg thus holds that "the cult of macho expectations" is the primary cause of *both* violent pornography *and* real-life sexualized violence (1985, 154). Even without any violent pornography, Feinberg maintains, sexualized violence persists as long as macho ideology does. Hence, we need to intervene on the level of culturally transmitted values and behaviors, one important vehicle being antimachismo moral education in schools.[7]

These arguments against the causal subordination claim merit a deeper analysis. Consider the supposed lack of empirical evidence. The 1979 report by the Williams Committee in the United Kingdom—headed by Bernhard Williams—found no conclusive evidence of harm caused by pornography (Williams 1981). However, the report has been criticized as incomplete by failing to include already-then existing research that established a link between sexualized violence and pornography (Itzin 1992a). In 1970, the US Commission on Obscenity and Pornography concluded that the available empirical evidence did not sufficiently establish a systematic link. In 1985, a second report (also known as the Meese Report) concluded quite to the contrary and found "strong support" for a causal link between pornography and sexual violence (Dwyer 1995, legal appendix). In the report, Edna Einsiedel discusses the then-available empirical evidence and concludes that the research demonstrates how the exposure to violent sexually explicit materials

(1) leads to a greater acceptance of rape myths and violence against women; (2) has more pronounced effects when the victim is shown enjoying the use of force or violence; (3) is arousing for rapists and for some males in the general population;

7. Another way to challenge the subordination claim would be to argue that because pornography is mere fantasy, it cannot have subordinating effects in the real world. I will postpone discussing this point until chapter 6 though.

and (4) has resulted in sexual aggression against women in the laboratory. (1992, 266)[8]

In reaction to the Meese Report, a powerful attack orchestrated by a Washington, DC, public relations firm ensued to discredit its findings (or as the company put it in a leaked letter: to deal with the "problems" the report generated [Itzin 1992a]). This campaign was successful in misrepresenting and discrediting the Commission's findings. Furthermore, it managed to distribute misinformation rather effectively because the report was initially published by an obscure Tennessee-based press and was at the time largely unavailable to the wider public (Itzin 1992a, 11; see also Russell 1993a). When assessing the evidence for and against the subordination claim, we must bear in mind that pornography is big business and, at least in the United States, the industry spends money on lobbying politicians and policymakers. Moreover, some feminist scholars have argued that two prominent feminist organizations campaigning *against* antipornography positions—Feminists Against Censorship in the United Kingdom and Feminist **Anti-Censorship** Taskforce in the United States—also grossly misrepresented antipornography positions and the available empirical evidence, which entrenched the

---

8. See Donnerstein et al. 1987; Itzin 1992c; Hald et al. 2010; Malamuth et al. 2000; Russell 2000; and Weaver 1992 for similar results. Not everyone agrees with these results: see Rubin 1993 and Segal 1990 for opposing views. For a more recent study about whether pornography consumption correlates with inegalitarian attitudes about women, see Kohut et al. 2016. The study found no increased correlation in such attitudes with pornography consumption. However, the study did not measure attitudes about women's sexuality, but rather whether consumers viewed themselves as feminists, whether they condoned women in positions of power, and whether they approved of abortion (among other things). It is important to bear in mind that one can harbor negative attitudes about women's sexuality while holding positive attitudes about (say) women in leadership roles. After all, sexualized violence against women and sexual harassment also happens to women in positions of power and in contexts of power. Furthermore, self-proclaimed feminists can and do perpetrate harassment and violence too.

opposition between anti- and pro-pornography advocates even further (Itzin 1992a).

Thinking about the apparent counterexamples of Denmark and Japan is also instructive. For a start, the evidence from Denmark that liberalization of pornographic materials lead to no increases in (and actually resulted in decreases of) rape has been widely discredited as methodologically flawed (Itzin 1992c). The original study by Kutchinsky (1970) that is still approvingly cited looked at the correlation between liberalization of pornography and *sex crimes*. However, the category of sex crimes involved much more than rape. For instance, in the relevant statistics rape was included alongside flashers and peeping toms. Importantly, looking at rape statistics alone does *not* support the view that the liberalization of pornography in Denmark correlated with decreased rates of reported rapes (Bart and Jozsa 1980; Bachy 1976)—in fact, at the time of the liberalization occurrences of reported rapes increased, although overall rates of sex crimes went down.

Furthermore, in an oft-cited book defending pornography, Nadine Strossen claims that "violence against women is uncommon" in Japan, despite the ready availability of "sexually oriented materials" (1995, 255). She offers no proper justification for her view though. In fact, feminist legal theorists discussing sexualized violence in Japan put forward a strikingly different picture. They have found "significant evidence" for such violence with the majority of women being abused by men they know (Burns 2005, 44). The criminal justice system consistently trivializes women's claims of sexual assaults, and the manner of recording crimes like rape differs greatly from that in the United States. Japanese statistics are limited to penile-vagina penetration, and (more bizarrely) they "generally exclude rape figures when the crime was perpetrated in conjunction with robbery— considered the more serious crime" (Burns 2005, 46). Moreover, prior to a change in law in 2000, Japanese rape statistics were limited to reports made within six months of the alleged incident, and an assault on a minor that "came to the attention of a doctor or teacher would not be included in the statistics" (Burns 2005, 46).

Women in Japan are also said to be deeply reluctant to report sexualized violence for a number of reasons. Rape myths are highly prevalent, and the construction of "normal" heterosexuality leads to pervasive victim blaming in cases of sexual assaults. Japan has a long history of state-sponsored and condoned brothels, which were considered necessary to provide males a place for sexual release given their supposed natural heterosexual urges that could not otherwise be controlled. According to cultural and legal scholars, much of the construction of male heterosexuality is framed around the idea that it is simply uncontrollable, which also informs much of Japanese sexual assault legislation. One particularly pernicious cultural construct is the idea of *sukebei*: "harmless, perverted, lecherous or 'dirty old man' framework of sexual desires and practices which, permeating class and status boundaries, is regarded as the fundamental nature of the (hetero)sexual male" (Burns 2005, 23). This construction of masculine sexuality underlies many practices, such as molesting women on commuter trains, purchasing women's used underwear, and other "fads in the realm of sexual fantasy produced and consumed at a staggering rate" (Burns 2005, 23). Connected to this idea of *sukebei* are gendered constructions of "good"/ordinary women and "deviant" women, where the *sukebei* behavior is thought to be directed only toward the latter. This generates some deeply problematic assumptions:

> One very significant consequence is the assumption that "ordinary" women are not targets of sexual assault . . . Therefore, those who have been targeted must have provoked their attacker, 'asked for it' [like sexually "deviant" women]. This makes the "blame the victim" narrative in Japan particularly pervasive and salient. (Burns 2005, 31)

Given the prevalence of such cultural narratives about gender, women are inhibited from reporting sexualized violence. Those who do report are often viewed as not credible by the police, prosecutors, and judges (Burns 2005, 52). Of course, none of this demonstrates that pornography is causally responsible for violence against women in Japan. It does, however, paint a very different picture from that put forward by critics of the subordination claim: high pornography consumption figures in Japan do in fact correlate with high rates of sexualized violence against women. This demonstrates that some critics base their arguments on false empirical claims. For instance, in her defense of pornography, Strossen (1995, 274) quotes the psychologist Shirley Feldman-Summers who takes the low Japanese rates of recorded rape to be explained by culturally induced *male* shame that prevents men from committing such crimes. Quite the contrary, the official low rates might more readily be explained by the silence surrounding rape due to *female* shame for having supposedly provoked an attack.

Feinberg's alternative analysis is also striking for a number of reasons. It buys into the false picture of there being "decent" and "deviant" chaps, where only the latter commit sexualized violence against women and children. This picture is flawed, and as one leading UK therapist working with sex offenders notes, "the men who offend are 'ordinary' men from every walk of life" (Wyre 1992, 241). Based on his extensive work with sex offenders, Wyre thinks that pornography consumption plays a significant part in shaping men's attitudes about women and children. The "deviancy model" assumed by Feinberg is inaccurate, and "all men have the capacity to be influenced by pornography" (Wyre 1992, 242). Then again, although Feinberg's explanation of inegalitarian macho values having a causal influence on sexualized violence has pretheoretical appeal, his discussion contains a striking lack of reflection about where these values come from. Since he maintains that macho ideology is something learned, not innate, causally efficacious macho values are grounded in socialization. But Feinberg does not consider what kind of socialization produces such an ideology. In being culturally transmitted, one might expect pornography to be one significant cultural means for transmitting macho values and socializing men accordingly (among others societal forces). In fact, communication and media specialists have argued so since the 1980s (Zillman and Weaver 1989; Weaver 1992. For more recent discussion of pornography's role in male gender socialization, see Ezzell 2014). This is conceivably even more so nowadays since the Internet has made access to pornographic materials incredibly easy.

Now, Feinberg accepts that "constant" exposure to pornography might have adverse causal effects and turn a "decent chap" into a violent macho (1985, 154). But he dismisses this as unlikely: after all, decent chaps have no predisposition to consume violent pornography, and thus such materials do not appeal to them. Other "foundational causes" must be at work for violent pornography to have any purchase at all (1985, 154). But Feinberg does not elucidate these foundational causes further, and at least some self-reports from male pornography consumers speak against this. Arguably one of the most objectionable producers of the kind of macho pornography that Feinberg probably would have found deeply troubling is Max Hardcore. Dines (2011) recounts stories of male viewers who began watching his materials out of curiosity given Hardcore's reputation. Some viewers remarked initially finding the materials deeply disgusting but having started to enjoy them upon longer exposure. This suggests to Dines that pornography clearly can affect men and shape their worldviews in harmful ways, which is not equivalent to saying that men are turned into rapists by pornography. Being influenced in manipulative ways to find extreme depictions of women's degradation enjoyable (which is a mainstay of Hardcore's work) is obviously also deeply worrying from a feminist perspective.

Aside from that, Feinberg critiques antipornography feminism for not demonstrating a reliable causal connection between pornography and the prevalence of sexualized violence. But he himself in turn offers *no* reliable empirical backing for the claim that macho ideology is the primary cause of both violent pornography and real-life sexualized violence. The very strong causal claims that Feinberg makes are at least as unsupported by social scientific evidence, if not more so, than the causal subordination claim. In terms of evidence, Feinberg merely offers a few citations from letters sent to *Penthouse* that fit his analysis of the macho culture. MacKinnon and Dworkin, by contrast, produced an impressive amount of expert evidence and first-person stories of pornography's harms during the early-1980s hearings that were part of passing the Minneapolis antipornography ordinance (reprinted in their 1997 work). Methodologically, Feinberg's philosophical work on pornography is precisely of the kind that I criticized in chapter 1: it makes use of a few examples that fit one's philosophical position mainly developed a priori, while discarding a wealth of empirical research that challenges one's view.

Finally, we might agree with Feinberg that macho values do not originate from violent pornography (although see Russell 2000 for the view that violent pornography can also create a predisposition to perpetrate sexualized violence). Nevertheless, if violent, inegalitarian pornography plays a role in reproducing such values and in maintaining a macho ideology, this should suffice to worry us about pornography's causal role in perpetuating a culture of sexualized violence against women. We need not establish that violent pornography *created* such a culture in order to find pornography a grave cause for concern—something that Feinberg fails to consider. For instance, Deborah Cameron and Elizabeth Frazer argue that even though empirical evidence does not support the view that pornography causes systematic sexualized violence in a copycat manner, pornography does seemingly contribute to the persistence of sexualized violence. Pornographic representations have the power to *shape* desire, even if it cannot create "evil" dispositions sui generis. This should give feminists cause for concern and suffices for criticizing pornographic representations (Cameron and Frazer 1992, 376). And as Susan Brison holds, even if pornography were a mere symptom of male dominance, this would not absolve it from responsibility. She draws an apt comparison to women's political representation: the low numbers of high-ranking female politicians may be just a symptom of patriarchy. This does not, however, mean that we should leave the political status quo as it is (Brison 2014, 94). Rather, symptoms of deeper problems merit feminist interventions too.

2.4. THE MEANING OF *CAUSE*

The above demonstrates that settling pertinent empirical issues is far from straightforward. As of yet, however, there is no conclusive proof that the causal subordination claim is *false*. Furthermore, there is compelling evidence that supports a systematic correlation between pornography and sexualized violence against women. This (I maintain) suffices for us to find at least some pornography troubling from a feminist perspective.

Many apparent disagreements may also hinge on misconceptions about what it is for pornography to cause sexualized violence. We must be careful to distinguish how pornography may causes changes in *attitudes* and in *behaviors* toward women. Sociologist Diana Russell defends the causal subordination claim with a multiple causation model of how pornography might cause rape. She claims that most critiques of the systematic causal connection between pornography consumption and sexualized violence against women have accepted an overly simplistic account of causation, where the former is both necessary and sufficient for the latter. This sort of "monkey see, monkey do" explanation is clearly empirically unsupported. However, Russell puts forward a multiple causation model, where some event may occur due to various causes any one of which is potentially sufficient but not necessary for the event, or necessary but not sufficient. Pornography may (a) predispose some men to rape and intensify such a predisposition in others; (b) it may undermine men's internal psychological inhibitions against acting out their desire to rape; or (c) pornography may undermine some social inhibitions against acting out that desire (Russell 2000, 62). Russell further holds that empirical evidence supports the view that pornography causally influences such attitudinal changes that together increase the likelihood of perpetrating rape. This sort of multifaceted explanatory framework, which was developed by looking at actual perpetrators' psychologies and actions, can help us see that the causal subordination claim is plausible albeit clearly not deterministic.

Anne Eaton (2007) also critiques the conception of *harm* typically employed in pornography debates. She formulates the harm hypothesis as follows: "pornography shapes the attitudes and conduct of its audience in ways that are injurious to women" (Eaton 2007, 677). This takes place when pornography insidiously shapes the emotional lives of its consumers by soliciting positive feelings for situations representing gender inequality, which in turn plays a role in maintaining systematic social injustice. This is akin to subliminal endorsement methods employed in advertisement: both male and female subjects retain information better if the information is presented in sexually arousing ways (May 1998, 72). The process by which such shaping of attitudes takes place, and that may lead to detrimental behavioral outputs, is clearly not deterministic. Eaton draws an analogy with smoking. It does not cause cancer in a deterministic sense: many nonsmokers develop lung cancer, and many smokers do not. So smoking is neither necessary nor sufficient to develop lung cancer. Nevertheless, we (the general public and medical experts) accept that smoking causes cancer. This is because it increases the *likelihood* of developing lung cancer—and this fact alone is enough to vindicate a causal connection between smoking and cancer. The sense of causation employed here is probabilistic:

> x is the cause of y if and only if (i) x occurs earlier than y and (ii) the probability of the occurrence of y is greater, given the occurrence of x, than the probability of the occurrence of y given not-x. (Eaton 2007, 696)

In a similar sense, it may be that pornography consumption increases the probability of sexualized violence against women. If this is so, we have vindicated a causal connection between pornography and women's subordination.

Eaton is careful to stress that we still lack empirical evidence to establish the matter. There are many issues that need to be considered, including the frequency of exposure to pornography, the strength of that exposure (how inegalitarian the pornographic depictions are), wider social forces and how gender egalitarian the consumers' social context is, and how all of these aspects interact. Still, critics have yet to show that the causal subordination claim is a nonstarter. Although Eaton does not explore this, one major problem with some of the earlier discussions is their unrealistically high expectations of empirical proof. And so, it is unwarranted to hold that unless definitive proof of the systematic causal connection is forthcoming, the subordination claim is utterly untenable. The idea that we need absolute certainty or the subordination claim folds precisely buys into such unrealistically high standards of scientific proof. In fact, definitive proof of pornography's harms is impossible to achieve. After all,

> given ethical considerations, evidence sufficiently defini-
> tive to satisfy this mandate [of conclusive proof for the causal

connection] will not be forthcoming. Obviously, any research protocol employing sexually abusive or violent behaviours as a response to viewing pornography cannot be sanctioned. Consequently, we *must* rely on the available research to develop an understanding of the behavioural consequences. (Weaver 1992, 301)

One should also bear in mind that for conclusive proof of the connection to be forthcoming, the evidence for there being a causal connection must be interpreted in opposition to a control group, where individuals have not consumed pornography. However, given how ubiquitous pornography consumption has become with the Internet, it is nearly impossible to find such a control group.

Finally, demonstrating a robust correlation between pornography and sexualized violence is not insignificant (Itzin 1992c, 559). After all, this does demonstrate a *connection* between the two. It does not demonstrate that pornography alone is responsible for sexualized violence against women—but, then again, advocates of the subordination claim do not think so either. MacKinnon's rhetoric can sometimes lend itself to an uncharitable reading, where pornography *alone* appears to cause women's subordination. But this is certainly not the case with Langton's more nuanced defense of the subordination claim. With correlation in mind, Adams (2000) argues that critics of the subordination claim are guilty of a double standard when it comes to the meaning of *cause*: in nonpornographic cases, we are willing to accept much lower standards of scientific proof of cause and are satisfied with strong correlation. Even critics accept that pornography can be a stimulus to sexual assault, despite not being deterministic in a "monkey see, monkey do" manner. The lack of determinism, however, does not in other cases hinder assignment of responsibility. Consider an example from Adams: an office-building parking lot was left unlit at night for a number of weeks due to the negligence of the building-management company. A user of the parking lot was viciously attacked at night, sued the management company for negligence and won the case. The building management was held partly responsible for the attack because their negligence facilitated it. In this instance, the unlit parking lot was the factor that stimulated the attack. The courts accepted that the negligence of the building management in part caused the attack, but such connections are typically denied in the case of pornography. This is the root of the double standard: "In nonpornographic cases [the courts] don't require overwhelming scientific research in support of the claim that, for example, leaving a parking lot dark has a high statistical correlation with people getting violently assaulted" (Adams 2000, 13). Nonetheless, such support is expected in pornographic cases.

2.5. PHILOSOPHICAL TENABILITY OF THE CONSTITUTIVE SUBORDINATION CLAIM

In addition to concerns about pornography causing subordination, some have worried about the philosophical underpinnings of Langton's constitutive subordination claim. For one thing, Louise Antony argues that Langton's claim ill fits Austin's view that determining the success of illocutions necessarily involves accepted background *conventions*. That is,

> the specifically illocutionary effects of a speech act are those effects that are *conventional* effects of that act of saying; they are effects that obtain *only because of* the background convention that defines the act as one of some particular illocutionary type. (Antony 2011, 392)

Although perlocutionary effects can obtain via nonconventional means, illocutionary effects cannot. By way of example: my uttering "I do" in a marriage ceremony may have all manner of perlocutionary effects on the audience (joy, fear, dismay, indifference) that do not hinge on any conventions about how one ought to feel in the situation. Whether my locution succeeds as an illocution though depends on conventionally governed conditions, like uttering the words at the right time. With this in mind, we can accept that pornography has some subordinating effects; but for those to be illocutionary effects, they must obtain *in virtue of* some specific background convention(s). However, subordination as a practice seemingly requires no such conventional backgrounds—there are "vastly many ways" to subordinate others (Antony 2011, 393). It seems then that Langton must settle for the view that pornography merely has the perlocutionary effect of subordinating women. Still, Antony holds that this in no sense diminishes the political case against pornography: pornography should give feminists grave cause for concern even if its bad effects are "*mere* effects" rather than "*illocutionary* effects" (Antony 2011, 387; see also Antony 2014 and Harel 2011).

Might illocutionary effects nevertheless be *worse* than "mere" effects? Some question this (e.g., Antony 2011, 2014; Harel 2011) and hold that an additional illocutionary story adds nothing normatively substantive to the perlocutionary harms done to women. I am not entirely convinced though. Let's assume for argument's sake that pornography has the pernicious perlocutionary effect of causing women's subordination. This is, of course, in and of itself a matter of moral and political concern. But if the illocutionary story holds, pornography does more: it constitutes an affront to women's equal citizenship. Subsequently, Langton (1993) holds that the subordination claim highlights a conflict between liberty (pornographers' freedom) and equality (women's civil rights). For instance, enacting a law that undermines my civil rights (e.g., takes away my right to vote) is prima facie worse than a law that "merely" interferes with me exercising those rights (e.g., a legal requirement to have a voter ID). The latter is worrisome for sure, but in that case my civil rights are still intact, and I can challenge practices that interfere with my ability to exercise those rights. If the illocutionary force of pornography is effective enough to undermine women's civil rights by, for instance, undermining their right to free speech altogether, there is something worrying about such exercitive illocutionary effects that go beyond "mere" effects. Thus, there is a normative difference whether the effects are illocutionary or "merely" perlocutionary. And (I contend) this is what Langton originally had in mind and why she took the illocutionary subordination claim to be distinctive and if true, deeply worrying.

Others (myself included; Mikkola 2008) have prima facie accepted the constitutive subordination claim but worried about its scope. Jennifer Saul argues that Langton must settle for a less radical claim: "*pornographic viewings* are *sometimes* the subordination of women" (2006b, 247). If pornographic works are considered speech acts, they must be utterances in contexts; and this, Saul argues, undermines Langton's subordination claim as she formulates it. After all, pornographic recordings (e.g., films) have no illocutionary force by themselves; rather, their force is context dependent. Saul makes her case with the example of Ethel's sign. Imagine that Ethel is in an environment where people communicate nonverbally. For convenience, Ethel makes useful multipurpose signs. One sign reads "I do," and Ethel uses it to perform various illocutionary speech acts (like marrying and confessing to a murder). The sign does not fix which speech acts Ethel performs in having no illocutionary force by itself. Neither does the context of writing (encoding) the sign because Ethel intended to use it in various future communications. Ethel's illocutionary speech acts, then, must be fixed by the contexts of using (decoding) the sign. Saul takes pornographic recordings to be like

Ethel's sign and to lack illocutionary force by themselves. Since pornographic recordings are involved in a variety of future viewings, their illocutionary force is not fixed by the context of encoding (production). Instead, it is fixed by the context of decoding: by actual pornographic viewings. However, some pornographic viewings are benevolent in that they do not (1) make the viewer more likely to treat women as inferior, (2) take pornographic viewings to be acts of subordinating women, and (3) treat pornographers as authoritative about sex (Saul 2006b, 244). An example would be a feminist critical viewing of pornography. But if *all* viewings subordinate women, even feminist critical engagements with pornography end up doing so, which seems wrongheaded. Thus, we should settle for the more qualified claim: only some viewings illocutionarily subordinate women, which substantially weakens Langton's constitutive subordination claim.

Claudia Bianchi (2008) defends Langton arguing that Saul focuses on the wrong context to fix pornography's illocutionary force; once we focus on the right one, Langton need not settle for Saul's more moderate thesis. For Bianchi, pornography's *intended* viewing contexts fix illocutionary force, not actual viewing contexts. Further, "[i]f a work of pornography is indeed intended as an illocutionary act of subordinating women . . . and *if* this intention is made available to the addressee, no benevolent viewing may change" pornography's illocutionary force (Bianchi 2008, 7). But, it seems to me that the antecedent is not obviously true. Langton admits that pornography may subordinate women although pornographers do not intend to subordinate women (1993, 313), while Saul holds that pornographers probably just intend to make money (2006b, 232). Bianchi disagrees: she contends that making money is probably the perlocutionary effect of pornographers' intention to subordinate women. Still, women's subordination could also be the perlocutionary effect of pornographers' intention to make money, and Bianchi must do more to show that she is right about pornographers' intentions. Actually, determining these intentions is very tricky on Bianchi's view: it would require "encyclopaedic knowledge of the world and of [pornographers'] desires, beliefs and intentions" (2008, 6)—something that strikes me as impossible to achieve.

Bianchi could claim in response that pornographers might not intend to subordinate women but, nevertheless, they do expect their works to be viewed in certain subordinating contexts. This, if true, supports her argument. Some odd consequences, however, follow from this move. For Langton, pornography is the illocutionary subordination of women if (1) pornographic speech plausibly has (or explains) subordinating effects; (2) viewers interpret pornographic speech as subordinating women; and (3) viewers consider pornographers as being authoritative about sex (1993, 310–311). For Bianchi's argument to work, pornographers would have to single out audiences that take pornographic viewings to satisfy these three conditions, and they would have to intend their works to be viewed by those audiences. Now, Saul argues that most audiences do not take pornographic viewings to be subordinating. The audiences that do are made up of antipornography feminists, who take pornographic viewings to be women's illocutionary subordination (Saul 2006b, 72). If Saul is right about this, the success of Bianchi's argument hinges on pornographers intending their works to be viewed by antipornography feminists. But I seriously doubt that producers on the whole have *this* intention. As a result, it is not possible to maintain the constitutive subordination claim relative to pornography as a kind. Rather, only some instances of pornographic speech can count as women's subordination.[9]

9. For a further critique of Bianchi's view, see my 2008 article. De Gaynesford (2009) provides an alternative discussion of Bianchi.

Above I focused on one complication: what pornographers *intend* to do with pornography is not obvious. I will discuss this point in later chapters too, which highlights an important methodological issue that we will return to time and again: many facets of the debate cannot be settled from the philosopher's armchair, and relying on intuitive and introspective philosophical methods won't do. However, there is another issue that merits more attention: pornography's *authority*. Consider the following line of argument put forward by Dyzenhaus (1992). Until now, we have focused on physical harm to women. But maybe there is a more fruitful alternative way to think about harm. Dyzenhaus holds that a more appropriate strategy would be to argue that forms of patriarchy and male dominance violate women's interests in being (and becoming) autonomous individuals. If antipornography feminists are right that pornography perniciously teaches both women and men lies about women's sexuality by erotizing inequality, this undermines women's sexual autonomy and self-determination. Doing so need not even involve sexualized violence against women because it renders women "willing" collaborators in their own subjugation. And so, we have another way to formulate the harm thesis: pornography illegitimately violates women's interest in autonomy, which liberals like J. S. Mill ([1869] 1974) take to be a fundamental interest of us as progressive beings. Subsequently, we need not demonstrate that pornography actually increases sexualized violence against women and thereby harms them. Rather, if we understand the subordination claim as being about rights violations and interest violations, we can sidestep questions about conflicting empirical evidence. In a slightly different vein, but also appealing to women and men's interest violations, May (1998) discusses pornography via the metaphor of pollution. Only rarely do individual pieces of pornography harm women in a manner that would make good the subordination claim. But cumulatively, pornography "pollutes" human interactions precisely because it hampers sexual autonomy and self-determination. Both women's and men's options are limited in sexual encounters, and pornography interferes with our human interest in healthy sexual interactions by affecting "attitudes that shape the sexual self-conceptions of men and women" (May 1998, 71). In this sense, pornography is like industrial pollution. No single instance is responsible for undermining socially and morally desirable sexual expression, but accumulated effects reinforce the subliminal and restrictive message about sex that pornography promulgates. Hence, pornography cumulatively undermines sexual autonomy.

In order to assess the above suggestions, we must consider whether pornography has the power to teach us about sexuality in insidious ways. That is, we must consider whether pornographers and pornographic speech have the requisite sort of authority to hamper sexual autonomy by seemingly polluting sexual lives. Recall that Langton provides three grounds for thinking that pornography subordinates: it is the best explanation for actual sexualized violence (for perlocutionary effects); pornography's audiences take it to subordinate women; and pornographic speech has authority over the domain of sex. Langton takes the last point to offer the strongest evidence for the subordination claim. If it holds, we may also make good the claim that pornography violates women's autonomy interests. For now, I will postpone discussing this point since it also pertains to the second central claim antipornography feminists have made: pornography silences women. Ultimately, if pornography does not have the requisite sort of authority, all of these claims—pornography hinders autonomy, and it subordinates and silences women—are undermined. Let's then turn to the issue of silencing to examine the matter further.

Chapter 3

Does Pornography Silence Women?

3.1. INTRODUCTION

One of Catharine MacKinnon's central claims is that pornography is not only words. Rather, pornographic speech does something harmful: it subordinates and silences women. The previous chapter examined Rae Langton's defense of the subordination claim. Langton argues that pornography is verdictive speech in ranking women as inferior sex objects and that it is exercitive speech—speech that confers or deprives powers and rights—in legitimating sexualized violence against women (Langton 1993, 307–308). What grants pornographic speech illocutionary force is its authoritativeness in the realm of sex. This might suggest that harmful pornographic speech should be countered by better speech, speech that undercuts pornography's false depictions of and lies about women's sexuality in order to undermine its authoritativeness. However, if pornographic speech has the power to silence women, such counterspeech looks set to fail. That is, pornography is said to be exercitive not only in legitimating sexualized violence but also in depriving women of important free speech rights—in silencing them. Call this the 'silencing claim'.

This claim has attracted a huge amount of philosophical interest over the past couple of decades, and the literature discussing it is by now extensive. In this chapter, I will consider how we should understand the silencing claim by carefully dissecting the relevant literature. I will further assess the philosophical and practical tenability of the silencing claim. The main philosophical lessons to arise from this chapter are as follows. First, even though some aspects of the silencing claim have pretheoretical plausibility, it remains to be established that pornographic speech is responsible for silencing women. Second, the silencing claim is often discussed by appealing to intuitive "gut-feelings" about specific cases. But this is not methodologically conducive to settling the matter.

3.2. THE SILENCING CLAIM

According to MacKinnon (1987, 1993), pornography silences women. In creating a worldview where violence is eroticized, violence becomes part of "ordinary" sex. This creates a climate where women are viewed as noncredible: when women try to speak out against sexualized violence or report assaults, they are often ridiculed, dismissed, not believed, and blamed for those assaults. This fits the idea that pornography *causes* women's silencing: thinking that one will not be taken seriously causes victims of sexual assaults to stay silent. But Langton has alone (1993) and together with Jennifer Hornsby (1998) made a stronger claim. Pornography also constitutes women's silencing; hence, there is a free speech argument *against* pornography. Drawing on Austin (1962), their idea is that the manufacture and consumption of pornographic speech may interfere with women's ability to perform certain actions with their speech, where this amounts to a peculiar kind of silencing. Recall Austin's view: the speaker's locution (the words uttered) can perform some illocutionary action (*in* uttering something the speaker's locution can *count* as øing), and the locution can have some perlocutionary effects (*by* uttering something the speaker can *cause* extra-linguistic effects).

Take the declaration "I now pronounce you a married couple." Provided that the speaker has the authority to wed people and the spouses-to-be are currently unmarried (among other things, though simplifying here for argument's sake), just in uttering the locution the speaker successfully performs an action other than simply voicing the appropriate words: they perform the act of marrying. This is—it *constitutes*—an illocutionary speech act, which is performed with the appropriate locution. The utterance also has various perlocutionary effects and it *causes* something extra-linguistic: for example, the couple may now be entitled to tax breaks.

Correspondingly, Langton argues, there are three types of silencing. *Locutionary silencing* takes place when no locutions are made (for instance, when I am gagged). *Perlocutionary frustration* takes place when the speaker voices the appropriate words but fails to secure their intended extra-linguistic effects. *Illocutionary disablement* takes place when the speaker utters the appropriate locution but fails thereby to perform their intended illocutionary act. For instance, imagine a judge passing a sentence, who utters the right words in the right context (e.g., "I find the defendant guilty" uttered in a court of law). The judge intends to perform the illocutionary act of sentencing, but imagine that unbeknownst to the judge, she has been disbarred during the proceedings and has lost her power to sentence the defendant. In this case, the intended illocution fails or (as Austin put it) misfires because a requisite felicity or success condition of *authority* relative to a domain is unmet. This failure on the illocutionary level will probably also result in perlocutionary frustration. If the judge has lost her authority to sentence people, her words will not secure the desired extra-linguistic effects: the defendant won't be imprisoned or detained as a result of the judge's utterance because the judge no longer has the power to enact sentencing.

In the above example, misfiring of the judge's intended illocution hinges on the lack of authority. But recall that illocutions may misfire for other reasons too. Take the already-familiar case of being an actor on stage and seeing a fire break out. I shout "Danger, fire!" intending to warn, but the audience takes this to be part of the play. Here we have an *uptake-failure* since the audience fails to recognize my intended illocution to warn. Note that this differs from the "boy who cried wolf"–type cases, where the audience takes up the intended illocution to warn but believes the warning is insincere. Taking sincere illocutions as insincere ones represents a different kind of failure for Austin: they are abuses, not misfires. (The distinction will be relevant shortly.)

How might pornographic speech silence women? Having speaker authority and securing uptake are central for illocutionary success, and pornographic speech may block the satisfaction of these felicity conditions. Pornography does not silence women in the locutionary sense. But, it may prevent women from performing some intended illocutionary actions with their speech. In particular, this may happen in sexual contexts, where pornographic speech is authoritative. And so, it may silence women's refusals of unwanted sex. First, pornography may shape men's conceptions of women's sexuality in ways that result in perlocutionary frustration of refusal. When faced with unwanted sex, the pernicious effects of pornographic speech may result in a woman's locution "No!" as being recognized as a refusal but simply ignored. Women's speech fails to have the desired extra-linguistic effects because perpetrators see no reason to respect women's wishes in the sexual domain. Second, pornographic speech may shape men's conceptions of women's sexuality by creating communicative conditions that result in the illocutionary disablement of refusals. In this case, pornographic speech prevents women from successfully performing the illocutionary speech act of refusing: if pornographic speech prevents the locution "No!" from being *taken to be* a refusal in a sexual context, due to which sex is forced on the speaker, she has not successfully performed the illocution of refusing the unwanted sex. This sort of uptake failure is exemplified (though not exclusively) in cases of the kind: "I thought she was being coy and meant *yes* when she said 'no.'" Women's speech is illocutionarily silenced when certain locutions with which they intend to perform actions like refusing sex misfire: when women's communicative efforts are systematically interfered with by pornographic speech. Despite making the right locution and having the intention to refuse, something about the speaker—something about her supposed role in a sexualized power dynamic—prevents her locution from achieving uptake. The speaker tries to refuse but fails because her illocutionary act was disabled by pornographic speech. This should not be merely incidental and idiosyncratic, but a symptom of something more systematic. Although the systematicity condition has been criticized as underdeveloped (McGowan et al. 2016), we can tentatively characterize it as follows: an instance of uptake-failure meets the condition "if it is nonidiosyncratic, it is brought about by systematic features of society, and others would make a similar mistake under similar circumstances" (McGowan et al. 2016, 76).

Let's specify this further with Hornsby's view that illocutionary speech acts are communicative. For her, a condition of linguistic communication is *reciprocity* (Hornsby 1995a, 1995b). This obtains when interlocutors "recognize one another's speech as it is meant to be taken," which ensures that the attempt to perform some speech act has been successful (1995b, 224). In this sense, communication is reciprocal and turns on the speaker being able to do with their words what they intend to and on the hearer recognizing the speaker's intention. We can now better understand what happens when illocutionary silencing happens: the promulgation of certain false views about women (and their sexuality) interferes with reciprocity, which is a precondition of communication. Such false views can render women relatively powerless in communicative exchanges. Their speech is not subsequently made ineffable (there is no locutionary silencing). Nevertheless, women's speech is in another sense inaudible: their ability to *communicate* has been hampered (Hornsby 1995a). Illocutionary silencing (or disablement) crucially involves such communicative interference.

The silencing claim pits pornographers' liberty to produce pornographic materials against women's liberty to perform important speech acts. Prima facie this undermines legal protections afforded to pornographic speech under the auspices of the US Constitution. Before discussing such legal issues in chapter 4, let's first consider influential philosophical critiques of the Hornsby-Langton silencing claim.

3.3. PHILOSOPHICAL TENABILITY OF THE SILENCING CLAIM

Some hold that the silencing claim is philosophically indefensible. This complaint typically turns on the following questions: Is pornography speech at all, or speech of the *kind* that the speech act approach assumes?[1] Are Langton and Hornsby faithful to Austin's original view—is their position tenable by *Austin's* own lights? In other words, debates about the philosophical cogency of the Hornsby-Langton view typically involve debates about who is right about Austin's speech act theory and what his theory is committed to.

Louise Antony argues that a good deal of pornography is not speech at all (although ultimately Antony thinks that the speech act approach fails on different grounds). Speech act theory is meant to illuminate verbal communication, but extending this model

---

1. Note that there is a further question about whether pornography is speech in a legal sense so as to deserve protection under constitutional free speech principles. I will discuss this in chapter 4.

"metaphorically to cover actions that do not involve speech" is a stretch too far (Antony 2011, 389). Antony's point is that much of pornography is pictorial and involves no words. But according to Austin, for some act of expression to be an illocutionary act, it must be a locutionary act: One cannot illocute without locuting, and pornographic pictorial representations do not locute. Whatever the courts have declared, by Austin's own lights much of pornography does not involve exercitive or verdictive utterances that could count as illocutionary silencing. At most we can say that the "message" of pornography might *implicitly* be exercitive or verdictive, but this (the argument goes) ill fits Austin's original account (Antony 2011, 390).[2]

Elsewhere Antony (2017) argues that taking some pornographic speech to be exercitive/verdictive is in tension with another oft-made antipornography claim: pornography tells *lies* about women. In telling lies about women, pornography is putatively reporting or describing some supposed way women are. Pornographic speech misrepresents women's "nature" as being inferior, of lower value, and as suited to service men's sexual needs. But antipornography feminism also holds that pornography *makes* this the case in ranking women as inferior and in legitimating violence against women. However, Antony argues, some use of language cannot simultaneously both falsely report something about women (describe some state of affairs) and make women fit the description (bring about that state of affairs). For instance, as the foreperson of a jury, my utterance "We find the defendant guilty" may either report or bring about a state of affairs. This depends on the context: if I utter it in the context of passing judgment in a court of law, it has illocutionary (performative) force. If I utter this to a friend after the trial, the utterance merely reports (describes) a state of affairs. But I cannot simultaneously do both in the same context. Or to put this differently: for pornography to tell lies about

---

2. Although for a view that there are covertly exercitive speech acts, see McGowan (2009b).

women, there must be some prior way that women are (e.g., women do not enjoy violent sex). But the supposed power that pornography has to shape sexuality conflicts with this. If it shapes both male and female sexuality, pornography no longer tells lies about women: it has constructed a reality where women *fit* the pornographic image. Pornography's reporting and constructing of women's sexuality are in tension with one another, and one of them must go. (Mikkola [2010] discusses this tension in MacKinnon; Jenkins [2017] offers an alternative formulation of this claim to be discussed in chapter 8.)

Perhaps surprisingly, Hornsby (2014) also argues that pornography is not speech, although we can use Austin's speech act theory to understand it. I say "surprisingly" because Hornsby, together with Langton, also defends the silencing claim against critics. (More on this shortly.) Hornsby's objection hinges on her general view of language briefly introduced above: the central function and point of language is *communication*. This is not equivalent to producing some (even meaningful) noises; rather, communication involves a "meeting of minds," where the hearer recognizes what the speaker is intending to say and to do with their words. This is the main thrust of legal free speech principles: to make sure that we can engage in meaningful communication with one another in order to advance democratic deliberation and knowledge-seeking activities. However, according to Hornsby, pornography is not communicative in this sense. First, we cannot isolate some message that is being communicated on some occasion; second, even if we could isolate the message, we cannot identify whether this is the message that the producer intended to convey; third, we cannot discern whether the consumers become aware of the intended and conveyed message (Hornsby 2014, 132). Pornography does alter its consumers' attitudes and beliefs, and it conceivably has effects like disabling women's speech, where the mechanism for achieving this is some sort of mental conditioning (Hornsby 2014, 132). But pornography does not constitute communicative illocutionary actions: it does not feature in reciprocal "meetings of minds." Since communication is the hallmark of speech, we should not think of (noncommunicative) pornography as speech.

Others have critiqued the silencing claim as not being faithful to Austin's original view in a different sense. For Hornsby and Langton (1998), when pornography prevents women's locution "No!" from securing the required uptake, the locution will fail to satisfy the required success conditions for *counting as* a refusal. This constitutes silencing of women's refusals in the illocutionary disablement sense.[3] However, some reject that uptake is necessary for illocutionary success. Since the Hornsby-Langton view takes securing of uptake to be necessary for successful illocutionary refusals, the argument goes, it has a misguided view of speech act theory and is thus philosophically indefensible. Alexander Bird, for instance, argues that uptake is unnecessary for successful illocutions in general and for successful illocutionary refusals in particular, where "uptake" means "the appreciation by an audience of the intended illocution of the speaker" (Bird 2002, 2).[4] Rather, for Bird, successful illocutions depend on "the words [locuted], their normal meaning and the context alone" (2002, 13). If this is right, securing uptake is neither here nor there. (Daniel Jacobson [1995] makes a similar claim; see Hornsby and Langton [1998] for a response.)

Consider Bird's argument in more detail. He distinguishes institutional illocutions from noninstitutional ones and argues that the former require no uptake for success. For institutional illocutionary

---

3. This also helps to explain why Hornsby thinks that speech act theory is still relevant when thinking about pornography: although pornography itself cannot be analyzed with such theory, its effects (like failures of refusals) can be.

4. In what follows, I take the expression "one's locution 'p' performs the illocution of øing" as shorthand for "one's locution 'p' *successfully* performs the illocution of øing." As I see it, unsuccessful performance of an illocution simply is a failure to perform that illocution (just as if one unsuccessfully performs the act of voting, one simply has not voted).

success, we simply require a locution (verbal or written) in its usual meaning in the relevant context to be executed in conformity with some established conventions. A judge performs the illocution of sentencing just in saying "I sentence the defendant to five years in prison" irrespective of whether the one being sentenced realizes this (Bird 2002, 7). The prisoner need not take up (or recognize) the judge's intended illocution for illocutionary success. In fact, that the judge is performing the act of sentencing need not be realized by anyone "so long as the judge performs his duty in accordance with the law and established procedures" (Bird 2002, 7)—although someone must recognize the judge's intentions for the right perlocutionary effects to follow. The same is allegedly true of noninstitutional illocutions and even of those that are "intimately bound up with communication" (Bird 2002, 8). To illustrate, Bird considers Jacques, the conceited chef. Jacques falsely views himself as a world-class chef and thinks that his customers cannot get enough of his cooking. The inflated and warped view of Jacques's cooking skills is the result of undue praise from overenthusiastic restaurant critics, friends, and family. This has had the pernicious effect that when Jacques offers his customers more food, and they refuse saying "No, thank you," Jacques thinks they want more. He simply thinks his customers are being coy about accepting more. So, "when Sara says 'No' intending to decline an offer of food, there is not even a flicker of uptake in Jacques. On the contrary, he takes this as a reason to give her yet more" (Bird 2002, 11). Sara intends to refuse, but Jacques fails to appreciate her intended illocution. On the Hornsby-Langton view, Jacques's failure to take up Sara's intended refusal means that Sara has not refused: she has merely tried to. By contrast, Bird claims, this "is not, I believe, how most people would read [the] case. She refused all right—only Jacques' arrogance and boorishness . . . prevented him from seeing that she was refusing" (2002, 11). Most people's intuitions (according to

Bird) count against the view that uptake is necessary for successful refusals.

I do not share this intuition though. As I see it, Bird is mistaken about the role of uptake since he does not sufficiently appreciate the communicative nature of refusals. Of course, successful illocution and communication are not equivalent. However, illocutionary refusals are not just intimately connected to communication; they are *essentially* communicative. Hornsby is right (I contend) that a hallmark of communication is reciprocity: when it fails, interlocutors are talking at cross-purposes. This is precisely what happens when illocutionary refusals misfire, which (as Hornsby and Langton originally argued) demonstrates such misfirings to involve communicative failures. When one is faced with unwanted sex (or food) and utters "No!" the usual way to read this situation is to take one's locution as intending to communicate something to someone else. The speaker aims to express herself to another with the view to producing some effects: that the hearer grasps the locution as a refusal and stops. The utterance does not simply express the speaker's disapproving opinion about the sexual advances. Rather, the locution is the verbal equivalent to kicking and punching one's adversary.

Imagine that this is all that one can do; perhaps one is gagged and, therefore, unable to make any locutions. Suppose further that the person has voluntarily been gagged. For instance, imagine that the protagonists are actors rehearsing for a play with a scene involving gagging. Now, suppose that the one playing the perpetrator has falsely come to believe that there is sexual chemistry between the actors, that his co-player has been flirting with him, and that she has expressed a desire to be gagged and "taken by force." For some reason, the misguided thespian thinks that this is precisely the moment to act on those (false) beliefs. He starts making his advances and, unable to speak, the co-actor begins to physically resist. However, the misguided actor takes the kicking and punching to be coy and implicit invitations for more. He has not appreciated that his co-actor is attempting to tell him to stop. On the Bird model of illocution, all that matters for successful refusal is physical resistance. After all, successful illocution depends on "the words [locuted], their normal meaning and the context alone" (Bird 2002, 13), where kicking and punching are physical counterparts to words. But to say that the co-actor refused, although she failed to communicate this due to which the misguided actor failed to register the refusal, strikes me as wrongheaded. A more plausible description of the situation is that the co-actor not only failed to communicate refusal but that she also failed to refuse: she merely unsuccessfully *tried* to refuse. If we are less ready in this case to grant that successful (though noncommunicated) refusal took place, we should revise our view of the parallel verbal case. After all, the locution "No!" has a dual aim: to refuse sex *and* to communicate this to the hearer. Insofar as this is the case, uptake is necessary for illocutionary success at least of refusals.

McGowan (2009a) identifies a different flaw in Bird's case: he takes Hornsby and Langton to claim that refusals are *purely* communicative, when they are merely highlighting the importance of communicating sexual refusals. If all that matters for illocutionary success is communication, McGowan holds, we get the wrong results. She offers the following example. Imagine that Cindy successfully communicates to Carl that Sally is unwilling to have sex with him. On the purely communicative view of illocutions, Cindy would have refused sex on Sally's behalf. However, Cindy's communication of the refusal would not count as Sally refusing sex with Carl because only Sally can issue such a refusal. If the silencing claim is committed to a purely communicative view, it looks prima facie implausible. But (McGowan holds and rightly so) this is not Hornsby and Langton's view. In taking refusing to be an excercitive speech act, it is a sort of communication-plus speech act, where "plus" highlights the relevance of speaker authority. That is, uptake is crucial for the communication part and authority for the "plus" part of the speech act. And the two can work in concert: sometimes what blocks uptake is precisely that one is not considered to be authoritative as a speaker. Just think back to the case of the actor trying to warn an audience about a fire. On Bird's view, just locuting "Danger, fire!" suffices for successful warning. But precisely because one's role as an actor prevents the audience from recognizing the intended illocutionary intention to warn, the locution does not count as a warning. In this case, there is a failure of uptake intertwined with speaker authority. All of these aspects are lost in Bird's view that successful illocutions depend on "the words [locuted], their normal meaning and the context alone" (2002, 13).

One might say in Bird's defense that what goes wrong with the above example and in cases of sexual attacks is that, although the speaker sincerely intends to warn/refuse, their interlocutor(s) take the warning/refusal to be insincere. Austin takes this sort of failure to be an abuse, as opposed to a misfire, of speech. Now, Bird thinks that this is a much more plausible account of what happens in cases of alleged illocutionary disablement (2002, 6–7). However, he fails to provide a convincing argument for putative misfirings of refusals being actual abuses of refusals. Consider a different case of warning that Bird takes to be analogous to refusing.

> A burglar enters a property at night. He has seen a clearly displayed sign: "Warning: premises patrolled by fierce dogs" but believes this is just a blind, intended to mislead people ... he later discovers his mistake when attacked by the patrolling dogs. The burglar has no right to claim that he was not in fact warned ... He was warned alright, but he failed to see that the warning was sincere. (2002, 10)

First of all, note that Bird runs together two different ways in which speech acts can be unsuccessful (or infelicitous): the sign is not taken as a *warning,* and the sign is not taken as a *sincere* warning. He begins by noting that the burglar believes the sign to be a blind—so he does not believe it to be a warning. But if this is the case, when the burglar encounters the dogs, the failure he discovers should not be that he should have taken the sign as a sincere warning. Rather, the mistake he should discover is that he should have taken the sign as a warning to begin with. (Independently of one another, Mikkola [2011] and McGowan et al. [2011] discuss this point in detail.) Presumably Bird's intended reading of this example is that the burglar takes the sign as a warning but thinks that it is insincere: the owners really are warning people not to enter, but they probably do not have fierce dogs. But now the failure in the burglary case becomes disanalogous to the failure in the sexual assault case and in the case of Jacques. Jacques did not believe that Sara's refusal was insincere since he did not believe Sara was refusing. He misinterprets Sara's behavior from the start. The locus of the failure is the primary interpretation of the relevant behavior, not whether that behavior is subsequently interpreted as sincere or not. If Jacques did not see Sara's locution as a refusal, he could not have seen it as an insincere refusal. The former is clearly a necessary precondition for the latter. The case of the burglar is different: if he believes the sign to be an insincere warning, he must have taken it as a warning to begin with. Here the failure does *not* pertain to the primary interpretation of the sign (whether it is a warning or not); rather, it pertains to how the warning sign is subsequently understood (whether it is sincere or not).

This disanalogy has significant consequences. Bird's arguments are aimed at convincing us that uptake is not necessary for illocutionary success. But the example of warning, which is meant to convince us of this, is an abuse. The Hornsby-Langton view does not analyze silencing of sexual refusals as abuses though, but as misfires.

Bird's critique ends up oscillating between abuses and misfires, and subsequently his argument misses its target: he argues that we can see why uptake failures are not necessary for misfires by appealing to evidence from abuses. Since these are two different *kinds* of infelicitous speech acts, we cannot use evidence from one to explicate the other. Otherwise we end up comparing apples and oranges. Now, Bird might, of course, think that Hornsby and Langton *should* analyze silencing of sexual refusals on the model of abuses, rather than as misfires. Actually, Bird holds, we can describe putative illocutionary disablements of refusals in ways that show them to be actual confusions between insincere and sincere refusals. And the latter description is supposedly "more psychologically plausible" (Bird 2002, 6), which is why the illocutionary disablement sense of silencing should be rejected. The evidence that Bird takes to prove his point comes from thinking about the culpability of rapists. I will turn to this line of argument next.

3.4. PRACTICAL CONSEQUENCES OF THE SILENCING CLAIM

Those critical of the silencing claim hold that there are further pressing grounds to reject it: it allegedly diminishes rapists' responsibility. Although the specifics of sexual assault legislation vary in different jurisdictions, a rape conviction must typically satisfy two jurisprudential conditions: the *actus reus* (the guilty act) and the *mens rea* (the guilty mind) requirements. What counts as the guilty act differs, and in some jurisdictions only a forced penile penetration of a vagina counts as rape, while other nonconsensual sex acts count as sexual assaults. But since rape falls under criminal law, a rape conviction must typically satisfy the guilty mind requirement: the guilty act must be intentionally, rather than accidentally, perpetrated.

(Just think of other crimes requiring intention too. For instance, it seems highly implausible that someone could accidentally rob a bank.) With these requirements in mind, some jurisdictions hold that if a man engages in sex with a woman *honestly* believing that she consented, however unreasonable this belief may be, he does not do so with "a guilty mind." Bluntly: he is being incredibly stupid and/ or reckless, but this does not suffice for a serious criminal conviction.[5] Now, Bird maintains that if the silencing claim holds, alleged perpetrators are less culpable or even exonerated in that they won't have committed rape. Daniel Jacobson also takes the phenomenon of illocutionary disablement to have the "strange and troubling consequence" that if women fail to illocute refusals and sex is forced on them, we "*cannot call this rape*" (1995, 77). This supposedly renders the Hornsby-Langton view practically indefensible. In fact, Bird takes these consequences to support the view that putative illocutionary misfires should be interpreted as actual abuses of refusals (where sincere refusals are interpreted as insincere).

However, this line of argument is deeply flawed. First, even if the silencing claim exonerates perpetrators, we have no reason to accept that putative illocutionary disablements of refusals are actual confusions between insincere and sincere refusals. Such "troubling" legal consequences do not demonstrate that the latter description is "more psychologically plausible" (Bird 2002, 6). Second, the silencing claim is in trouble *only if* the lack of refusal entails consent. After all, the determination of rape does not turn on whether the victim refused but on whether they consented to sex. For example, in English law, if the victim did not consent, the *actus reus* of rape is satisfied—whether the victim refused is neither here nor there. So, we must not conflate consent with nonrefusal: a failure to illocute refusal does not entail that one has illocuted consent to sex instead.

5. For more on the *mens rea* requirement, see Archard (1999) and Baron (2001).

Granted, neither Bird nor Jacobson explicitly state that consent is entailed by the absence of refusal. But the "if no refusal, then no rape" argument only gets off the ground and seems plausible if we accept this implicit and false extra premise (that nonrefusal entails consent).[6] Third, *contra* Jacobson, even if the *mens rea* requirement is not satisfied, this does not entail that rape did not take place. Consider the infamous English case of *R v. Cogan and Leak* ([1976] QB 217). Mr. Leak persuaded Mr. Cogan to have sex with Mrs. Leak while he watched. Leak further convinced Cogan that his wife liked having sex forced on her and that she consented to Cogan doing so. In fact, Leak arranged this to punish his wife who had refused the previous day to give him money while he was drunk. Both Cogan and Leak acknowledged that Mrs. Leak was sobbing while Cogan was assaulting her. Nonetheless, Cogan took her to be consenting because Mr. Leak said so. The presiding judge admitted that intoxication seemed to be the only reason for taking the sobbing and distress mistakenly as consent. But given English law, Cogan was acquitted of rape: however unreasonable, Cogan's mistaken belief that Mrs. Leak had consented was an honest one, and Cogan failed to satisfy the *mens rea* requirement. However, Mr. Leak was found guilty of aiding and abetting rape: the court held that even though Cogan could not legally be found guilty of rape, rape had nonetheless taken place and this was due to Mr. Leak's actions. So, even in the eyes of the law, it may be impossible to sentence someone and yet acknowledge that rape took place. Bird and Jacobson's critiques, then, rely on false legal premises.

Nellie Wieland (2007) has put forward a more sophisticated variant of the above argument. The silencing claim takes pornographers as authoritative convention setters in sexual discourse or "the language of sex": women face illocutionary silencing because their "No!"

---

6. I discuss these points further in my (2011 article); independently of my discussion, so does McGowan et al. (2011).

is taken to mean *yes*. However, accepting this (according to Wieland) diminishes perpetrators' culpability because they cannot satisfy the *mens rea* requirement:

> *if* there is a convention of women meaning *yes* by uttering "no" in relevant [sexual] contexts, then it is no longer the case that men *mis*interpret women as meaning *yes* by uttering "no" in contexts of unwanted sexual encounters; but rather, men correctly interpret "no" as meaning *yes* in these contexts given the establishment of the convention. The result is that these speakers have *no words* to express their refusal of an unwanted sexual encounter. (Wieland 2007, 445)

If pornographic speech is responsible for such a meaning switch so that women's attempted refusals are honestly taken as granting consent, the *mens rea* requirement will not be fulfilled. In fact, Wieland continues, if the convention set by pornography (that "no" means *yes*) is stable and not easily countered, it makes women illocutionarily silenced and perpetrators interpretatively disabled. If the silencing claim holds, pornography makes women unable to voice refusals and their attackers unable to understand refusals, which leaves us with no "reason for thinking that a rapist should be able to understand a victim's meaning that *p* by uttering 'x'" (Wieland 2007, 452). This allegedly excuses rape.

Wieland is right to claim that if Hornsby and Langton are correct about women's illocutionary disablement, this ill fits legislation outlawing rape that requires *mens rea* for conviction. Wieland even accepts that women have been silenced if the perpetrator can reasonably claim to having obtained consent. But, she holds, "this is crazy and has got to be wrong" (2007, 453). I agree that this is crazy and wrong. Still, Wieland's argument does not speak against the silencing claim or shows that *it* is wrong. Rather, a law that allows a defense along the lines of "I honestly thought she meant *yes* when she said 'no' " is wrong. When philosophy clashes with the law, this might give us good reasons to reformulate the latter. So, pointing out that illocutionary disablement legally diminishes the *mens rea* of perpetrators does not yet count against Hornsby and Langton. Doing so would require a further independent argument that establishes the adequacy of our current *mens rea* requirement and shows it to be worth preserving. In the absence of such an argument, though, if pornographers are able to create conventions where women's "no" means *yes*, we should seriously take this into account when formulating rape and sexual assault legislation by rethinking the *mens rea* requirement. Just think of the case of *R v. Cogan and Leak:* What would correct the mistake that Cogan was exonerated for the rape? Giving up the silencing claim seems wrongheaded; rather, the mistake would be corrected by taking the claim seriously and reforming the relevant legislation to undermine the "I honestly thought she meant *yes* when she said 'no' " defense. In fact, Wieland's argument seemingly *supports* the silencing claim: if interpretative disablement is widespread and at least partly due to pornographic speech, the effects of such speech are even more pernicious than antipornography feminists initially realized. It demonstrates the need for sexual communication education to eradicate illocutionary silencing *and* interpretative disablement. That said, although Wieland's analysis of interpretative disablement has pretheoretical appeal, it is probably due to various factors rather than just pornographic speech. (Just think of the *Cogan* case.) The link to pornographic speech thus remains to be established.

Others have raised doubts about whether the linguistic conventions Wieland identifies do obtain (although some discuss this point without directly referring to Wieland). First, Antony holds that even if pornography degrades, dehumanizes, and insults women, it does not obviously result in illocutionary silencing. This is because "the erotic effect" of pornographic materials hinges on "representations of things being done to women *against their will*" (Antony 2011, 398). That is, unless women's refusals are taken to be refusals, the intended erotic effects won't obtain. Such effects require perpetrators to have the ability to recognize refusals and not to suffer from interpretative disablement. Bluntly: the kinds of erotic effects that violent, inegalitarian pornography celebrates are premised on men understanding women's "No!" as a *no*, which counts against there being a meaning switch. Second, Angela Grünberg offers a slightly different elucidation of the meaning switch, where "the hearer takes the sense and reference of the word 'no' *not* to be the meaning that it conventionally has" (2014, 182). That is, we have a meaning switch because the hearer and the speaker in a sense occupy different contexts: the speaker operates within the conventional context (where "no" means *no*), whereas the hearer operates within a fictional "context of sex" (where "no" means *yes*). And so, when a woman utters "no" intending to refuse, the hearer takes her to be operating in a fictional context governed by pornographic meanings where "no" means *yes*. Arguably, though, this mistake isn't unavoidable. The perpetrator should epistemically be in a position to see that their context is not the conventional one. And so, perpetrators are not absolved from responsibility: after all, most of us most of the time can tell the difference between fictional and nonfictional contexts. Third, Maitra and McGowan (2010) doubt the pervasiveness of the proposed meaning switch: even though the no-means-*yes* convention might be operative in pornographic contexts, it takes a lot of effort for that convention to spread in the required manner. For the convention to obtain more generally, it would have to be "a regularity in behaviour among a population in certain current situations . . . where it is common knowledge in that population that everyone conforms to that regularity, everyone expects everyone else to conform, and so on" (Maitra and McGowan 2010, 169). But this simply does not hold; for one thing, women who say "No!" meaning *no* do not conform to the convention. Wieland's meaning switch is a hypothetical case; but it does not exonerate actual perpetrators of sexualized violence insofar as the meaning switch actually fails to obtain.[7]

Maitra and McGowan (2010) and Maitra (2004) further discuss the view that if pornography interferes with communication in a manner that produces systematic illocutionary and interpretative disablement, perpetrators cannot be held responsible for their actions—rather, pornography is somehow the responsible party. They, nevertheless, reject this. Imagine that while driving I am distracted by my passengers and this causes a serious accident. Despite the causal explanatory chains leading to my passengers, I am no less responsible for the subsequent accident. The same goes for pornography: even if it plays a causal role in generating communicative disablement, perpetrators of sexualized violence are no less individually responsible for their actions. Or rather: if such disablement were ubiquitous and could not be helped, perpetrators would be absolved from responsibility. But this is simply not the case because the force of pornography is not deterministic.

3.5. ALTERNATIVE ACCOUNTS OF SILENCING

The main thrust of the Hornsby-Langton account is that silencing in the illocutionary disablement sense involves communicative interference: the hearer fails to recognize the speaker's illocutionary intention (what sort of a speech act the speaker aims to perform), where this is brought about in a systematic manner by pornographic speech. This is a novel sense of silencing in addition to the more familiar case

---

7. McGowan et al. (2011) further argue that Wieland is wrong to analyze the Hornsby-Langton account in terms of a meaning switch. Rather, more central to Hornsby and Langton are communicative failures of refusals.

of perlocutionary frustration, where a woman's "No!" is recognized as a refusal but ignored. Above I looked at two lines of argument against the Hornsby-Langton view: it is philosophically untenable in not being faithful to Austin's original view, and it is practically unsupportable because illocutionary silencing allegedly diminishes rapists' culpability. Both lines of attack, I contend, fail, and we have no good grounds to abandon the idea of illocutionary disablement just yet (although we are still to establish that pornography specifically generates such disablement). In discussing the Hornsby-Langton view of sexual refusals, Mary Kate McGowan has identified yet further ways in which women's refusals might be silenced. McGowan does not argue that the Hornsby-Langton analysis is implausible; rather, it is incomplete.

Let's look at possible further ways in which pornography may silence women next. McGowan holds that it is odd to call perlocutionary frustration a type of silencing at all precisely because the speaker's linguistic intentions were recognized (albeit ignored). In fact, for her, perlocutionary frustration is not a type of silencing. Still, McGowan holds that there are ways in which sexual refusals might be silenced in addition to illocutionary disablement. McGowan (2009a) develops (what I call) *authority-failure silencing* that is constituted by the hearer's failure to grant the speaker authority over some relevant domain. What goes wrong in failed sexual refusals is that the speaker fails to exercise her authority over the domain of sexual access to her body. Elsewhere McGowan (2014) argues for *sincerity silencing*. Pornography may shape men's conceptions of women's sexuality in ways that, when faced with unwanted sex, women's locution "No!" is taken as an insincere refusal. This is a variant of the "I thought she was being coy and meant *yes* when she said 'no'" case. To clarify: in the illocutionary disablement sense of silencing, the perpetrator does not take a woman's "No!" as a refusal at all. In the sincerity silencing case, they take "No!" as a refusal but think that the woman is not *sincerely* refusing. In the former case, we have a failure of the speaker's illocutionary intention condition, in the latter, a failure of the speaker's sincerity condition. McGowan (2017) explicates a still further type of silencing: *true feelings-recognition failure*. This is a case where

> a woman says "No," sincerely intending to refuse sex, but although the addressee recognizes her sincere refusal, the addressee nevertheless falsely believes that refusing is not what the speaker's "deep self" really wants. Suppose, for example, that the addressee believes that the woman will change her mind as soon as she realizes how amazing he is. (McGowan 2017, 49)

Such a case, McGowan holds, is distinct in kind from the other types of silencing in that the illocutionary intention, authority, and sincerity conditions have been fulfilled.

These alternative types of silencing raise two questions though: Are the above genuinely different types of silencing or variants of the same type? And is pornographic speech responsible for any of them? With the latter issue in mind, McGowan (2017) suggests that pornography causes the requisite types of silencing: it conceivably causes its consumers to have false beliefs, and it sexually conditions them in ways that hinder the recognition of the relevant conditions (intention, authority, sincerity, and true feelings conditions). McGowan further considers pornography's constitutive role in silencing. She holds that pornography enacts norms that silence. For instance, relative to true feelings-recognition silencing, pornography enacts norms that comply with certain rape myths (e.g., women really want sex even when they think otherwise). Deep down women want to be "taken by force," but they have simply been gender socialized to hide this. Abiding by norms like this may then "systematically prevent the recognition of the speaker's true feelings of refusal" (McGowan 2017, 56). Now, these ways of bringing about silencing may certainly be grounded in pornography consumption; but as of yet, the empirical evidence does not back up the claim that pornography *in particular* causes and constitutes these types of silencing. Plenty of gendered norms and role expectations conceivably interfere with the satisfaction of the above conditions. One might point out that these types of silencing were commonplace well before the onset of contemporary pornography production and consumption on mass scale. In fact, a central case of silencing that McGowan (and Maitra) make use of comes from Jane Austen's *Pride and Prejudice*, which in no way connects to pornographic materials. A more convincing case, then, must be made of pornography's role in women's silencing.

Furthermore, I am not entirely convinced that McGowan has offered genuinely alternative *types* of silencing. Her view is that authority silencing is a distinct phenomenon to that identified by Hornsby and Langton (failure to recognize a speaker's illocutionary intention). But, as I noted earlier, uptake and speaker authority often work in concert: many uptake failures turn on the hearer not taking the speaker to be authoritative over some relevant domain. As Langton (1993, 322) originally put it, something about the speaker—about her social role or position—prevents the hearer from grasping her illocutionary intention. This homes in precisely on the type of silencing that McGowan takes to be an alternative to illocutionary silencing. It seems to me rather more plausible to say that illocutionary silencing and authority failure silencing are the *same type* of silencing, but our explanations of what goes wrong in particular instances hinges on different aspects of the phenomenon. Or, not recognizing illocutionary intention and not recognizing speaker authority are part and parcel of the same failure in a sense that there is no clear break between them. Moreover, I am not convinced that the failure to recognize the speaker's true feelings is a genuinely distinct type of silencing. Instead, it strikes me as a variant of authority silencing: the hearer does not take me as authoritative about my "true feelings," and the hearer thinks that they know what I really want better than I do. In short, I disagree with McGowan that in this case the authority condition has been fulfilled and that "the speaker's exercise of authority is recognized" (McGowan 2017, 49). In a case where sex is forced on someone because the perpetrator thinks that the victim really "deep down" does want sex, I do not see how the exercise of authority over one's body is recognized. Actually, this phenomenon also strikes me as a variant of Hornsby and Langton's original type of silencing, although McGowan provides helpful details of how such silencing may be brought about.

What about sincerity silencing? It is different in kind from illocutionary silencing. However, I am less convinced that sincerity silencing comes apart from perlocutionary frustration, where a woman's "No!" is recognized as a refusal but simply ignored. Sincerity silencing does essentially the same: the perpetrator ignores the refusal because they think the refusal is insincere. But it is not obvious to me that this is substantively different from perlocutionary frustration. Think about why women's refusals might be ignored. One rather obvious (and, I fear, frequent) reason is that the refusal is taken to be insincere. Other cases involve straightforwardly ignoring the refusal even when it is recognized as sincere. But both are variants of the same case: refusals are recognized as refusals but (for different reasons) ignored. Pointing out that one of these cases involves a failure to satisfy the sincerity condition does not yet carve out a substantively different and novel type of silencing in social space. If there is no substantive difference here, McGowan's alternative type of silencing is in trouble. She denies that perlocutionary frustration of refusals counts as silencing. But if her account of sincerity silencing turns out to be a variant of perlocutionary frustration, she will have to deny that sincerity silencing is an alternative type of silencing or she must admit that perlocutionary frustration is a kind of silencing.[8]

3.6. PORNOGRAPHY'S AUTHORITY

The above does not yet establish that pornography in particular undergirds illocutionary disablement. For instance, gender norms, expectations, romance novels, and media in general also enact communicative conditions that seemingly interfere with women's ability to do things with their words and men's ability to understand women's utterances. To show pornography's role in (re)creating such communicative conditions, we need to establish that pornography is somehow—as Langton puts it—authoritative over the domain of sex. Quite a lot hinges on establishing authoritativeness. It not only supports the silencing claim but also the subordination claim, along with the view that pornography hampers women's autonomy (section 2.5.). However, the idea that pornography and pornographers are in some requisite sense authoritative has generated much resistance. I next discuss some important contributions to the debate.

Langton takes there to be empirical evidence for pornography's authoritativeness insofar as young people (and young men in particular) are increasingly treating pornography as sex education. In a recent paper, Langton (2017) discusses the 2013 report from the UK Office of the Children's Commissioner (Maddy et al. 2013). This large-scale report found that many respondents take pornography to educate them about sex and that such education is in many ways

---

8. Maitra (2009) develops the silencing claim by drawing on Paul Grice, rather than Austin. However, although her position is inspired by discussions that link silencing and pornography, Maitra's explicit aim is not to argue for or discuss such a link. Rather, she proposes an alternative account of silencing in general that may be due to many different factors, like racist hate speech.

problematic. Consumption of pornography was linked to hetero-sexual boys' unrealistic expectations about sex with corresponding feelings in girls that they must submit to boys' expectations irrespective of their own wishes. (For similar results, see Paul 2005.) The report offers compelling evidence for the claim that many young people consider pornographic materials to offer authoritative guidance on sex.[9]

However, Antony holds that this sense of *authority* is not that of Austin's. 'Authority' as Langton's employs it can only be used to determine whether pornography as a pernicious type of sex education has perlocutionary effects (Antony 2011, 396; see also section 2.5 in the previous chapter). But this is not the sense of *authority* Austin had in mind when thinking about illocutionary speech acts; rather, his sense was about linguistic competence and about authority as a competent language user. Judith Butler (1997) also argues that the appeal to authority fails, irrespective of any empirical issues and whether pornography has real-world effects on people. Her view pertains to the internal workings of language: there is a "gap" between speech (or speakers' intentions) and its effects on recipients because speech can always be "resignified." Meanings are not stable in the sense presumed by advocates of the speech act theory because the conventions governing speech are always open to subversion. One of the most celebrated examples is that of 'queer': it has undergone a resignification from a pejorative term to proud self-identification. The act of appropriating the term subverted the earlier problematic meaning.

---

9. It is worth noting that the educational value of pornography is likely to differ significantly for heterosexual and nonheterosexual youth. Gender nonconforming youth and those who fall outside of heteronormative sexualities more often find pornographic depictions of nonheteronormative sexualities valuable educationally and in legitimating their identities (Albury 2014). Disability activists have also welcomed pornography with atypically functioning bodies in order to disrupt the stereotype of "disabled" people as asexual. In these ways, pornography is also authoritative but in beneficial ways—something Langton does not discuss. I will return to the emancipatory potential of pornography in chapter 7.

And so, bluntly put, whatever meaning-intentions pornographers might have, they lack the authority to enforce those intentions because audiences can always engage in reappropriation or subversion of pornographic meanings. For instance, feminist audiences can "turn the tables" and "read" pornographic materials in subversive ways, thus disrupting pornography's pernicious meanings. The sheer possibility of subverting pornographic meanings shows it to lack the requisite sort of authority presupposed by the speech act approach: if it were to have it, its authority would be "divine."

Langton (2009b,) denies that her approach assumes a divine conception of authority, where speakers' intentions always transpire in their intended effects. (See also Schwartzman 2002 for a critique of Butler.) She accepts that feminists can offer subversive readings of pornography but holds that this does not undermine the silencing claim, because silencing is a context-dependent phenomenon. So even though in some contexts subversively interpreted pornographic materials do not silence, in other contexts they may well do. Furthermore, Langton takes Butler's hopes for deconstructive and subversive readings of pornography to be hyperbolic:

> It is not easy to see how such readings are supposed to reveal to pornography's usual consumers, and their partners, the "unrealizability," the self-defeatingness, of pornography's norms. How does a reading of pornography "against itself" help those women who are abused and exploited in its making? How does it affect those men who want their sex lives, and their partners, to resemble ever more closely what pornography offers them? (Langton 2009b, 115)

For Langton, pornography's authority is greater than the force of deconstruction. An argument to the best explanation demonstrates this: perlocutionary effects on our normative beliefs about sex and our subsequent actions are better explained by assuming that pornography has authority context dependently than by assuming that "pornography has no authority" (Langton 2009b, 111).

Even though I share Langton's skepticism about the efficacy of deconstruction, her critique of Butler does not entirely succeed. Langton draws an opposition between pornography having no authority and pornography having authority (in a context) and proceeds to reject the former view. However, this way of demarcating the disagreement isn't entirely right. As I see it, Butler does not hold that pornography has no *force*; she simply denies that this force is somehow unique to pornography. Or to put the point differently: Butler does not deny that pornography has *power* to (re)produce meanings. Antony helpfully elucidates the nature of pornography's power to be "a matter of being able to arrange contingencies, to make things be the way you want" (2017, 79). Pornographic meanings cannot be (re)produced without discursive force and power. But Butler's point is that pornography is not alone in having such power: even those in oppressed social positions have power—otherwise resistance would be impossible. Still, pornography does not have *authority* in the sense of having some special purview over the (re)production of meanings; after all, feminist readings can (re)produce and subvert pornographic meanings. In her response to Butler, however, Langton fails to note this subtle distinction between power and authority, and the two end up talking past one another.

One might critique Langton for confusing authority with power in other ways too (Antony 2014, 2017; Drabek 2016). Being authoritative as a speaker to enact women's subordination and silencing can only take place within some established and institutionalized conventions; but since in pornography such conventions are missing, Langton's approach is undermined. Antony (2014) elucidates this with a distinction between conventional and de facto subordination.

(Although Antony makes her argument relative to the subordination claim, it also applies to the silencing claim.) Conventional subordination requires authority relative to some domain; for instance, being a legislator in Pretoria during Apartheid came with authority in the requisite sense to enact laws that deprived black South Africans voting rights. This sort of authority is necessary for performing exercitive speech acts, and it is institutionally governed. An ordinary white South African could have made the same locutions, but they would not thereby enact discriminatory laws. Still, ordinary white South Africans had *power* over black South Africans by virtue of the social and political structures in place. They were powerful in being able effectively to treat black South Africans as inferior, despite lacking the necessary conventionally governed authority over some relevant domain(s). This suggests that we should shift our focus: Langton takes pornographers to have authority over the domain of sex in offering pernicious sex education. But since there are no clear conventions framing this sort of authority in the required sense, we must look to pornography's audiences to see what is really doing the work. This is where power comes in:

> [S]haping the beliefs and attitudes of men is not the full extent of the power of the pornographers. Insofar as the members of pornography's audience are powerful—insofar as pornography exists within a patriarchal society—the consumers of pornography have the ability to shape reality itself. Expecting certain behavior from women, they can coerce women into displaying it. (Antony 2014, 163)

In short, pornography's authority is rather limited, and it is separate from the kind of authority typically required to make verdictive and exercitive speech acts. Instead, the background structures that give consumers power to shape social reality in certain ways are of central importance. For Antony, focusing on this part of the story neverthe-less in no sense hinges on Austin's speech act theory.

A similar thought seemingly undergirds Nancy Bauer's (2015) critique of Langton. Bauer asks: Why is it that pornography appar-ently makes people see the world in a certain way and thus has perlo-cutionary effects in the world? Why is it that consumers "acquiesce to the pornographer's point of view" (Bauer 2015, 80)? These effects for Bauer cannot be explained in terms of pornographers' authority. Instead, a more fruitful feminist analysis requires that we refocus our attentions away from speakers and their illocutionary intentions to-ward hearers and why certain perlocutionary effects are possible. Bluntly: problematic perlocutionary effects in the "real world" are not due to producers' authority but due to consumers granting pornographic speech particular powers to shape actual social rela-tions. Leslie Green's (1998) critique of the silencing claim echoes this thought as well. Pornography has power not by virtue of what it says but rather as a function of "the whole social context in which it occurs" (Green 1998, 294).[10] Moreover, pornography has no au-thority over women—its jurisdiction only covers men and boys. The only way in which pornography could be authoritative, Green posits, is if pornography managed to establish some effective pornographic norms to govern sexual relations generally. However, he doubts the existence and efficacy of such norms insofar as the "standard use" of pornography is not to treat it as authoritative about sex but as offering consumers "masturbation materials" (Green 1998, 296).

Langton (1998) has responded to Green in a manner that (I hold) also responds to Antony and Bauer. At times, Langton does

---

10. Linda LeMoncheck also holds that the reason pornographic lies about women—that women are "natural" sexual subordinates of men—have any purchase is that such lies are already part of gendered stereotypes and role expectations (1997, 130). This is where pornography's power derives from.

run power and authority together in a manner that suggests she is conflating the two. However, looking at her response to Green dispels this concern. Langton accepts that pornography is not authoritative to (most) women in the sense of providing pernicious sex education. But even though pornography's authority only extends to some men and boys, it can still subordinate women. This depends on whether the group that takes pornography to be authoritative also holds social power—and, as it stands, typical consumers of pornography (namely, men) do hold social power. Langton draws the following analogy: imagine a powerful religious organization has authority over a small but socially powerful minority. Now imagine that this organization condemns homosexuality and has the authority to convince its followers that homosexuality is a sin. Even though the church in this case does not have the authority to hire and fire those with differing views, the socially powerful members of the society convinced by the church's message can enact such subordinating practices. That is, they have the power to make the church's teachings "real" in the world. In this sense, even those who reject the church's authority are still indirectly under its jurisdiction. So we can see a sort of two-tier way in which subordination is enacted: first from the church to the ruling group via the former's authority; then from the group to the wider society via the exercise of social power. Power and authority work in concert. This tells us two important things about Langton's speech act approach: she does not always conflate power and authority; and even if pornography's authority is limited and consumers' power is more influential, it does not suffice to focus on the latter alone. A deeper social explanation of pornography's effects in the world should also bear in mind the sort of authority that pornography has over sex. Irrespective of whether pornographers wish to be authoritative about sex, they are so for many—especially for young men. And even if pornographers' authority derives from less conventionally regulated and more diffuse social arrangements, this does not undermine Langton's claim that pornography has authority over the domain of sex. We must simply remember that producers' authority is intertwined with consumers' (social) power—something that Langton (1998) is acutely aware of, albeit being something that she misses in her response to Butler (as I argued above).[11]

More recently, Langton (2017) has distinguished epistemic and practical authority, which may further diffuse the charge that Langton conflates power and authority. Practical authority is necessary for making exercitive speech acts (just think of parents' having such authority over their children). Epistemic authority is about being or being perceived to be an expert about some domain. One can have practical authority even when others reject one's authority. If I have a certain institutional status to enact laws, I have the authority to enact laws irrespective of whether others respect or acknowledge this authority. Epistemic authority is subtly different, and it hinges on others recognizing me as an expert in some area. Langton takes pornography to have both types of authority insofar as young people self-report turning to pornography for information about sex. But note importantly that epistemic authority depends on the power that consumers grant pornography as a source of information. Bluntly: if no one took pornography to be informative about sex, it would not be taken to have epistemic authority—pornographers would not be considered experts about sex. Here, too, we can see the subtle difference between pornographers' authority to enact something (e.g., subordinating norms) and their power to shape our social realities.

---

11. We might have further reasons to favor the focus on power over authority. After all, as some hold, pornography has the power to deprive women of sexual autonomy. In fact, pornography appears to hamper *men's* sexual autonomy too (Ezzell 2014), which very vividly illustrates its power to shape our lives. In the light of this, we need not settle how authoritative pornographers are in order to see pornography's power to mold real-life circumstances.

One might argue in Langton's defense that there is still a further sense of authority that does not fall prey to some of the above critiques. McGowan (2003) argues that the sort of authority required to make exercitive speech acts need not be governed by institutionalized conventions, such as in the case of enacting laws. She draws a distinction between Austinian and conversational exercitives. Although the exercise of the former requires that some conventionally and institutionally governed background conditions are in place, the latter does not. Ordinary conversations are governed by loose conventions, and ordinary speaker authority fixes what is permissible within such conversations. Moreover, this involves exercitive speech acts, albeit not obviously. For instance, if I say to someone, "My neighbor's cat Lucky keeps sneaking into my house," I have made Lucky the most salient cat in this conversation. This (according to McGowan) is a conversational exercitive, and I have fixed what is permissible in the conversation to follow. If my interlocutor then replies, "That cat is crazy," taking 'that cat' to refer to some cat other than Lucky, they have in a very ordinary sense done something conversationally impermissible. In a sense, my interlocutor has made an impermissible "move" in our conversation. Understanding pornography with such conversational exercitives in mind avoids the problem of institutionalized authority because we need not hold that pornographic speech is governed by institutionalized conventions. That said, McGowan is careful to stress that she is arguing for a possible way to understand the exercitive force of pornography—not that she is arguing for the *truth* of the thesis. Still, McGowan is right to point out that there are perfectly ordinary ways in which we authorize certain moves in everyday communication, and so, the apparent lack of pornography's institutionalized authority does not yet undermine the speech act approach. Drawing on this idea, Langton has more recently suggested that we should understand what pornography does on a pragmatic model, where its illocutionary force hinges on pornography altering normative facts about what is permissible and possible in a conversational context. Subsequently, Langton admits that this would enable us to see how speech can change beliefs and norms without requiring that the speakers satisfy strong Austinian felicity conditions for exercitives (Langton 2012, 84).

3.7. METHODOLOGICAL LESSONS

In this chapter, I have considered the silencing claim that Langton and Hornsby have influentially advanced. First, despite extensive literature discussing this claim, it remains to be established that pornographic speech is responsible for women's silencing. In fact, philosophical debates about silencing often have merely a tenuous connection to pornography. Second, the silencing claim is regularly discussed by appealing to intuitive gut-feelings about specific cases. This is especially so with respect to debates about the success conditions of refusals. Intuitions even play a role in the dispute between Bird and me about the role of uptake in the illocutionary success of refusals. Now, although I too have appealed to intuitions to justify a particular view (namely that uptake is necessary for illocutionary success of refusals since refusing is an essentially communicative act), ultimately I do not find this move methodologically conducive to settling the matter. As it stands, much of the debate ends up trading intuitions, and it seems highly unlikely that we can achieve some consensus on which intuitions will be the "right" ones given how idiosyncratic they tend to be and how greatly our background beliefs and commitments influence the assessment of examples used. Methodologically, I would thus counsel against relying on intuitions as justifications for "our" views about silencing: immediate gut-feelings about particular cases may afford valuable starting points for further inquiry but do not afford particularly reliable and helpful ways to settle disputes. One upshot of this is that the focus on refusals when discussing the silencing claim might be inflated and not conducive to drawing conclusions about pornography in a meaningful sense.

There is a further methodological consideration that I wish to flag. A number of critiques considered in this chapter made the claim that the feminist speech act theoretic appropriation of Austin is in some sense not faithful to the original. Of course, faithfully reconstructing others' views and arguments is highly prized in analytically oriented philosophy and legitimately so. But one might wonder: Does it really matter to the plausibility of Langton and Hornsby's approach whether they followed Austin to the letter? After all, one might find their arguments that are in the *spirit* of Austin nevertheless highly compelling, even if they are merely "Austinian." Just think of the difference between someone doing moral philosophy that follows Kant to the letter and someone doing moral philosophy in a Kantian spirit. Both are legitimate philosophical enterprises. One might then say that the difference between (say) Langton and Antony is that Antony follows Austin to the letter, but Langton only in spirit. Both are worthwhile philosophical projects to engage in and both can tell us something insightful about pornography.

If this is a compelling diagnosis of the source of the disagreement, then some interlocutors in the debates conceivably end up talking past one another—they are engaging in subtly different philosophical projects. For instance, Antony's objections to Langton's treatment of Austin would miss their mark and, at most, we can reproach Langton for not having explicitly noted that she is not intending to follow Austin to the letter. However, this highlights an important further aspect of philosophical debates pertaining to the silencing claim: parties to the debate must be more explicit about their metaphilosophical commitments. That is, if Langton intended to follow Austin in spirit only, she needs to explicitly note this and consider why an Austinian approach nevertheless delivers the desired gains. The silencing claim has generated a substantive philosophical literature and is one of the most debated aspects in philosophical pornography debates. But if those engaged in the debate are undertaking different projects and thus end up talking past one another, we are left with a frustrating situation where the dispute risks becoming merely parochial. Insofar as it is desirable for feminist philosophy to hit the ground running (so to speak) and have an impact on actual societal debates, we would do well to avoid purely insular disputes.

Chapter 4

Free, Regulated, or
Prohibited Speech?

4.1. INTRODUCTION

The previous two chapters considered whether pornography is and/or causes women's subordination and silencing. These issues are usually debated in connection with legal concerns: whether the subordination and silencing claims undermine a free speech defense of pornography. If pornography does what antipornography feminism claims it does, we have a strong legal case for restricting pornography. And, importantly, appealing to the central liberal value of free expression cannot mitigate the incurred harms. The previous chapters discussed the subordination and silencing claims divorced from this legal issue. This chapter considers whether we can plausibly defend legal restrictions on pornography that are compatible with liberalism.

Some preliminaries are in order. Most crucially, we must bear in mind that *regulating* the manufacture, distribution and/or consumption of pornography is not equivalent to *prohibiting* pornography via censorship.[1] Not clearly distinguishing these possible legal responses

---

1. Unhelpfully, different authors use the relevant terms differently. For instance, Kristol (1997) discusses "liberal censorship" of pornography by which he does *not* mean an outright ban that criminalizes pornography production and consumption. Rather, he means

to pornography entrenches the supposed—though misguided—opposition between prudish, antiporn censorship feminism and "pro-sex" liberal champions of free expression. Moreover, regulating some x is not *eo ipso* illiberal. First, the manufacture of goods is regulated in all sorts of ways via (for instance) employment and environmental laws. After all, authorities are justified in closing down dangerous factories that do not comply with health and safety measures, and dangerous work practices cannot be defended by appealing to freedom of action. Second, the distribution of many goods is regulated without this being prima facie an affront to liberty. For instance, in many jurisdictions alcohol can be purchased only from specialized outlets (this is the case to varying degrees in Finland, Sweden, the Netherlands, Canada, and Norway to name but a few examples). In many places, the same goes for tobacco products, and (to the best of my knowledge) legalized cannabis distribution is everywhere restricted to authorized dispensers. Hence, even though this limits our freedom to purchase alcohol, tobacco, or cannabis wherever and whenever, the restrictions are not unreasonable given further legal and societal considerations—we may be inconvenienced, but this is defensible within a liberal framework. Third, the consumption of various goods can be legitimately constrained. In many jurisdictions, smoking is only allowed in designated areas to safeguard nonsmokers. There is a huge difference between prohibiting the consumption of some product (like making smoking illegal) and restricting consumption (like restricting where one can publicly smoke).

What about pornography then? Staunch legal moralists would argue that since we must prevent citizens from engaging in actions

---

pornography regulations compatible with liberalism. And Chester and Dickey outline in their introduction to a collection on feminism and censorship a number of different ways in which feminists tend to understand censorship: "For some women this [term] pertains to state censorship alone; for some it denotes the silencing of oppositional voices ... for others it represents an acceptable method of controlling material" (1988, 1).

that offend prevailing standards of decency and since pornography is indecent and offensive, there is a prima facie justification for outright censorship or prohibition of pornography. Thoroughgoing libertarians would reject any infringements on our liberty of thought and action and would argue that *nothing* should be done about pornography—this is a private matter and of no concern to the state. Antipornography feminism is sometimes equated with legal moralism (Dority 1991), and liberal defenders of pornography are sometimes painted in this libertarian light (Held 2014). However, it is a mistake to draw the opposition in this manner. Feminists and liberals typically reject both extremes, whether they oppose pornography or not. State censorship of materials on the basis of indecency is a blunt instrument that even opponents of pornography view with deep skepticism (Easton 1994, 70–78). And hardly any party to the debate eschews all forms of regulation or intervention—liberal philosophers typically do not hold that *nothing* should be done about pornography or that it is a thoroughly harmless private affair. For instance, if pornography production puts performers in harm's way, we have perfectly legitimate liberal grounds to legally regulate manufacture by (say) coercing production companies to create safer working environments. Between the two extremes, which are practically nonexistent in contemporary philosophical discussions, are many more nuanced views. This chapter then asks two broad questions: Are pornography regulations permissible? If so, in what form? In discussing these issues I endeavor to show the following. First, in disentangling what different feminist and liberal views are committed to, we can see that the supposedly firm opposition between feminist pro-regulation and liberal antiregulation positions is not so firm after all. Instead, there is much common ground between allegedly opposing sides. Second, some pornography regulations are permissible, even within a liberal framework *and* on paternalistic grounds. Third, although we have grounds to regulate pornography, criminalizing pornography production, distribution, and consumption is the wrong response to pornography's problems.

I should say at the outset that much of this chapter focuses on legal discussions pertaining to the United States. This is due to contingent reasons: the relevant philosophical literature tends to be US-focused. As the task of this chapter is to consider debates in legal and political philosophy, I cannot undertake a jurisprudential investigation of different legal systems in order to compare the situations. I will, however, endeavor to address other legal contexts where appropriate along the way.

4.2. PORNOGRAPHY AND THE HARM PRINCIPLE

J. S. Mill's famous harm principle figures prominently in philosophical discussions over pornography. This central liberal principle holds that the state cannot legitimately restrict freedom of opinion and action if there is no harm to *others*. Paternalistic restrictions on freedom of action—ones justified on the basis of those restrictions being good for the individual actors concerned—are usually viewed as illiberal. For instance, restricting smoking in public places is typically justified on the basis of passive smoking being harmful to bystanders. Some people may decide to smoke against their better judgment, but this is a burden of autonomous decision-making that competent adults must bear: we can educate people about the dangers of smoking, but we cannot legitimately prohibit smoking on the grounds that this would be good for the smokers themselves. Such paternalistic justifications (liberals hold) are unacceptable. Liberals typically value freedom (of speech and action) to secure democratic functioning, to foster individuality and autonomy, and to facilitate moral independence of citizens (e.g., Mill [1869] 1974;

R. Dworkin 1981; Scanlon 1972). And so, being a matter of free expression, pornography cannot legitimately be regulated, unless we can show that its manufacture and/or consumption significantly harms others. If the manufacture and consumption of pornography generate no such harms, the state cannot interfere with people's freedoms to partake in and consume pornography however morally depraved other citizens may find this. Now, antipornography feminism (see chaps. 1–3) holds that pornography does harm others— it is *not* a harmless private matter. Pornography subordinates and silences women as a group, which prima facie undermines a liberal free speech–based defense of pornography. In subordinating women, pornography is an affront to women's equality. In systematically interfering with women's communicative capabilities by disabling their illocutionary speech acts, pornography violates women's right to free speech. If we accept the subordination and silencing claims, a defense of pornographic speech that appeals to pornographers' free speech rights does not suffice to mitigate pornography's harms.

In order to understand this better, let me spell out the free speech defense in more detail by sketching some relevant legal background. The First Amendment of the US Constitution states that the US Congress "shall make no law . . . abridging the freedom of speech." Importantly, this does not entail that anything goes—as Stanley Fish (1993) puts it, there is no absolute freedom of speech, and this is a good thing too. In short, not everything that we ordinarily think of as speech counts *legally* as speech. The speech/nonspeech distinction in law does not track its ordinary, everyday counterpart. Some spoken words count legally as nonspeech: for example, perjury, verbal threats, fraud, and conspiracy (Schauer 1979). In legal jargon, they are *not covered* by the First Amendment and raise no free speech concerns whatsoever. If I lie in court, I cannot defend my actions by appealing to my right to free speech.

Perjury is a crime: although it is speech in the ordinary sense, it does not count legally as speech in the sense that is relevant for free speech protections.

This is not the only relevant distinction though. Within the legal category of speech, some speech is *protected* while other speech is *unprotected*. That is, speech that is covered by the First Amendment may still be regulable (unprotected) if it presents a "clear and present danger" to others. Although Mill probably did not have the US Constitution in mind, he offers an apt illustration. The opinion that corn dealers are starvers of the poor (by hiking up corn prices) should be protected when expressed in a newspaper article. But it does not deserve protection when uttered to an angry mob outside a corn dealer's house—this constitutes *incitement* to violence, which presents a clear and present danger to life and limb. In this sense, some (legal) speech may legitimately be regulable: for instance, the freedom to organize a Nazi demonstration may be legitimately restricted because of the danger it poses to public order, though not on the basis of its objectionable content. Typically, offensiveness does not justify restricting speech. Instead, there must be some demonstrable harm to others or to society at large that some speech generates (or is likely to generate) in order to ground regulation. Protected speech is regulable by the strongest demonstration of harm only. Or to put the point differently: a change in the status of some speech from protected to unprotected speech demands highly stringent demonstration of harm. Furthermore, this must be done in a content-*neutral* way. Liberal principles customarily dictate that speech cannot be regulated based on what it says, however repugnant we may find it. Rather, regulations must be based on demonstrable harms, and they must be in a content-neutral spirit that does not condemn the speech based on the ideas that it expresses. To grasp the content-neutral/content-specific distinction further, compare a citywide ban on all advertisement billboards and just on billboards advertising cigarettes, respectively.

Now let's return to pornography. Since the liberalization of pornographic materials in the United States (in the 1970s), antipornography feminism has not objected to what pornography depicts; such objections have no legal bite precisely because they would advance content-specific restrictions on speech. Instead, feminists have argued that pornography does something harmful and that these harms are sufficiently grave to justify removing pornography from under the purview of protected speech. As a result, pornography could justifiably be regulated in some (as of yet unspecified) sense. This is what the Dworkin-MacKinnon ordinances intended to do: the basic idea was that our laws should recognize "the concrete violations of civil rights done through pornography as practices of sex discrimination and [to give] survivors access to civil court for relief through a law they could use themselves" (MacKinnon 2000, 131). The ordinance would have given those trafficked into or coerced to perform in pornography, those who have had pornography forced on them, and those who are survivors of assaults caused by pornography consumption the opportunity to seek legal recourse for the harms done to them. And, importantly, the ordinance would have prevented a free speech *defense* of pornography. Bluntly: as long as pornography counts as protected speech, free speech considerations will be overriding. But if pornography's protected status were undercut, free speech considerations would no longer be put first. Subsequently, pornography would be more akin to Nazi demonstrations: both would be regulable on the basis of harms done to their recipients or to the society at large. This is not equivalent to banning the production and distribution of pornographic materials. Hence, antipornography feminism is not tantamount to pro-censorship feminism. MacKinnon and Dworkin—the purported champions of repressive and illiberal antipornography measures—did not advocate criminalization or outright censorship of pornography, nor did they advance a moralistic condemnation of pornography.[2]

However, as we already know, the ordinance was struck down as unconstitutional. In the opinion of Judge Easterbrook, even though pornography causes harms, this only demonstrates its power as speech. Thus, the ordinance was deemed unconstitutional in advocating content-specific restrictions on speech: it suggested that pornographic speech expresses a distinctive point of view in claiming that it "presents" women in certain ways (as dehumanized sex objects). Pornography puts forward and advocates a certain view about women, sexuality, and supposedly proper gender roles. Still, even if we deeply disagree with the content of the expressed views, this does not justify legal proscription. Besides, pornography is hardly alone in depicting women in objectionable ways: many other media along with religious scriptures do so as well (Stark 1997). An antipornography position would need to make a case for pornography's exceptionalism in this regard in order to remove legal protections.[3]

2. Falsely equating MacKinnon's position with a pro-censorship position persists; see, e.g., Simmons Bradley (2014, 262).

3. To specify further: pornographic materials in the United States are legally protected provided that they pass the (so-called) Miller test. This legal test regulates the distribution and consumption of *obscene* materials, which are not protected by the First Amendment. So somewhat oddly, there are two distinct legal parameters against which pornographic works are measured in the United States. If some pornographic work counts as speech in the relevant sense, it deserves First Amendment protection. If, however, it counts as obscene, the work loses this protection. The Miller test for obscenity is a *conjunction* of three conditions: if an average person applying community standards finds a work as a whole to appeal to prurient (sexually arousing) interests; the work depicts in a clearly offensive way sexual conduct; and the work as a whole lacks any serious literary, artistic, political, or scientific value, then it counts as obscene. De facto, the test does little to no work in restricting the production and distribution of pornographic materials. Antipornography measures advocated by MacKinnon and Dworkin were precisely put forward as alternatives to such unhelpful and vague obscenity-based measures.

Apart from such constitutional concerns, some feminists have taken issue with the underlying rationale of the ordinance and with its implications. Feminists critical of the Dworkin-MacKinnon ordinance do not find pornography wholly unproblematic. But they worry that removing pornography from under free speech protections won't be conducive to general feminist aims. Applying the ordinance would still have involved much legal interpretation. This would have given individual judges the power to decide what materials count as graphic, sexually explicit dehumanization of women (or of men used in the place of women). Some of those judges would have been deeply conservative and probably would have found materials depicting queer sexualities and sexualities that do not fit "community standards" (like BDSM literature) to be pornography in the relevant sense (Califia 1994; Nielson 1988). Even materials promoting prima facie nonpornographic feminist issues (e.g., information about abortion and birth control) might end up being restricted (Carse 1995). The scope of the ordinance was too wide and too much hostage to individual biases: it made no principled distinction between egalitarian pornography and erotica, and so could effectively cover sexually explicit materials that are premised on equality (Frug 2000; Ross 2000). Furthermore, some argue, the ordinance perpetuates sex-negative and gender-stereotypic views: for instance, that sex is bad for women; only heterosexual sex in monogamous marriage relationships is acceptable; and that women are victims, who need to be protected from "libidinal" men (Cornell 2000b; Hunter and Law 1997). Perpetuating such views again plays directly into the hands of pornography's conservative opponents, who also tend to be antifeminist. It is worth bearing in mind that Mayor Hudnut, who championed the adoption of the Dworkin-MacKinnon ordinance in Indianapolis, was a religious conservative with a dismal record of promoting gender justice. And although the ordinance was anticensorship in letter, some argue that it was not so in spirit (Strossen 1995, chap.3). The ordinance allowed a form of censorship in disguise by permitting governmental coercion: as government officials, judges would still have a substantial role to play in the outcomes of particular civil cases premised on the ordinance (Strossen 1995, 67). As noted, there are good reasons to be wary of such a situation. Finally, despite rejecting the Dworkin-MacKinnon ordinance, many feminists are still in favor of some forms of legal recourse. Laurie Shrage, for instance, holds that "the methods of legal recourse appropriate in the case of pornography should be ones that enable women in the industry to defend their rights as workers, not ones that take away their work" (2005, 58). This again highlights the mistake to juxtapose pro- and antipornography positions as being about liberal unrestricted freedom versus feminist censorship to produce and consume pornographic materials.

Liberal philosophers typically object to the ordinance because the causal subordination claim is said to be untenable (chapter 2): because there is no definitive empirical evidence that pornography consumption causes systematic sexualized violence against women. That said, this does not mean that these philosophers are *against* regulating pornography. Some argue that Mill's classic liberal position, once properly understood in the light of his feminism, would have been rather sympathetic to even censoring pornography. Dyzenhaus (1992) holds that since pornography is an affront to women's autonomy and so violates a central interest that we as progressive beings have, liberals can legitimately prohibit pornography. Instead of framing the harm principle in terms of sexualized violence, we can formulate it in terms of interest-violations. Hence, pornography harms women by hampering their interest in autonomous agency. [4] *Contra* Dyzenhaus, Vernon (1996) argues that pornography on a Millian picture commits a different sin that justifies

4. See Skipper (1993) for a critique of Dyzenhaus.

interference: it keeps in place barbaric social conditions that are contrary to civilization. And Scoccia (1996) argues that a liberal commitment to free speech does not preclude censoring pornography if it affects consumers' psychologies in nonrational ways. Bluntly: a ban can be justified if pornography conditions men's psychologies in pernicious ways and by creating violent desires through this conditioning. Now, although other liberals vehemently reject censorship and critique the Dworkin-MacKinnon ordinance, they seldom hold that *nothing* should be done about pornography. Many prominent liberal philosophers take pornography to be odious and to generate incidental harms, although they find the feminist case for pornography causing systematic violence against women lacking. Still, these harms should be countered by means other than prohibiting pornography production and consumption. Some have been in favor of restricting distribution via zoning (limiting public displays of pornography to specific areas) to safeguard nonconsenting adults and children from being unwittingly exposed to pornographic materials (Feinberg 1985; R. Dworkin 1981). Such restrictions do "damage" consumers of pornography by inflicting on them inconvenience, expense, and embarrassment (R. Dworkin 1981, 198). But none of these are serious enough to amount to objectionable and illiberal state encroachments upon citizens' basic liberties.

4.3. PATERNALISTIC JUSTIFICATIONS FOR REGULATION

The above demonstrates that regulating pornography need not be in tension with liberalism. It also shows that the idea of there being a stark opposition between pro-censorship feminism and pro-pornography liberalism is misguided. However, I briefly noted above that paternalistic regulations of pornography might also be permissible. What might ground their permissibility? First, legal paternalism—the view that the state can legitimately interfere with some actions of competent adults for their own good—is not always impermissible. The legal obligation to wear a motorcycle helmet is a case in point. One might then argue that if pornography consumption "corrupts the souls" of otherwise competent adults or hampers human flourishing, we have a prima facie justification for restricting it on paternalistic grounds. Second, if Langton is right about pornography's power to shape younger consumers who are still incompetent in the domain of sex, this may justify restricting young people's access to pornography. After all, Mill's liberalism is designed to apply only to human beings who possess mature "faculties" (Mill 1974). Let's consider these views in turn.

Soft-paternalistic interference with our freedom to consume pornography may be warranted, if pornographic sex education hampers rational agency: namely, if it interferes with our freedom to exercise our own rational capacities in deciding what to think and how to live. For instance, Stephen Kershnar (2004) considers whether "violation pornography" that depicts unjust sex acts might hamper human flourishing.[5] If we understand flourishing in terms of pleasure or desire fulfillment, one might think that viewing pornographic materials is compatible with—even conducive to—flourishing. Then again, if we think about flourishing in terms of attaining knowledge, having meaningful relationships or exercising rational agency, the situation gets murkier. If pornography tells lies about women and generates false beliefs in its consumers, its consumption seems to erode human

---

5. Kershnar's view of what counts as violation pornography again illustrates how different theorists understand objectionable pornography differently. For him, unjust sex acts include adultery, rape, and adult-child sex. Why depictions of adultery would count as unjust sex though, eludes me. I expect that many contemporary critics of pornography do not view depictions of adultery objectionable or morally on a par with depictions of sexualized violence.

flourishing in that it interferes with knowledge attainment and leads to irrationality. One might hold that we should be safeguarded from being influenced by forces that threaten such flourishing though, which would support soft-paternalistic measures to undercut pornography's pernicious message and prevent consumers from forming false beliefs about women and sexuality. Consider a parallel with advertisements glamorizing smoking. They are not usually condoned on free speech grounds because they are said to amount to pro-smoking propaganda. Falling prey to such propaganda may not only physically harm us by increasing the probability of developing certain illnesses; doing so may also harm smokers by facilitating addictions that hamper future rational agency. If (at least some) pornography functions as a kind of sexual propaganda that generates false beliefs about sexuality and if the development of such beliefs hampers consumers' reasoning abilities, there is a case for restricting pornography consumption for our own good—in order to prevent practical irrationality. Furthermore, the available evidence suggests that pornography does interfere with some consumers' freedom to exercise their rational capacities insofar as heavy pornography consumption correlates with the acceptance of rape myths and with callous views about women in general (see chapter 2).

By the same token, there is increasing evidence that consumption of pornography does not in the long run increase pleasure, *contra* first appearances. At least some pornography seemingly alienates men from their sexuality and constructs men's sexual expectations in ways that hamper sexual self-determination (Baker 1992; Brod 1988; Dines 2011; May 1998; Paul 2005; Wyre 1992). Empirical research confirms that heavy pornography consumption interferes with (heterosexual) men's ability to enjoy sex with actual partners. Pornography "provides men a sexual script that shapes the ways they view and enact their sexual selves, and the more pornography a man consumes, the more he comes to depend on it for that enactment"

(Ezzell 2014, 25). If sexual pleasure and sexual self-determination are part of human flourishing, pornography consumption hampers both women's *and* men's flourishing. Finally, Internet pornography addiction is said to be a fast-growing problem (Griffiths 2001; Paul 2005; see also Sweet 1992). Although some deny that this is a genuine phenomenon, many firsthand stories suggest that Internet pornography is addictive just as Internet gambling is. At any rate, it seems incontrovertible that a compulsion to consume pornography for up to ten hours a day is akin to addiction (Paul 2005).

Nevertheless, what type of regulation might subsequently be warranted is still an open question: Prohibiting pornography or restricting its availability? The former is surely too draconian, even if we accept that pornography consumption hampers rational agency in being addictive. Lots of benign activities like sports can be addictive without therefore meriting a governmental ban. The latter option faces many practical problems due to the Internet. As is well known, the surface web that is covered by common search engines does not cover all online traffic. The rest operate "in the shadows" (deep or dark web) and must typically be accessed with special software. Regulating all of these webs is near impossible: for instance, even if one cannot host a website with certain content in one's country of residence, one can usually effortlessly access similar websites hosted in other countries. So even if the distribution of certain particularly inegalitarian pornographic materials could be restricted within some legal jurisdiction, the consumption of those materials in the same jurisdiction is much harder to control. Moreover, judgments about which materials ought to be restricted are contentious. Once again, the worry is that leaving this to politicians (or, worse, to lobbyists) results in deeply misguided policies. The concern is not unfounded: in 2014, the UK government issued a list of sex acts to be banned in UK-produced pornography that many in the industry have critiqued. It includes face sitting (as potentially life-threatening), urolagnia (known as "water sports"), and female ejaculation. Although consumers in the United Kingdom can still view materials with these acts, materials produced there cannot easily contain them. The idea behind the ban is to undercut pornography's pernicious message about "proper" sex. However, those drafting the list failed to realize that many sex acts on the list do not usually feature in some of the most virulent industrial pornography, which was the supposed target of the ban. Rather, acts like female ejaculation are a mainstay of alternative pornographic materials that also aim to undercut pernicious ideas about sex found in much of industrial pornography that one can find on the Internet for free. (I will return to these issues in chapters 5 and 7.)

The above are not the only types of governmental regulation though. Prior to Internet pornography, age restrictions to see certain films or to enter particular premises were in place. Since such restrictions now look less likely to be effective, one might prefer public campaigns or nudging. This is a public policy practice that aims to reinforce positive behavior by indirectly suggesting that some course of action is good for us. For instance, campaigns that encourage healthy living practices, rather than bans on junk food, are of this kind. This type of governmental interference would support forms of sex education that alert us to how pornography might hamper sex lives and relationships, and how sex in pornography differs from sex in the "real world." Spelling out precisely what sorts of nudges and what type of education would have the desired effects is a huge point of contention. Still, even prominent liberal philosophers who critiqued the Dworkin-MacKinnon ordinance held that such noncoercive countermeasures are fully acceptable within a liberal framework (R. Dworkin 1981; Feinberg 1985). They share much more with anticensorship antipornography feminism than might at first seem.

The above dealt with soft-paternalistic regulation of pornography for competent adults. But what should we do about younger consumers who are less competent or, worse, wholly incompetent in the domain of sex? Are there grounds to governmentally restrict pornography for such consumers in less soft ways? I think there are. If pornography consumption hampers the *exercise* of reliable reasoning processes, it plausibly hampers the *development* of such processes. And as things stand, pornography does not conceivably enhance the development of young people's sexual self-determination in desirable ways. Or at least this is the case for the huge number of young people exposed to the run-of-mill, inegalitarian, industrial porn that the Internet is saturated with. (Just think back to Langton's discussion of the 2013 report from the UK Office of the Children's Commissioner from section 3.6.) We might then argue that the development of healthy sexual autonomy and bodily integrity are interests that should be legally guaranteed. Although not in connection to pornography, Thomas Scanlon holds that we have an interest "in having a good environment for the formation of [our] beliefs and desires" (1978–9, 527). According to Scanlon, media audiences have a positive autonomy interest in being free from manipulation, which is why it is legitimate to restrict subliminal advertising messages: they interfere with personal autonomy in producing beliefs and desires that the audiences have no control over. If at least some pornography for some inexperienced consumers functions like subliminal sexual propaganda, it would be legitimate to restrict its distribution and to control pornography's consumption insofar as it goes against consumers' positive autonomy interest to be free from subliminal manipulation.

I am sympathetic to this line of argument and hold that it speaks for not only soft nudges but also for harder controls on the availability of pornography. For example, legislation could coerce search engines and Internet sites with pornographic materials to implement truly effective measures to keep those under eighteen out. To the bemusement of many, this is precisely what the co-chairman and -founder of Vivid Entertainment Group (the world's largest producer of pornography) Steven Hirsch called for in 2008. He accused

Google and Yahoo! of implementing insufficient filters to protect children and minors from adult content and pornographic materials.[6] Now, one might view Hirsch's motives in a somewhat cynical light. After all, free Internet pornography diminishes profits for big production companies, and so they have an interest in curbing too easy access to pornography. Still, such corporate agendas curiously coincide with those of antipornography activism, which asserts that the availability of free Internet pornography prevents young people from developing healthy sexual selves and relationships. Moreover, calls from those in the industry to curb the ubiquity of Internet pornography suggests that doing so might be much easier than is sometimes assumed. That said, I submit, Scanlon's view that media audiences have a positive autonomy interest in being free from subliminal manipulation seemingly extends beyond the media. In addition to some restrictions on the accessibility of pornography, much improved educational programs about sexuality and relationships are required. In other words, young people have an additional autonomy interest in being free from other forms of manipulation in the domain of sex. Without improved sex and relationship education, legal restrictions on young people's access to pornography are likely to be ineffective and perhaps even counterproductive. More needs to be said about the form that this education should take, which I am not able to do here. However, one major point to emerge from my present discussion is that in supporting paternalistic regulations of pornography, we should not only focus on restricting access to pornography: rather, legal regulations also encompass educational programs and nudging that are permissible from a liberal perspective.

6. Cade Metz, "Pr0n Baron Challenges Google and Yahoo! to Build Better Child Locks," *The Register*, February 15, 2008, http://www.theregister.co.uk/2008/02/15/vivid_slaps_google_yahoo/. Accessed August 8, 2018.

4.4. PORNOGRAPHY AS UNCOVERED SPEECH

As long as pornographic materials are protected by liberal free speech principles, regulating them will be arduous. However, some have argued that we can reconceptualize pornography within existing legal parameters and remove it from the scope of protected speech without compromising our commitment to free speech. If pornography counts as uncovered speech, regulating it raises no free speech concerns whatsoever.[7] A number of possible routes have been suggested. We could argue that pornography is (1) discriminatory conduct; (2) parallel to verbal contracts; (3) legally nonspeech given its content; (4) hate speech or incitement to violence against women; or (5) group defamation. Let's consider these views next.

(1) For MacKinnon, pornography is a practice of sex discrimination. Taking this point seriously, Antony (2017) holds that Langton could have employed Austin's speech act theory in a more fruitful way to remove pornography's First Amendment protections. Instead of arguing that pornography is both speech *and* action, Langton should have argued that pornography amounts to discriminatory conduct that merely involves speech. The First Amendment does not protect discriminatory conduct even if it is performed with words. Hanging a "Whites Only" sign in a café is a case in point. It constitutes an illegal act of racial discrimination and cannot be defended by appealing to free speech rights. However, Langton follows MacKinnon in rejecting the view that pornography constitutes discriminatory conduct only. Puzzlingly though, MacKinnon (1987) does not argue for this and takes the justification for the rejection to be obvious.

---

7. Note that in the previous chapter we considered whether pornography is speech in the sense relevant for Austin's speech act theory. The arguments here are subtly different and concern the *legal* definition of speech, which is a separate issue.

(2) According Maitra and McGowan (2007), we need not argue that pornography is just discriminatory conduct in order to remove (at least some) pornography from the purview of the First Amendment—we can do so with Langton's speech act theoretic understanding of pornography too. The main gist of their case rests on the recognition that certain *significantly obligation-enacting utterances* already fall outside the scope of the First Amendment. Such utterances include (among others) verbal contracts and "Whites Only" signs. If I make a verbal contract, I have enacted an obligation to fulfill whatever the contract dictates. If I then fail to do my part, I cannot defend my (in)action by appealing to free speech considerations. The relevant sorts of utterances must also enact significant rather than trivial obligations: if I fail to fulfill the terms of the agreement, my failure is legally actionable. Compare this to a case where I promise a friend to lend them a book but forget to bring it over. My utterance has enacted an obligation but not a significant one: not meeting my obligation is not actionable by law. With this in mind, Maitra and McGowan argue that if (some) pornographic materials do what MacKinnon and Langton claim them to do, these materials fall into the category of significantly obligation-enacting utterances and this renders them *uncovered* speech. Langton claims that pornographic speech is verdictive and exercitive: it legitimates women's discrimination, and it deprives women important powers and rights. If some pornography does this, it enacts changes in obligations: for instance, "in legitimating discriminatory behavior toward women, it enacts changes with respect to the obligation to refrain from such behavior" (Maitra and McGowan 2007, 65). These obligations are also significant: they are legally actionable insofar as sex discrimination is legally actionable. And so, we can see that *if* MacKinnon and Langton are right about what pornography does, it falls outside the scope of the First Amendment and regulating it raises no free speech concerns. Maitra and McGowan stress that they do not argue pornography

(as a whole or in part) counts as significantly obligation enacting. Their point is just that even if we follow the speech act analysis of pornography, at least some pornography might not warrant First Amendment protections.

(3) Frederick Schauer (1979) argues that pornography does not constitute speech in the relevant legal sense to merit protection. Although courts have declared pornography to be speech, looking at the First Amendment carefully shows that this is a mistake. In a nutshell, something is speech "in the constitutional sense if and only if it has *a certain kind of value*: value as the process and result of intellectual communication. There are many other kinds of value, but this is the only one protected by the first amendment" (Schauer 1979, 927).[8] In not having the appropriate kind of value *qua* process and result of intellectual communication, pornography is not speech in the relevant sense. Why does Schauer think pornography lacks this value? The communication of ideas is the essential purpose of constitutionally protected speech; or more precisely, communication in this sense pertains to communication of "mental stimulus": an attempt by the speaker to influence their audiences in some specific fashion (Schauer 1979, 921). And here we can see a break with "hardcore" pornography: it is "designed to produce a purely physical effect" (Schauer 1979, 922). This being the case, such pornography is actually more akin to sexual activity than to any communicative process. A piece of pornography is a "sexual surrogate" that merely takes pictorial or linguistic form (Schauer 1979, 922). And so, pornography does not constitute communication in a cognitive sense— a sense required for communication of ideas protected by the First Amendment. Schauer proclaims:

---

8. See also Sunstein (1986) for an argument that pornography counts legally as "low-value" speech and thus it can legitimately be regulated without this conflicting with the US Constitution.

The purveyor of the pornography is in the business solely of providing sexual pleasure; it is unrealistic to presume that he is anything but indifferent to the method by which pleasure is provided and profit secured. Similarly, there is no reason to believe that the recipient desires anything other than sexual stimulation. (1979, 923)

Thus, the point of excluding such pornography from the legal category of speech boils down to it having physical effects and *nothing else* (Schauer 1979, 925). Having sex is not a free speech issue though.

(4) Aminatta Forna (1992) proposes an understanding of pornography analogous to racial hate speech (see also Itzin 1992b). On this model, we could introduce a criminal offense of incitement to sexual hatred that would be parallel to the offense of incitement to racial hatred. This type of speech goes beyond mere advocacy for a view; rather, it aims to induce action in its recipients by emotive or noncognitive means. A typical way to decide the matter appeals to the "clear and present danger" test: whether one's utterance aims to induce action that presents an immediate danger to others. Just think back to Mill's example of corn dealers being starvers of the poor uttered to an angry mob outside a corn dealer's house; if I make the very same utterances to my cat at home, I will not have incited violence. Pornography, the thought goes, incites its viewers to commit acts of sexualized violence against women: it celebrates, endorses, and recommends such violence in noncognitive ways that go beyond mere advocacy (Adams 2000; see also Easton 1994, chap. 14). And since inciting someone to commit a criminal act is illegal, pornography production would be criminalized and would not warrant free speech protections.

(5) We encountered the idea that pornography defames women in chapter 1: according to some antipornography feminists, pornography amounts to sexual propaganda or a sort of false advertisement

about women (Longino 1980; Hill 1987; Tong 1982). Defamation involves circulating false claims that harm their recipients' reputation. For instance, if I fail to be promoted because my co-worker circulated false claims about my competence, I have been defamed. Defamation is not a criminal offense, but civilly actionable: I can subsequently sue my co-worker for damages. And it falls outside of free speech legislation—my co-worker cannot defend their actions by appealing to free speech rights. With respect to pornography, the idea is that the lies pornography circulates about women harm their reputation. These lies portray women in a certain light, which generally decreases their credibility and hampers women's social opportunities. Hence, the idea goes, pornographers could be sued for having produced particular materials that circulate harmful lies about women as a group, where this cannot be defended on free speech grounds.[9]

How plausible are these ways of removing pornography's free speech protections? I contend that none are without problems. First, the proposals of Antony, on the one hand, and Maitra and McGowan, on the other hand, hinge on contentious empirical premises. Success of each proposal requires that MacKinnon and Langton are right about what (at least some) pornography does. But, establishing this is notoriously difficult and deeply contested.

Second, Schauer's conception of what pornography is and what "purveyors" of pornography do is contentious (if not downright false). These purveyors are a hugely diverse group of individuals with many different aims and intentions. Taking them "solely" to

---

9. Jeremy Waldron (2012) has more recently put forward a view of hate speech on the model of group libel. In the course of his discussion, Waldron suggests that this model could also apply to pornography and make sense of the idea that it constitutes a form of group defamation or libel. Nevertheless, Waldron does not develop this view in detail. There are reasons to be prima facie wary of this move though. As Waldron thinks that group libel is a criminal offense, extending his model to cover pornography would effectively criminalize at least some pornography. For reasons to be discussed shortly, I am not in favor of criminalizing pornography.

provide sexual pleasure with no concern for methods used is dubious. For a start, one might point out that many of these purveyors are selling us a product. But in so doing, it seems odd to assume that producers are "indifferent to the method by which pleasure is provided and profit secured" (Schauer 1979, 923). Capitalist market competition seemingly speaks against this assumption. Furthermore, recent years have seen a significant increase in self-proclaimed feminist pornography made by female producers. These producers explicitly intend to create egalitarian pornography, rather than (what on the Dworkin-MacKinnon definition would count as) erotica. Considering such works is instructive to demonstrate Schauer's flawed assumption. When asked why she directs pornographic films, Petra Joy (one of the best known independent feminist pornographers and a former antipornography activist) states that she aims to portray a realistic picture of sexuality and to provide an alternative female perspective to mainstream pornography's male point of view.[10] Sinnamon Love, who describes herself as a black feminist pornographer, aims only to work with directors and production companies that "portray black female sexuality in ways that I feel are expansive, progressive, and interesting" (Love 2013, 103). She strives to provide "more positive images of black men and women in sexual situations that don't require stereotypes to get the point across" (2013, 103–104). Candida Royalle (2000), an ex-performer turned director, recounts that she started directing pornographic films to undercut the exploitation and sexist depictions of women in mainstream pornography. Royalle refuses to use common industry tropes in her films, such as facial ejaculations known as "money shots" (since without them,

---

10. This interview was published in a now defunct Berlin-based magazine, *Feigenblatt* in its autumn 2010 Special Film edition titled "Die 60 besten Sexfilme für Anspruchsvolle" ("The 60 Best Sex-Films for the Discerning"). Translations from German to English are mine.

pornographic works are not thought to sell). These producers intend to subvert and provide alternatives to the mainstream porn industry as well as to portray a more realistic picture of sexuality in general and of racialized/female sexuality in particular. Following Schauer then, to say that these producers have no other intention but to solicit a physical (sexual) effect and that they are unconcerned with the way to do this strikes me as seriously misguided.[11]

Third, not all feminists of color welcome the parallel between pornography and racist hate speech (Mercer 2000; Osman 1988; Parmar 1988). Equating the two ends up drawing an unhelpful analogy between racial hatred and male dominance. This suggests that women suffer harms and violence analogous to enslaved people of color, but the analogy is unwarranted because different types of oppression and violence cannot be equated. Such an approach often also ends up masking and marginalizing the situation of women of color. For a start, it can fail to theorize the role that racism plays in the presentation of black women in pornography since their treatment would become a matter of sexism and male dominance. Appreciating the intersections of sexism and racism in pornography becomes impossible if we think that pornography is just about the former. Instead, a more nuanced approach that recognizes the multifacetedness of social identities is needed. Bluntly, some pornographic materials (and perhaps even genres) do not only involve male dominance but also racial hatred. Understanding pornography on the incitement to sexualized violence model, however, ignores racism inherent in some virulent pornography, and thus perpetuates the idea that pornography is just about sexism—that it is a "white issue." This leaves the oppression of

---

11. One might further question Schauer's equation of pornography with sex. This is echoed in Melinda Vadas's work (2005) that takes pornography consumption to be equivalent to having sex with (e.g.) pieces of paper. I will discuss the plausibility of this claim in chapter 8.

women of color in and via pornography undertheorized (Mayall and Russell 1993).

The incitement to sexualized violence model faces further legal difficulties in that it would criminalize pornography. As I see it, this result is both undesirable and impractical. Consider the latter point first. Intention is key to the crime of incitement to racial hatred. Typically, one cannot be found guilty of accidentally inciting racial hatred; recall that a criminal conviction usually requires that perpetrators satisfy the *mens rea* requirement (see chapter 3). But do pornographers generally intend to move consumers to commit acts of sexualized violence against women? This seems highly unlikely. Or, even if some do, most conceivably intend to make money. At most, this proposal could legislate against some small subset of particularly inegalitarian pornography. And even then establishing that the makers *intended* to incite sexualized violence against women would be incredibly difficult to pull off—after all, we have no direct access to others' mental states to settle the matter. More generally, though, I take criminalization to be the wrong response to pornography's problems. To begin with, I do not take all pornography to be on a par and hold that some pornography can be liberatory (though I will postpone considering this in detail until chapter 7). We cannot and should not criminalize all pornography; but if we only criminalize some, this opens up the door to legal interpretation. Such interpretation will be contentious and hostage to much individual bias on the part of the judiciary. It is far from obvious to me that those making decisions about which pornography is objectionable and warrants criminalization will make the right decisions. (Recall the discussion of the Dworkin-MacKinnon ordinance and the UK list of banned sex acts.)

Fourth, the defamation claim has generated resistance from liberal perspectives. In practical terms, it is extremely difficult to establish that a group's reputation has been tarnished severely enough in the requisite sense for the defamation approach to succeed (Feinberg

1985, 148–149; May 1998, 66–67). In the case of pornography, we would have to establish that an individual's reputation *qua* woman has been tarnished by pornography. Empirically establishing this looks near impossible; and what does it even mean to have one's reputation as a woman tarnished? Settling this conceivably turns on the apparent lies that pornography tells about women. But pornography is surely not alone in doing so—just think of the images of women put forward by much of mainstream media, films, and romance novels. There must be some principled manner to distinguish these harms from those done by pornography, but the prospects of spelling this out in a manner that avoids an ad hoc moralistic condemnation of pornography look unpromising. That pornography tells lies about women is also contentious. If pornography successfully constructs women's "nature" in its image, it tells *truths* about women's sexuality—the constructionist claim is in tension with the defamation claim. Then again, if pornography is sheer fantasy, it won't be propositional in the requisite sense since it makes no truth claims about women. All fantastical materials are in some sense false, and they fail to correspond to reality; but they are not false in the same sense as nonfantastical materials are—just compare a science fiction story with a disproven scientific theory (Soble 1985). If pornography is more akin to the former than to the latter, the defamation approach cannot get off the ground. (I will discuss the fantasy element of pornography further in chapter 6.)

4.5. LEGAL COVERAGE OF ILLOCUTIONARY SPEECH ACTS

Above I argued against attempts to establish that pornography counts as uncovered speech. But this is not the only pertinent issue about coverage: the free speech argument against pornography maintains that our ability to perform certain *illocutionary* speech acts (like refusals) merits legal protection. If this does not hold, the antipornography case is undermined. Some philosophers claim that there is, indeed, no legal obligation to protect the right to perform illocutions (Antony 2011; Green 1998). To think otherwise rests on a "dangerous confusion" (R. Dworkin 1993): one that confuses a negative liberty to be free *from interference* with a positive liberty *to have* the freedom to do something. Freedom to illocute is of the latter kind. But there is a difference between the state legally protecting activities that we have a right to and the state legally enabling or facilitating the exercise of those activities. Even if my legal right to free speech is protected, the state is under no obligation to ensure that my speech is heard or understood.

The dispute boils down to this: Hornsby and Langton take the scope of legally protected speech to extend to (some) illocutions; their critics deny this. The dispute is about the proper scope of the First Amendment, and whether the limits of protected speech extend to speech acts like refusals. Who is correct? This depends on how we frame the coverage question, and there are two options. First, given the existing free speech principle in one's jurisdiction, where should illocutionary speech acts fall? Second, which free speech principle ought we endorse, and where should illocutionary speech acts subsequently fall? One diagnosis of the dispute between Hornsby and Langton, on the one hand, and their opponents, on the other hand, is that different sides ask different questions. Critics of the speech act approach typically have the former question in mind; Hornsby and Langton's position is less clear. In defending their view that freedom to illocute merits free speech protections, they write:

> We should say at the outset that we do not take ourselves to be
> involved in the interpretation of the U.S. Constitution as such.
> Our claims here are claims about how free speech should be

conceived if the value of protecting it is to be fully intelligible.
(Hornsby and Langton 1998, 23)

Hornsby and Langton are seemingly asking the second question, while their critics address the first one. Perhaps the entire debate is misguided because interlocutors are talking at cross-purposes.

In order to salvage the debate, we might appeal to two lines of argument. I do not aim to argue for their plausibility. Still, looking at the suggestions on offer once again reminds us of the importance of being clear about our metaphilosophical commitments and about which questions we are asking. First, Alex Davies argues that we can make an alternative silencing argument that does not shift the debate away from the conception of free speech endorsed by the critics of Hornsby and Langton (the conception that does not extend to illocutionary speech acts). Davies examines the influence of rape myths on creating a hostile environment in courtroom settings, which prevents assaulted women from making certain statements. In particular, this turns on how defense attorneys frame their questions. They are loaded in ways that prevent victims from making their desired statements, where this amounts to silencing of the sort that violates the women's free speech rights. The acceptance of rape myths smuggles into the conversation presuppositions that make it impossible for women to make the statements that they are looking to make. For example, imagine that after initially struggling against one's attacker, the victim finds herself violently pinned down on the floor. Out of fear, she stops struggling. In cross-examination she is then asked, "You did not take advantage of subsequent opportunities to resist, is that correct?" to which the assaulted woman can say neither yes nor no. This is because both answers count against her by buying into prevalent rape myths—like women must have consented if they did not struggle against their attackers (Davies 2016, 512). The attacked is silenced in the courtroom in being unable to make the statements that she wants to make given (a) how questions are framed and (b) how her answers are interpreted due to prevalent rape myths. This analysis fits Hornby's view of communicative illocutionary acts introduced in chapter 3. Our ability to effectively communicate with one another is at the heart of free speech protections. And so: "If caring about free speech is a matter of caring about people's powers of communication, about an ability to do illocutionary things, then there is reason to stop the cumulative process of silencing" (Hornsby 1995b, 229). Women in courtroom settings facing cross-examination of the above kind are precisely facing questioning that intends to scramble communication and to interfere with their ability to communicate. Hence, if safeguarding communication is a central task of free speech legislation and women are silenced in the above ways that hampers communication, the silencing claim so formulated has not changed the terms of the debate.

In a similar vein, Caroline West (2003) defends the free speech argument against pornography. As noted, the liberal aim to protect free expression amounts to protecting speakers' freedom to communicate ideas and opinions. Since freedom of speech aims to safeguard communication and communication requires reciprocity (as Hornsby holds; see section 3.2.), free speech considerations demand a minimal comprehension requirement. It would be illegitimate to demand that the state ensures my utterances are understood. Still, *were speakers to speak, and were hearers to want to hear the idea the speaker expressed by so speaking,* [it is required that] *there is no agent whose actions prevent hearers from comprehending that idea*" (West 2003, 408). This comprehension requirement does not embody a positive right to be understood; it involves a negative right that no one *blocks* comprehension. This is a perfectly acceptable liberal requirement and expresses a negative liberty to be free from interference. Thus, West holds, the silencing claim does not dangerously confuse negative and positive liberty. Of course, the role of pornography as the "scrambler" of communication would have to be established. Still, West aims to establish that bringing communicative illocutionary speech acts under free speech protections is not an illegitimate move and that doing so is compatible with existing liberal free speech principles.

4.6. FREEDOM OR EQUALITY?

Above I spelled out two ways to extend free speech protections to illocutionary speech acts. Some critics of the speech act approach take a still further issue with it: even if the silencing claim holds, it does not support a *free speech* argument against pornography. In short: silencing in the illocutionary disablement sense is about autonomy and equal citizenship, not about our right to free speech. Legal free speech considerations are simply irrelevant when thinking about refusing sex or engaging in political protest (Bird 2002; Jacobson 2001). For instance, black South Africans being denied the vote is not a free speech issue; it is a civil rights violation. The same goes for a same-sex couple unable to marry in uttering "I do": if the legal jurisdiction in which they make their utterances does not recognize same-sex unions, they cannot perform their intended illocutions with their words. But, again, the problem does not hinge on free speech concerns—it turns on being denied equal civil rights.

We might concede this. But might there still be a way to undermine a liberal argument *for* pornography? Langton (1990) does so by making use of Ronald Dworkin's own liberalism. She argues that Dworkin's liberalism is not only compatible with prohibiting pornography but prohibition is also demanded by it. Dworkin famously argues for a right to pornography. He discusses principle- and goal-based justifications for a prohibitive legal approach. First, Dworkin argues against the goal-based approach, which turns on whether pornography causes some social ills severe enough to merit prohibition: that is, we would have grounds to prohibit pornography if its production and consumption are "bad for the community as a whole" (R. Dworkin 1981, 177). The goal of prohibition would be to undercut social ills and to promote general social utility. However, Dworkin takes the goal-based justification to hinge on contingently held political and moral convictions of policymakers, which is too weak to justify the prohibition of pornography. (And, as we have seen, he further denies that the subordination claim substantiates pornography's causal role in producing such social ills.) Second, Dworkin considers the stronger principle-based justification and asks: "Do people have moral or political rights such that it would be wrong to prohibit them from . . . [producing or consuming pornography] even if the community would be better off . . . if they did not?" (1981, 194). His answer is yes: people have a right to moral independence, which makes pornography prohibition wrongful. This right roughly consists in the following. Just because policymakers and fellow citizens find my way of life ignoble and wrong, I have the right *not* to suffer disadvantages in the distribution of social goods and opportunities just because others disagree with my way of life (1981, 194). Our right to moral independence trumps social utility that might be derived from prohibiting pornography. Or more precisely: this right demands a permissive government policy toward the consumption of pornography, although some restrictions on public displays of pornographic materials (like zoning) are allowed (section 4.2.). In sum, we do not have grounds to prohibit pornography on either goal-based or principle-based ways: in the former case, the justification for prohibition would hinge on contingently held moral convictions of policymakers; in the latter, our right to moral independence (or our "right" to pornography) trumps possible social utility derived from prohibition.

Langton makes her case by looking at Dworkin's political philosophy more broadly and the role that rights play in Dworkin's overall framework. The starting point of Dworkin's entire position is a liberal principle of equality, which holds that governments should treat citizens as equals and governments should treat citizens' different conceptions of the good life as equally worthy of respect (R. Dworkin 1978). This conception of equality is central to Dworkin's political philosophy, and it is embodied in arguments from principle. Such arguments are fundamentally rights-based, and they play a special role in protecting individuals from (what Dworkin terms) "external preferences" other individuals may have. These preferences are ones that a citizen has for assigning goods and opportunities *to others*; that is, they are external to one's own preferences. We can now see how this relates to moral independence: this right protects individual agents against others' external preferences. For instance, imagine that someone has a preference for assigning me fewer opportunities due to my religious convictions—namely, because they believe that my conception of the good life is not worthy of respect. My right to moral independence safeguards me against such preferences: it makes assigning me fewer opportunities on the basis of external preferences *wrongful*. Hence, liberties like the freedom of religion are derived from our right to equality because egalitarian considerations demand that external preferences be discounted *even if* the majority of my fellow citizens hold them. Relative to pornography, the reasoning goes as follows: even if most people want to see pornography prohibited because they think pornography consumption is ignoble and it reflects a conception of the good life that deserves less respect, I have a right to pornography given my right to moral independence. Pornography prohibitions would be based on moralistic external preferences that others attempt to impose on me; but my right to moral independence protects me against policies based on moralistic external preferences of this sort.

With this in mind, Langton argues that Dworkin's position should support the prohibition of pornography. Following Dworkin's argument, Langton makes the following moves. A permissive policy on pornography seemingly harms women. First, women do not have equal social status; and second, as MacKinnon holds, pornography contributes significantly to women's continued subordination (Langton 1990, 333). The former claim is uncontroversial. Although the second claim is contentious, even many critics of MacKinnon accepted it (just think of Judge Easterbrook). Now does a permissive policy that harms women also violate their rights? This hinges on the kinds of preferences that the permissive policy is based on. If these preferences are self-directed, there is no right's violation. But if the preferences are external, the situation is very different. Langton holds that this is precisely the case: the permissive policy on pornography is based on *men's* external preference for pornography—preference that hampers women's equal citizenship and leads to diminished assignment of opportunities. Do women then have a right against the right to pornography? On Langton's reconstruction of Dworkin, the answer is yes. Men's external preference undergirding a permissive policy on pornography is sexist and embodies a macho ideology, as Feinberg put it (see section 2.3.). According to Dworkin, however, we can discard external preferences as justifications for a policy when those preferences are based on a strong and pervasive prejudice against a disadvantaged group. Men's external preference for pornography can be discarded as justifying a permissive policy on pornography in that those preferences are based on a strong and pervasive prejudice against women. Women therefore have a rights-based claim against pornography: women's rights *trump* a permissive policy on pornography insofar as that policy is justified by prejudicial external preferences. Dworkin's permissive policy on pornography conflicts with his own principle of equality—and so, women have a right against pornography, instead of pornography consumers having a right to pornography (Langton 1990, 346). This provides a strong liberal justification for regulating pornography, though Langton stresses that her argument does not establish prohibition or censorship as the appropriate way to regulate pornography (1990, 313–314).

4.7. UPSHOT

In this chapter, I have considered whether pornography regulations are permissible and if so, in what form. In so doing, we have seen that no party to the debate takes all regulations to be impermissible and that prominent liberal positions do not argue for unencumbered and free production, distribution, and consumption of pornography. This shows that the simple opposition between antipornography pro-censorship feminism and pro-pornography antiregulation liberalism is misguided.

An important upshot of this chapter, then, is that regulating pornography is permissible even within a liberal framework. This still leaves open important practical questions. For one thing, even if philosophical arguments make a convincing case for regulating pornography, this does not tell us what the best way to do so is, all things considered. There are many worries about who decides the specific shape of our public policies and how we can tell which strategies will work the best. The wealth of Internet pornography makes this all the more complicated. Attempts to block apparently objectionable materials online often fail to restrict precisely those materials that lawmakers aim to restrict—instead, such attempts can block access to materials deemed pornographic that we might wish to promote, like information about marginalized sexualities and identities. As I suggested above, for precisely such reasons measures that criminalize some (or all) pornography should be avoided. Nonetheless, regulating access to pornography is not always illegitimate and restricting the distribution of pornography is permissible given its apparent power to shape our sexual lives. Or so I maintain.

Not everyone agrees, and some hold that we ought to have more open debate: to fight pornography and its effects head-on in the open "marketplace of ideas." This would involve (for instance) educational efforts, consciousness raising, protest, and the creation of alternative erotic possibilities (Carse 1995). I do not disagree with these measures in addition to some pornography restrictions. But advocating solely such a "more speech" strategy is naive. Human beings are influenced in many subtle and insidious ways by public stereotypes, which have been shown to be highly predictive of discriminatory behavior (Brownstein and Saul 2016). More speech may then be ineffective because women's speech may be perlocutionarily frustrated, even if it is not illocutionarily disabled: women's locutions may be taken in their intended sense (as refusals) but simply ignored by hearers who are influenced by broader sexist and prejudicial messages. This won't render women equal participants in the marketplace of ideas, because their speech is simply ignored. And problematically, hearers may not realize that they have not given women's speech the required gravitas because they are influenced by unconscious attitudes like implicit bias that are automatic, associative, affective, and arational. The appropriate remedy against problematic pornographic speech is thus unlikely to be just more of any old speech. Rather, there is a need for a particular *kind* of speech, and the challenge will be to elucidate this kind. One suggestion is that there is beneficial pornographic speech that undercuts the effects of pernicious pornographic speech—a suggestion that I am sympathetic to and will return to in chapters to come.

Chapter 5

Pornographic Knowledge and Sexual Objectification

5.1. INTRODUCTION

Chapter 2 dealt with the subordination claim: the manufacture and consumption of pornography play a causal role in perpetuating systematic sexualized violence against women. This is not the only sense in which pornography seemingly harms women. Feminists often critique pornography for being a major force in women's sexual objectification. Most basically, objectification amounts to viewing and/or treating a person as a thing or an object to be used. With this in mind, antipornography feminism not only claims that pornography production objectifies female performers; rather, men's consumption of pornography also ends up objectifying women *as a group* by conditioning men to view and treat women as objects to be used for their sexual ends (Assiter 1988; Langton 1995; MacKinnon 1987; Vadas 2005; for an overview, see Papadaki 2015a).

Connected to this, Rae Langton (2009c) has more recently made an interesting suggestion that pornography produces a distinctive kind of *maker's knowledge* about women. This is also relevant for free speech debates about pornography (see chapter 4). Following J. S. Mill's liberalism, the generation of knowledge is one justification for free speech. Hence, there may be a knowledge-based *defense* of pornography: if pornography creates knowledge, there is a putative case for allowing it. Langton argues that pornography indeed produces knowledge about women, where the mechanism of knowledge production is women's objectification. In so doing, pornography produces a peculiar kind of knowledge that "not only aims at truth, but *makes* its truth" (Langton 2009c, 292). Nevertheless, this kind of projected and self-fulfilling pornographic knowledge is harmful in that it destroys women's sexual autonomy.[1] The knowledge-based defense of pornography is therefore undermined.

This chapter considers sexual objectification and its connection to pornographic knowledge. It examines what sexual objectification amounts to and allegedly does, and whether pornographic maker's knowledge is harmful, as Langton claims. The philosophical lessons to emerge from my discussion are as follows. First, even though we can make sense of the claim that pornography objectifies women, assessment of whether this claim is true typically involves a problematic focus on what pornography depicts in a decontextualized fashion. This is problematic since it is remarkably difficult to draw moral and ethical conclusions from apparently objectifying pornographic depictions alone. Second, even though some pornographic materials surely involve objectionable objectification of women and problematic requisite maker's knowledge, other materials plausibly do not. Determination of which materials are worrisome and which are not, again, depends on background social conditions and contexts. This then undermines Langton's view that pornographic maker's knowledge is always harmful in undermining women's sexual autonomy.

---

1. Langton is not alone in claiming that pornography hinders women's autonomy. Although not in connection to pornographic knowledge, other philosophers, too, take industrial, mainstream images of women's sexuality to hinder women's power to articulate their own conceptions of the good life (e.g., Dyzenhaus 1992; Easton 1994).

5.2. WHAT IS SEXUAL OBJECTIFICATION?

Sexual objectification of women is often viewed as one the most pernicious aspects of pornography. This raises a number of philosophically pertinent issues. First, what does objectification amount to? Second, why exactly is sexual objectification morally problematic? Third, since pornography seemingly involves *sexual* objectification of women, what makes objectification specifically sexual?

Let's consider these questions by looking at two prominent feminist accounts from MacKinnon and Martha Nussbaum. First, what is objectification? MacKinnon understands objectification to be dehumanizing and to involve *reductive* objectification, whereby—as Lina Papadaki puts it—"the objectified individual's humanity is reduced or diminished as she ends up acquiring the status of a thing (a being that no longer is a person)" (2015b, 96). This draws on a familiar Kantian idea that objectification involves diminishing, reducing, or lowering a person's humanity to the status of an object (for detailed discussions of this view, see Herman 2002; Papadaki 2007, 2015a; Shrage 2005). MacKinnon (1987) holds that in pornography women are made into sex objects and as objects they lack autonomy, subjectivity, agency, and self-determination. Nussbaum, by contrast, advances a *nonreductive* conception of objectification: it involves ignoring or not properly acknowledging someone's humanity. In a well-known article, Nussbaum examines 'objectification' as a loose cluster term. Or more specifically, objectification seemingly involves treating a person as an object, and such treatment involves seven possible features:

- *instrumentality*: treating a person as a tool for the objectifier's purposes;
- *denial of autonomy*: treating a person as lacking in autonomy and self-determination;

- *inertness*: treating a person as lacking in agency;
- *fungibility*: treating a person as interchangeable with other objects;
- *violability*: treating a person as lacking in boundary-integrity;
- *ownership*: treating a person as something that can be bought or sold;
- *denial of subjectivity*: treating a person as something whose experiences and feelings need not be taken into account. (Nussbaum 1995, 257)[2]

For Nussbaum, objectification can take place even if only one of the seven features is present, though in most cases objectification involves more than just one feature (1995, 258). Still, Nussbaum takes the denial of autonomy and instrumentalization to be the most morally exigent features. They are also connected in that noninstrumentally treating a person seemingly entails that their autonomy is recognized (Nussbaum 1995, 264).

What makes sexual objectification morally problematic? For MacKinnon, objectification is always morally objectionable: since it is dehumanizing and dehumanization is always morally wrong, so is objectification. *Contra* MacKinnon, Nussbaum does not hold that every instance of objectification—even of sexual objectification—is morally problematic. For her, "context is everything . . . in many if not all cases, the difference between an objectionable and a benign use of objectification will be made by the overall context of the human relationship" in which objectification takes place (Nussbaum 1995, 271). Objectification may even be a "wonderful" part of sexual lives (256). Features of benign objectification for Nussbaum encompass

---

2. Langton has added three more features to Nussbaum's list: reduction to body (a person is identified with their body parts); reduction to appearance (treating a person in terms of how they look); and silencing (treating a person as lacking the capacity to speak) (2009a, 228–229).

the absence of instrumentalization and that objectification is "symmetrical and mutual—and in both cases undertaken in a context of mutual respect and rough social equality" (275). Furthermore, "there is no malign or destructive intent" on the part of the objectifier (281), and a person's humanity is still acknowledged and respected (Papadaki 2010, 31). Negative or objectionable objectification, however, takes place when equality, respect, and consent are absent. At least based on some of Nussbaum's remarks, this sort of objectification is dehumanizing: "What is made sexy ... is precisely the act of turning a creature whom in one dim corner of one's mind one knows to be human into a thing, a something rather than a someone" (Nussbaum 1995, 281). However, Papadaki (2015b) takes Nussbaum's objectionable objectification ultimately to involve a slightly different phenomenon: negative objectification for Nussbaum involves merely ignoring or not properly acknowledging someone's humanity—it is about *disrespecting*, rather than destroying, the objectified individual's humanity. Nussbaum's conception then is weaker than MacKinnon's.[3]

3. Papadaki takes this to demonstrate that MacKinnon and Nussbaum's conceptions of *objectification* are in tension with one another. Stock (2015) disagrees: she argues that Nussbaum and MacKinnon are instead undertaking different projects. Nussbaum (according to Stock) is engaged in elucidating the concept of *objectification* and how the term 'objectification' is applied in everyday contexts. MacKinnon is aiming to explicate a specific phenomenon that is pretheoretically problematic. And so, the success of the former project hinges on "whether it captures all the significant contexts in which the concept is ordinarily applied," while in the latter whether the proposed account of objectification "offers explanatory value: a useful way of grouping observed phenomena in the world, at least partly with a view to effective moral criticism" (Stock 2015, 195). Although not in response to Stock, Bauer (2015, chap. 3) argues against Nussbaum-type analyses that seek to specify criteria for the application of 'objectification'. Rather than first elucidate the term 'sexual objectification' in order to make sense of people's experiences, feminist analyses of sexual objectification should start from ordinary intuitions and experiences of those facing and witnessing objectification—in short, we should start with affected persons' experiences. Feminist strategies like Nussbaum's (according to Bauer) fail to track the *relevant* phenomenon in the most reliable manner, and engaging in further conceptual analysis distracts feminist philosophers and prevents them from making sense of sexual objectification as a social fact.

Objectification need not have the absolute power to destroy women's humanity or reduce them to objects.[4]

For Nussbaum, objectification is always morally problematic *under some conditions*; but whether these conditions hold depends on the overall context in which objectification takes place. To explicate this, Nussbaum unfortunately and confusingly writes: "the instrumental treatment of human beings as tools of the purposes of another is always morally problematic; if it does not take place in a larger context of regard for humanity, it is a central form of the morally objectionable" (1995, 289). So, Nussbaum identifies instrumentalization as the most worrisome feature of objectification in being *always* morally problematic, while other features of objectification can be morally mitigated. And, nonetheless, Nussbaum holds that *even* instrumentalization can be morally mitigated if it takes place "in a larger context of regard for humanity." How can we make sense of this? In short, Nussbaum draws a distinction between instrumental use and *mere* instrumental use. The former is not problematic in all contexts. Consider Nussbaum's example to illustrate:

> If I am lying around with my lover on the bed, and use his stomach as a pillow there seems to be nothing at all baneful about this, provided that I do so with his consent . . . and without causing him pain, provided, as well, that I do so in the context of a relationship in which he is generally treated as more than a pillow. (1995, 265)

And so, we can make sense of the above claim: instrumentalization in a strong sense involves treating someone as a mere instrument

---

4. See also McLeod (2002) for a critique of the view that objectification must be somehow "absolute" in order to be morally problematic.

for one's ends, which is always morally wrong as this ends up being dehumanizing. Instrumentalization in a weaker sense, where the objectified person's humanity has not been negated, is not. Settling whether instrumentalization involves the strong or the weak form depends on the context, and whether the context is characterized by mutual respect and rough social equality (as Nussbaum puts it).

Having considered what objectification amounts to and what makes it morally objectionable, we still need to consider what makes objectification sexual. Perhaps surprisingly, answering this question is not straightforward. Still, depending on how we cash this out, our assessment of which instances are morally problematic and in what sense will differ. Nussbaum offers indirectly at least three answers: first, she claims that objectification occurs when "a human being is regarded and/or treated as an object, *in the context of a sexual relationship*" (1995, 254; italics mine). Second, she alludes to problematic instrumentalization involving someone being used to gratify another's sexual needs (270). And third, the problem with pornography is that it "depicts a thorough-going fungibility and commodification of sex partners, and, in the process, severs sex from any deep connection with self-expression or emotion" (283). Hence, what seems to make objectification specifically sexual hinges on the context (sexual situation), purpose (sexual gratification), or mode (commodified view of sex). MacKinnon also fails to provide a clear answer, although at times she appears to be committed to the second view: "A person . . . is a free and rational agent whose existence is an end in itself, as opposed to instrumental. In pornography women exist to the *end* of male pleasure" (1987, 173).

A closer look reveals that sexual context is the wrong characteristic to focus on. Langton is implicitly committed to this in describing Kant's view of sexual objectification (to which MacKinnon and A. Dworkin too seem to be wedded) as follows:

[I]n sexual contexts, women are treated as things to the extent that women are treated as merely bodies, as merely sensory appearances, as not free, as items that can be possessed, as items whose value is merely instrumental. (1995, 153)

But clearly women can be so treated in many contexts, and this view connects instrumental use and sexuality only contingently (it just so happens that *this time* objectification took place in a sexual context, rather than in some other context). But when feminists talk about sexual objectification, they are seemingly talking about a phenomenon where objectification and sexuality are not just accidentally and incidentally related. Furthermore, unless there is a tighter modal connection between objectification and it being sexual, we end up condemning the wrong thing when we condemn objectionable sexual objectification. What makes incidental cases objectionable will be either that they involve general objectification or that the objectification takes place in a sexual context. But both of these yield misguided critiques. First, objectification takes place in many contexts and per se poses no particular worry for feminists. That is, feminists may certainly be concerned about general, generic objectification, but one need not be a feminist to find such treatment objectionable (just think of Kant who was hugely concerned with objectifying treatment of others but was hardly a feminist). If the target of sexual objectification is just objectification in general, this seems to miss issues pertinent to feminists. Second, if the target of critique ends up being the sexual context, we again end up critiquing the wrong thing. There is surely nothing problematic about sexual contexts per se, unless one holds a dim view about sex as (for instance) always debasing humanity. As this conception of sex just looks pretheoretically false, focusing on the sexual context when critiquing sexual objectification misdirects feminist critical attention. Furthermore, this sort of misdirection unhelpfully buys into the caricature of antipornography feminism as being sex-negative and prudish.

Now, focusing on the mode—on pornography treating sex as something that can be traded against a monetary value—also ends up putting forward a misguided critique. Feminist condemnations of sexual objectification turn into condemnations of particular conceptions of *sex*: namely, of sex that is severed from "a deep connection" with one's partner, which (in my view) is overly romanticized. Nussbaum makes precisely such a move when she claims that pornography problematically "depicts a thoroughgoing fungibility and commodification of sex partners, and, in the process, severs sex from any deep connection with self-expression or emotion" (1995, 283). Claire Dines's critique of the pornography industry also hinges on such a romanticized view: "Porn sex is not about making love, as the feelings and emotions we normally associate with such an act—connection, empathy, tenderness, caring, affection—are replaced by those more often connected with hate—fear, disgust, anger, loathing, and contempt" (2011, xxiv). Dines further writes: "Missing from porn is anything that looks or feels remotely like intimacy and connection, the two ingredients that make sex interesting and exciting in the real world" (2011, 68). I suspect that not everyone agrees with this description of what makes sex interesting in the real world—and it is possible to disagree with Dines without being in thrall to a sexist sexual ideology. Claims like these demonstrate a significant difference in many antipornography and feminist pornography positions: the two camps disagree about the *role of sex* in our emotional lives and relationships. Nevertheless, they typically agree that exploitative and unethical pornography portrays women in deeply worrisome ways—a point of agreement that unfortunately gets obscured by radically different conceptions of sex.

Judith Hill provides another way to see why the commodification of sex in pornography does not quite explicate what makes objectification sexual (and objectionable). Hill considers whether "victim pornography" degrades all women, which is defined as the "graphic depiction of situations in which women are degraded by sexual activity" and where this activity is presented as entertaining (1987, 44). Although pornography may depict women being treated as mere means, these depictions are not morally reprehensible: "The fact that much of pornography *depicts* women being treated as means only, does not entail that pornographic material itself *treats* women as means only" (45). In order for degradation to take place, actual women must be so treated and pornography must be responsible for the treatment. Nevertheless, Hill goes on to claim that since the pornography industry makes a profit by circulating deep and vicious lies about women, it degrades women in a different sense. The morally relevant point is "not that pornography may incite men to rape women. The point is that the pornography industry blithely perpetuates derogatory myths, blithely lies, about the nature of women, for its own financial gain" (49). I have much sympathy with this critique of pornography. But it, too, suggests that capitalist markets, rather than women's sexual objectification, are to blame. Objectification is again only incidentally sexual and objectionable insofar as it takes place within industrial, profit-driven contexts.

Having rejected context and mode as that which makes objectification sexual, we are left with the purpose: objectification is essentially tied to instrumental use of someone as a mere tool for another's *sexual ends* (e.g., sexual gratification). To see this more clearly, distinguish different instrumental uses. Imagine a case where one is drugged and has their mouth swabbed so that one's DNA can be extracted for scientific research, when (for some reason) the person would not have consented to its extraction. In this case, the person has been used as a mere tool for scientific purposes. This differs from a case where a drugged person has sex forced on them: in this case, they have been used as a mere tool—they have been instrumentalized—for sexual ends. We can further illustrate the idea by thinking about mere instrumental use in a sexual context that is nonetheless nonsexual. Think of someone who engages in sexual activity but with nonsexual ends in mind: for instance, imagine someone who has sex solely for the purpose of reproduction in order to comply with religious teachings or to satisfy God's will of populating the world with followers of one's religion. (Bearing in mind that reproduction and sexuality are clearly distinct: one can reproduce without any sexual activity and engage in sexual activity without any intention to reproduce.) In this case, the person would treat another as a mere instrument for their ends that are to do with reproduction and religion. The treatment is objectifying for sure, and it takes place in a sexual context; but it is not sexually objectifying insofar as the other is not instrumentalized for sexual ends. Consequently, this yields an account of what makes sexual objectification *sexual*: if the ends for which one is used are sexual (as opposed to, say, religious), one's objectification is specifically sexual too.

5.3. PORNOGRAPHIC MAKER'S KNOWLEDGE

Above I outlined prominent feminist conceptions of *sexual objectification*. Being a book in philosophy, one might expect me to consider next how plausible these conceptions are. In what follows, I won't tackle their plausibility directly. Rather, I will consider the role that objectification plays in putative pornographic knowledge and whether the latter is harmful (as Langton claims). I will return to dehumanizing objectification and consider its plausibility at the end of the chapter.

Langton connects objectification to a kind of knowledge pornography allegedly generates. Pornography conceivably produces maker's knowledge, which is a special kind of knowledge that makers have by virtue of creating something (Langton 2009c, 289). Maker's knowledge functions like a blueprint, rather than a mirror—just think of the sort of knowledge that (say) architects have of the buildings they have designed. Pornography, too, creates maker's knowledge. Or better, pornographers have a special kind of knowledge about their creations akin to architects' knowledge. Pornographic (or architectural) maker's knowledge is distinctive in being self-fulfilling. The world arranges itself to fit the pornographic "design," which involves a kind of desire-driven projection. In order for such projection to work, the maker must have some substantial social power or the design must echo the desires of the socially dominant group(s). This idea draws heavily on MacKinnon's social ontology, where reality (in general as well as the "truth" about sex) is constructed from the dominant perspective. Since men are the dominant social group, it is constructed from *their* perspective. The mechanism of construction is objectification: male power has the ability to create "the world in its own image, the image of its desires" through women's objectification (MacKinnon 1989b, 118). This does not generate falsehoods, illusion, or deception about how things are. Rather, the world comes to fit how the powerful want the world to be:

> [For MacKinnon] when the powerful desire that p, they come to believe that p . . . instead of belief arranging itself to fit the world, the world arranges itself to fit the belief. When the powerful believe that p, things alter to make it the case that p. (Langton 2009c, 283)

A nonpornographic example of such projection-driven construction is the golem effect: when the teaching staff has lowered expectations about an individual's academic performance, it leads to poorer performance results by the individual, given how the staff subsequently treats the student.

With respect to pornography, projection is said to work roughly as follows. Pornography falsely portrays women as sexually submissive, and this conditions male desire to find dominance and submission "sexy." As MacKinnon puts it, pornography eroticizes the dominance and submission dynamic: "It makes hierarchy sexy and calls that 'the truth about sex' or just a mirror of reality. Through this process pornography constructs what a woman is as what men want from sex" (1987, 171). The prevalent masculinist perspective desires women to be submissive and since this is the perspective of the dominant group, men have the power to *project* and *enforce* their desires and perspectives onto the world (make their desires "real" in the world). This perspective, then, takes women *in fact* to be submissive: it is believed that sexual submissiveness is an independently existing fact about women's supposed sexual nature. In other words, pornography puts forward a certain blueprint about women's sexuality, which is not just an illusion but becomes real via enforcement. Just think about women, who self-report feeling pressure to conform to a pornographic image of sexuality to avoid certain social sanctions (Bauer 2015, chap. 4). This generates problematic maker's knowledge about women in suggesting that sexual submissiveness is the alleged truth about women's sexuality.[5] For Langton, pornographic knowledge so generated constitutes a kind of gendered harm. Part of the harm involved is in the *shape* of women that pornography projects: that is, its vision of women enjoying rape, being inferior, and sexually servile. Another part of the harm is the *shaping* itself: in having the power to shape sexuality, pornography takes away women's power to

---

5. MacKinnon further claims that to look at the world objectively is to objectify. I will not explore the connection between objectification and objectivity here though, as this does not specifically pertain to pornography debates. See Haslanger (1993) for an illuminating discussion of the connection.

determine their own sexuality. In short, the harm of pornographic maker's knowledge boils down to it destroying women's sexual autonomy.

At least some social scientific research supports the view that sexual objectification harms women in related ways: sexual objectification is causally linked to men's perceptions of women as being incompetent and not credible, generally speaking. Female self-objectification is further linked to lowered grade point averages and problems with sexual satisfaction and intellectual development (Tarrant 2014). Nonetheless, various media outlets conceivably promulgate sexual objectification with such adverse effects. This raises questions about how plausible the connection between *pornographic* knowledge and objectification is. Let's consider this issue next by looking at three questions in detail: (1) Does pornography have the role that Langton's view presupposes it to have? (2) Is pornographic knowledge *maker's* knowledge? (3) Might some pornographic knowledge be *nonharmful* maker's knowledge? To anticipate, I will ultimate claim that although some pornography surely involves problematic maker's knowledge, who the maker is makes a huge difference—and so, not all pornography generates harmful maker's knowledge.

5.3.1. The Role of Pornography

Is pornography responsible for generating harmful maker's knowledge about women? One might worry that pornography's role in women's objectification is exaggerated. Many sexually nonexplicit materials (e.g., advertisements, literature, other media) contain objectifying portrayals of women and, some argue, given that romance novels and advertising are likely to be more widespread than inegalitarian violent pornography, they play a greater role in problematic objectification (Cocks 1989; Coward 1984; see also Eaton 2012 who considers women's objectification relative to the artistic genre of female nude). Although this seemed true a couple of decades ago, it is nowadays doubtful given how ubiquitous Internet pornography has become.

Nonetheless, one might contest the assertion that pornography objectifies *only* women. It is not uncommon to hear in everyday discussions that pornography objectifies *male* performers because they are more reduced to their body parts than female performers. In line with this, two Amsterdam-based communication scientists, **Marleen** Klaassen and Jochen Peter, have recently conducted a content analysis of pornography's putative objectification. They focused on two key features from Nussbaum's definition of *objectification*. First, on the frequency of instrumentalization, such as instances of close-up shots of body parts, manual stimulation of sexual organs, oral stimulation, and achieving orgasms; second, on markers of (de)humanization that included the frequency of initiating sex, seeking sex for one's own pleasure, and close-up shots of faces. The authors then conducted a quantitative content analysis of mainstream pornographic videos on four popular and free on-line platforms (Pornhub, RedTube, YouPorn, xHamster) selecting the top-100 most-viewed videos in February 2013 of each site (400 videos in total). The selected videos had been viewed from 300,000 to over 52,600,000 times, which (as the authors mildly put it) confirms their popularity. The findings of this research purportedly support the pretheoretical view that in pornography male performers are objectified. In summarizing their findings, Klaassen and Peter write:

[W]omen were more likely to be instrumentalized than men [in mainstream pornographic Internet videos], as indicated by a strong focus on women's sexual body parts as well as on sex acts and orgasms in which men rather than women gained sexual pleasure. However, there was no evidence of a general dehumanization of women. Notably, men were more likely to be dehumanized than women in that men's faces were rarely shown. (2015, 727)

One might, however, worry that this is too quick. For one thing, consider the frequency of initiating sex and seeking sex for one's own pleasure, which are markers of humanization. One might grant that in much of mainstream pornography women do initiate sex, rather than have sex forced or coerced on them. However, this may not be innocuous in that it can reinforce a view of women as always ready and available for sex. That is, there is a difference between portraying women positively as sexually self-determining and problematically as hypersexualized and insatiable. Hence, pointing out that mainstream Internet pornography includes depictions of women initiating sex does not yet show that these depictions portray women positively as self-determining in a sexual context.

One might further wonder if background social and political conditions make a difference as to whether the failure to display men's faces counts as dehumanizing on Nussbaum's account. Being reduced to one's body parts does not figure as a social cost for men, and thus, being so treated does not have the same social and moral significance for all genders.[6] Compare racial slurs directed at persons racialized as white and as black. Given background social inequalities and histories of racial oppression not all racial slurs are on a par: racial slurs about white people have much less bite given their relatively privileged social position occupancy. Similar considerations should make a difference to our assessment of pornographic objectification too: even if both male and female performers are reduced to their body parts, given patriarchal and sexist background conditions, the

---

6. And given intersectionality, the meanings may differ even further given other identity facets and within gender categories too.

resultant objectification is likely to be different in *kind*. Bluntly: even when male performers' heads are cut off and the camera focuses just on their genitalia, this does not generate widespread and persistent conceptions about men being there "just for fucking." And even when such conceptions are generated, this tends to work for men's benefit, rather than being something that incurs social sanctions. (Just think of the common phenomenon of sexually promiscuous females being branded "sluts" and males being hailed as "studs.") Thus, the same surface actions (cutting off of faces, racial slurs) can have very different social *meanings* given broader background conditions and circumstances. Trying to grasp the significance of pornographic depictions without considering wider social and cultural conditions is likely to yield misguided results.

Furthermore, Langton (2009a) has argued that one way of treating another as an object involves an explicit *affirmation* of their autonomy. For instance, autonomy affirmation is a necessary feature of sadistic rape. Sadistic rapists want their victims to fight back and thereby affirm that they are subjects rather than inert things. Inert objects cannot partake in their own violation, only subjects with agency can. And sadistic rape is precisely aimed at exploiting the victim's autonomous subjecthood in order to violate it. In this case, objectification *depends on* the affirmation of autonomy (2009a, 225). To connect this idea to the above content analysis, consider two senses of autonomy denial: first, nonattribution of autonomy; second, violation or hampering of autonomy. Langton takes the former primarily to be an attitude, while the latter is more action: it involves an active deed that prevents another from doing what they choose (2009a, 233). These senses are distinct. Some depictions can superficially attribute autonomy to women in pornography in that they (for instance) apparently seek sex for their own pleasure. But such depictions may still end up violating the autonomy of actual women by creating expectations about women's sexuality in pornography's consumers. And so, it is insufficient to claim that mainstream Internet pornography does not dehumanize women in the sense of involving autonomy denial just by looking at what is depicted. This is because pornographic autonomy violations need not take the form of depicting forced or coerced sex, which would involve the nonattribution of autonomy. Rather, autonomy violation can take the second form, where autonomy is first attributed precisely in order to be subsequently assaulted.

The take-home message is that although pornography is certainly not alone in depicting women in problematic ways and although men may also be depicted in worrisome ways in pornography, objectification of differently gendered individuals is not morally on a par. As Nussbaum holds, background contexts make a great deal of difference, and to examine prima facie objectifying pornographic depictions in a social vacuum is likely to miss aspects relevant for the moral assessment of pornographic works and depictions.

5.3.2. Pornographic Knowledge as Maker's Knowledge

Above I considered a challenge to Langton's view that pornography generates maker's knowledge by examining the putative role that pornography plays in women's objectification. One might challenge the existence of pornographic maker's knowledge in other ways too. Next I will consider whether all pornographic knowledge is *maker's* knowledge. To begin with, one might appeal to pornographic intentions to challenge this view. Maker's knowledge must be intentional: architects do not design buildings accidentally, and architectural blueprints typically are intentionally the way they are. Having a specific vision and aiming one's product design to realize that vision are intentional moves. Still, antipornography feminism also at times holds that pornography or pornographers need not intentionally aim to degrade or objectify women. Rather, depictions of women and their sexuality can be degrading and objectifying without being so intended and without any intentional ill will. But the idea of pornographic maker's knowledge is in tension with the view that pornography can promote problematic images of women and sexuality without intending to promote such images. If pornography involves harmful maker's knowledge, the harmful images promulgated in and by pornography must be intended as harmful or as images that celebrate or endorse women's degradation. If this intention is absent, it makes no sense to talk about pornographic *maker's* knowledge (though of course pornography may still generate some other kind of harmful knowledge).

Discussions in previous chapters raised difficulties with determining pornographic intentions from the philosopher's armchair, and I will return to this topic in chapters to come. However, even from the philosophical armchair, it does seem warranted to say that some pornographers do intentionally promote harmful visions of women's sexuality—visions that celebrate women's sexual submissiveness and endorse not taking consent seriously. Max Hardcore strikes me as a clear example.[7] Fortunately, not all producers are like him. Consider the work of pornographers who self-identify as feminists.[8] These makers explicitly intend to produce egalitarian pornography, rather than, what on Langton's and MacKinnon's views would count as, erotica (see section 1.3). One of the most famous

---

7. The 2001 documentary film *Hardcore* by Stephen Walker provides a vivid albeit highly disturbing illustration. The film follows a British single mother, Felicity, trying to make a career in the US pornography industry. By far one of the most upsetting scenes involves an encounter Felicity has with Hardcore at a filming set. The documentary makers ended up removing Felicity from the set due to Hardcore's predatory, manipulative, and abusive behavior. The scene quite clearly shows that Felicity's consent to performing and engaging in sexual acts that she was uncomfortable with was of no concern to Hardcore.

8. For an excellent guide to feminist pornography, see http://www.feministpornguide.com/. This site is maintained by one of the most well-known directors in the genre, Ms. Naughty. I will discuss feminist pornography in more detail in chapter 7.

examples is the 2009 film *Dirty Diaries* consisting of twelve shorts of "feminist porn" (https://en.wikipedia.org/wiki/Dirty_Diaries/). An instructive ten-point manifesto accompanies the film. This manifesto urges the creation of alternatives to the mainstream pornography industry by making different kinds of "sexy films." Other manifesto points include fighting against prevalent beauty myths, capitalism, patriarchy in general and in the mainstream pornography industry, and censorship that represses images of liberated female sexuality. They also include fighting for a change in our conceptions of and judgments about female sexuality, women's reproductive and bodily control, and diversity in expressions of sexuality. *Dirty Diaries* is not the only example of this kind. In chapter 4, I also noted the examples of Petra Joy, Sinnamon Love, and Candida Royalle. These producers intend to provide alternatives to and to subvert the mainstream pornography industry as well as to portray a less distorted picture of sexuality in general and of racialized/female sexuality in particular. Feminist pornographers often hold that much of mainstream industrial pornography is sexist (e.g. Arrowsmith 2013). But (they maintain) we should not therefore oppose pornography per se. Rather, we should oppose exploitative and unethical pornography. Feminist producers aim to show (among other things) that exploitative mainstream industrial pornography gets things *wrong*. They aim to represent female sexuality more authentically in order to undercut unrealistic representations found in the run-of-the-mill mainstream imagery. Feminist pornography might, then, have a claim to telling educationally valuable truths about gender and sexuality. In this case, it too produces pornographic knowledge, but not *maker's* knowledge. Rather, feminist pornography has a claim to being a more standard sort of knowledge that mirrors reality.

Nevertheless, a proper assessment of this suggestion requires us to take issue with what is authentic sexuality: if it is accurately represented in feminist pornographers' works, these works involve more standard kind of knowledge, rather than maker's knowledge. But the prospects of making good this move are poor. An elucidation of authentic or "true" sexuality of any kind is impossible, I contend, given the extent and influence of socialization, cultural traditions, even indoctrination, and taboos in shaping human sexual lives. With this in mind, some antipornography claims about what pornography does strike me as deeply misguided (although I think that antipornography feminism is not alone in disseminating misguided views about authentic sexuality). Dines claims that in "pornland"

> an authentic sexuality—one that develops organically out of life experiences, one's peer group, personality traits, family and community affiliations–is replaced by generic porn sexuality limited in creativity and lacking any sense of love, respect, or connection to another human being. (2011, xi)

Given what we know about coercive mechanisms that families, communities, and even the law exercise to make people conform to heteronormative sexual expectations, I see little reason to believe that an authentic sexuality would "organically" develop in the course of sexual maturation without pornography. Even though I would welcome curbing the power that inegalitarian, industrial pornography has to construct sexuality, we have good reasons to doubt that in its absence our sexual lives will magically become gender just. Furthermore, although I have no doubts that unethical pornographic-production patterns persist, focusing on those alone is like discussing current food-production practices *solely* by focusing on industrial, cruel, and unethical practices. Chauntelle Anne Tibbals offers a more recent sociological study of current trends in the US pornography industry and concludes:

[A]lthough it comes in many different forms, politically charged considerations regarding authenticity and ethics seem ubiquitous to adult content production and consumption today. Ethics generally refers to the fair treatment of adult performers in their respective workplaces, as well as ethical representations of sex in content. Authenticity refers to the "realness" of content, and various debates regarding what constitutes "real" sex and sex-related representations are ongoing. (2014, 133)

This helpfully enables us to distinguish different ways in which depictions of sex can be authentic: authenticity may be about how sex would "really" be were it not for pernicious pornography, or it can be about how sexuality is manifested outside of pornographic contexts. Hence, even though no such thing as a truly authentic nonconstructed sexuality exists in my view, ethically focused pornography that aims to depict sexuality in alternative ways to exploitative, industrial pornography may nevertheless have a claim to depicting more authentic sexuality in avoiding warped depictions of sexuality (like depictions that condone and endorse ignoring consent in sexual situations, or that, *contra* standard pornography tropes, most women do not enjoy facial ejaculations). This would render the generated knowledge a more standard kind of knowledge in challenging deformed depictions of sex that are found in inegalitarian, industrial pornography.

5.3.3. *Pornographic Knowledge as Nonharmful Maker's Knowledge*

Above I considered the possibility that some pornography might not involve maker's knowledge. There is, however, yet another way to challenge Langton's knowledge-based argument against pornography. We might accept that pornography involves maker's knowledge. But if some instances of sexual objectification can be morally benign (as argued for by Green 2000; Nussbaum 1995; Soble 2002), some resultant instances of pornographic maker's knowledge can be so too—some such knowledge will be *nonharmful*.[9]

Not everyone accepts the antecedent though. For instance, Papadaki (2010) holds that we should reject Nussbaum's account of benign objectification because calling cases where people's humanity is merely disrespected (rather than destroyed) 'objectification' makes the notion too broad. This may prevent feminists from effectively fighting negative objectification, and so it would be preferable to restrict objectification to cover the morally problematic cases only. Bauer (2015) agrees and thinks that Nussbaum's extended understanding empties the concept *sexual objectification* of any political "oomph." Patricia Marino (2008) also questions the idea of benign objectification. As she sees it, symmetry and mutuality do not mitigate objectification: if sexual actors ignore their partners' desires and wishes symmetrically, Marino asks, "how could this improve [instrumental] use that is otherwise problematic?" (2008, 353). That said, something else might: when instrumental use does not violate autonomy in that a person has genuinely consented to instrumental sexual use. However, in this case what matters for genuine consent is background social and political equality. And so, under the right background conditions, consensual instrumental use is possible, and it would be morally benign. Marino nonetheless holds that given the prevalence of sexism, this sort of genuine consent may currently be impossible (2008, 360–361; see also Bauer 2015, chap. 4 for a discussion of the "allure" of self-objectification that might make genuine consent presently unattainable).

---

9. In fact, I think that some pornographic maker's knowledge can be emancipatory and not merely nonharmful. I will postpone discussing pornography's emancipatory potential until chapter 7 though.

Claiming that genuine consent is de facto impossible without gender justice strikes me as too strong. The example of BDSM further undermines this view and challenges the idea that seemingly objectifying sexual practices cannot be consented to (e.g., Califia 1994). BDSM communities typically have detailed and stringently followed rules that govern sexual encounters (though of course these rules of conduct are not watertight). It is customary for the participants in BDSM "play" to discuss the details of their encounters beforehand and to make sure that the participants are aware of the sexual practices that their partners wish to engage in. They also agree on certain strictly enforced safe words, which signify the end of play. Some BDSM advocates argue that their sexual practices are among the most consensual to be found. Nonpractitioners (the argument goes) fail to understand what goes on in such practices, and therefore find them degrading, objectifying, and violent based on the surface activities depicted (Rubin 1993). Therefore, if the moral status of objectification in pornography hinges on whether participants have genuinely consented to being objectified, it is a mistake to focus just on whether pornographic *depictions* are objectifying. Our assessment of pornographic imagery must consider the contexts of making, viewing, and distributing pornographic materials. Given the context, some such materials may actually enhance women's sexual autonomy or (at the very least) not hinder it.

Another way to challenge the idea that pornographic maker's knowledge is always harmful is to think about whether feminist pornography involves morally problematic objectification of women. That is, we can accept that some pornography objectifies women in pernicious ways—but perhaps feminist pornography avoids this. This would be possible if the shape (i.e., the vision) of women that feminist pornography portrays is not insidious, and if the shaping of sexuality does not undermine women's sexual autonomy. Assessing these claims is not, however, easy with philosophical tools. Evaluating whether the vision of women put forward in particular pornographic works or genres is insidious cannot be undertaken with a priori philosophical methods; rather, doing so requires tools from film and cultural studies. Still, the example of *Dirty Diaries* and its accompanying manifesto points speak against the view that the vision of women put forward is one of servility and inferiority to the extent that pornography *simpliciter* counts as the subordination of women. This example also speaks against the second claim about shaping: part of the project of feminist pornography is to urge women to shape themselves instead of patriarchal conceptions of women's sexuality doing the work. Feminist pornography aims to increase options available to women in the shaping process. In this case, it involves maker's knowledge too, but not the harm that Langton identifies. Furthermore, Langton holds that the shaping of sexuality is harmful insofar as the projected vision of female sexuality "becomes, in contexts of oppression, a self-fulfilling one" (2009c, 307). But note here the key point about projection becoming self-fulfilling in *contexts of oppression*. Although Langton does not clarify what exactly she means, I suspect that Langton had in mind current background social conditions that are generally speaking patriarchal and sexist. Social injustice is (fortunately) like a frictionless plane: the latter does not exist in reality and, in a similar sense, absolute injustice that leaves no room for resistance and escape is infrequent. Even in contexts of oppression, then, the power of oppressive pornography is not absolute. There is room for emancipatory, feminist pornography too. And so, if the construction of sexuality takes place within subcultural contexts that are feminist and emancipatory, where women are positively depicted as sexually self-determining, this can generate nonharmful pornographic maker's knowledge.

Above I mentioned Langton's view that one way of treating another as an object involves an explicit autonomy affirmation. With this in mind, one might object that perhaps feminist pornography ends up denying women's autonomy in a parallel fashion. It first affirms it via an alternative vision of sexually autonomous women in control of their bodies and desires; but this ends up undermining women's power to shape their own sexual lives. One projected social construction of women's sexuality (a mainstream one) has simply been replaced by another (a putatively feminist one). I suggested above that some mainstream depictions can superficially attribute autonomy to women in that (for instance) women in pornography apparently seek sex for their own pleasure. But such depictions may still end up violating actual women's autonomy by creating certain expectations about sexuality in pornography's consumers. Might the same then be true of putatively feminist pornography, which would make it no less worrying than its mainstream industrial counterpart? I think not. Although both put forward a certain shape or vision of gender, the projected visions are substantially different. Even though Langton may be right that one way to objectify another involves an affirmation of their autonomy, whether feminist pornography involves this move is another matter. In order to show that it does, Langton must show that the vision of women that feminist pornography projects is in the end insidious and corrupt. However, it is not possible to demonstrate this by appealing to intuitions. A proper analysis of this point would require alternative investigative methods that consider actual pornography production and pornographic products more carefully. Still, given that one major point of feminist pornography is to avoid common pornography tropes (like money shots and gagging/choking oral sex), the shape of women's sexuality depicted differs substantially depending on who does the depicting. Furthermore, the expectations generated in the viewers of feminist pornography are likely to be very different to those generated by much of industrial mainstream pornography. This is (I would speculate) due to background political commitments of those who seek out feminist pornography. Unlike much of easily available Internet pornography, self-proclaimed feminist pornography is much harder to come by freely online. Consumers of such materials are (roughly put) more discerning, and they go to greater lengths to find materials that satisfy not only certain sexual appetites but that also fit the consumers' pre-existing political commitments. Just compare consumers of feminist, ethical pornography with any other ethical consumerism: given people's political and ethical views, some go to great lengths to ensure that their consumption patterns are as ethical as possible. Pornography consumption in this sense is no different.

5.4. THE CONSTRUCTION OF SEXUALITY

Earlier chapters considered pornography's putative causal influence on (re)producing systematic sexualized violence against women. Above I examined pornography's apparent causal role in women's objectification. There may, however, be a still further way to think about what pornography does. MacKinnon writes:

> To be sexually objectified means having a social meaning imposed on your being that defines you as to be sexually used . . . and then using you that way . . . Pornography creates an accessible sexual object, the possession and consumption of which is male sexuality, to be possessed and consumed as which is female sexuality. This is not because pornography depicts objectified sex but because it creates the experience of a sexuality which is itself objectified. (1989a, 329)

The idea here is that pornography plays a central role in the construction of sexuality.[10] In fact, pornography not only constructs women's

---

10. Let me clarify: although pornography supposedly plays a central causal role in this construction, antipornography feminists like MacKinnon do not therefore hold that

sexuality, but it also constructs women's "natures" (or what it is to be a woman) more generally. This hinges on MacKinnon's general theory of gender as a theory of sexuality (for feminist theories of gender and sex, see Mikkola 2017a). Gender difference for MacKinnon is not a matter of having any particular psychological orientation or displaying some specific behavioral patterns; rather, it is a function of sexuality that is hierarchal in sexist societies. Roughly, the social meaning of sex (i.e., gender) hinges on sexual objectification of women in that women are viewed and treated as objects for the satisfaction of men's desires. Masculinity is defined as sexual dominance, femininity as sexual submissiveness: genders are "created through the eroticization of dominance and submission. The man/ woman difference and the dominance/submission dynamic define each other. This is the social meaning of sex" (MacKinnon 1989b, 113). Of course, there is nothing natural about such hierarchical sexuality. Male and female sexualities are both defined from a male point of view, which is conditioned by pornography in that it tells deep and vicious lies about women supposedly being submissive (MacKinnon 1989b, chap. 7).[11]

Timo Jütten has more recently developed such a MacKinnon-inspired account of construction, which he terms "the imposition account": "the defining feature of sexual objectification is the

pornography alone is responsible for women's subordination. It is one of the forces that subordinates women, but a full explanation of subordination hinges on various other phenomena connected to male dominance too. Nevertheless, MacKinnon seems to think that since women's putative "natures" have been constructed in insidious ways, this undergirds different subordinating forces, like sexual harassment and the lack of credibility.

11. One might immediately wonder how women's constructed nature as sex objects squares with the idea that pornography tells lies about women being for men's sexual satisfaction. After all, if pornography constructs women's nature as being object-like, it no longer *lies* about women when they are depicted as object-like (McGowan 2005; Mikkola 2010). I briefly touched on this point in chapter 3, and I will discuss it in more detail in chapter 8. For now, I will focus on examining the role that sexual objectification supposedly plays in this construction.

imposition of a social meaning on women, which marks them out as proper objects of instrumentalizing attitudes and treatment that undermine their autonomy and equal social standing" (2016, 28). Irrespective of any actual instrumentalization that may subsequently follow, such an imposition of a social meaning on women is wrongful in and of itself—and this is what makes sexual objectification wrongful. Jütten's conception of *sexual objectification* is meant to be distinct from Nussbaum's in that even though the imposition of meaning and instrumentalization are typically connected, they need not be. Rather, imposition of the social meaning "sex object" is a necessary and sufficient condition for sexual objectification. Morally impermissible instrumentalization is neither a necessary nor a sufficient condition for it, but an additional harm and wrong that is made possible by sexual objectification. (Jütten 2016, 29–30)

How does (objectionable) sexual objectification harm women? Understood in the imposition sense, it is an affront to women's autonomy and equal social standing because sexual objectification allegedly hampers self-presentation. This idea of self-presentation draws on the works of Thomas Nagel and David Velleman and refers to us intentionally creating "public images of ourselves by selecting which aspects of ourselves we expose to others and which we conceal from them" (Jütten 2016, 33). Self-presentation depends on two social conditions: first, "on our ability to be self-presenters at all"; second, "on socially available meanings in terms of which we can present ourselves" (Jütten 2016, 34). If we are unable to self-present because we cannot fulfill the first condition, our autonomous agency is imperiled. If our inability to self-present hinges on the inability to satisfy the second condition, our equal social standing is under threat. This is what sexual objectification of women does: when social meanings are imposed on women, sexual objectification hampers women's capacity to self-present (Jütten 2016, 35)—it limits women's opportunities for self-presentation and therefore threatens their autonomous agency and equal social status. This is because, when women are viewed as sex objects whose nature and worth are defined from the perspective of male sexuality, their opportunities as autonomous and equal self-presenting agents are undermined, which attacks women's social standing.

There are grounds to find this view worrisome though, which indirectly shows MacKinnon's original view to be questionable too. First, the imposition account is too strong and overstated; second, pornography's role in it is questionable. The imposition account makes sexual objectification the linchpin of gender injustice per se. For instance, sexual objectification imposes the view of women as men's sexual servants, where this "socializes men and women into gendered role expectations that teach them to assume their sexual and social roles as superiors and subordinates" (Jütten 2016, 40). Furthermore, it is sexual objectification that grounds women's vulnerability in general because women can be "reduced to sex object status at any time when their sexual attributes are made dominant in their public image" (Jütten 2016, 42). And finally: "all practices and media that participate in the construction of gender roles through sexual objectification undermine women's opportunities for self-presentation, because they construct what the social status of women is on the basis of men's interests" (Jütten 2016, 46). The worry here is that sexual objectification and being expected to be a sexual servant for men are surely not alone in grounding ways in which women's opportunities for self-presentation are hampered. Just think of the ways in which women are expected to do service work (both in public and private), various ways in which work and family lives are divided along gendered lines, and the different ways in which women are economically and socially vulnerable. To say that gendered roles and identities *all* ultimately hinge on women being viewed as men's sexual servants and on women being reduced to sex objects strikes me as exaggerated, and gender roles and identities are conceivably constructed though various mechanisms (not through sexual objectification alone). Again, think of the expectation that women undertake the bulk of household chores and caretaking roles. Is this ultimately undergirded by the view that women are men's sexual servants? Not obviously: women may be viewed as men's servants, but in a manner that does not simply hinge on the view that "women are properly valued and treated in terms of their sexual attractiveness and availability" (Jütter 2016, 45). Being viewed as servile and as sexually servile are not equivalent and running the two together in such a sweeping manner is an overstatement. Reducing the social reality of gendered oppression to sexual objectification in Jütten's sense is not a particularly compelling social explanation of a complex phenomenon that is historically and culturally specific.

Moreover, does pornography have the power to undermine women's equal social status in Jütten's sense? The story apparently goes like this. Pornography generates and imposes sexual social meanings available to men and to women, but these are not on a par: the available social meanings in the realm of sex for women are impoverished and having such impoverished meanings imposed on women undermines their equal citizenship. As sexual objectification is by definition morally exigent, consenting to objectification is morally irrelevant: women's status as sex objects "licenses the same attitudes and behaviors whether it is imposed or embraced" (Jütten 2016, 47–48). Furthermore, Jütten claims that de facto women's choices may often be driven by socioeconomic "desperation"—and even when this is not the case, it still apparently "remains difficult for women to defend their equal social standing when they adopt sexualized self-images" (Jütten 2016, 48). Jütten qualifies this claim in a footnote stating: "I am not suggesting that women necessarily make these decisions consciously. Decisions about dress, makeup, mannerisms, and speech are made on the basis of conventions that are deeply embedded in class-specific socialization processes"

(2016, 48 fn. 67). This story, however, suggests that women are help-less dupes, who cannot resist what is imposed upon them, and that pornography has a huge amount of power to enact all manner of gendered conventions and norms. This strikes me as false, which is plainly obvious from the fact that socialization is not deterministic and not solely driven by pornography.

Then again, assume for argument's sake that Jütten is right. If pornography and other media have such power to impose social meanings that threaten women's equal citizenship in hampering ways to be self-presenting, this ends up threatening *everyone's* equal citizenship. After all, women are not alone in being influenced by social conventions; men, too, come under the purview of imposed social meanings that define them as providers, leaders, and "sexual studs." Prima facie this ends up threatening men's opportunities to be self-presenting too. The sexual meanings imposed on men differ in content and valuation. But, as noted earlier, run-of-the-mill industrial pornography also presents men with diminished sexual scripts and constructs male sexuality in truncated ways that seemingly threaten men's self-presentation as well. Consequently, the problem with pornography is not that some are constructed as sex objects. Rather the problem becomes the *imposition* of sexual meanings irrespective of content. In this case, focusing on sexual objectification focuses on the wrong aspect of the story. Rather, we should single out imposition of meanings for moral condemnation—but then, there is no special sense in which women alone are affected by it.

The point of the above discussion, in short, is this: even though I do not dispute that our sexual lives and selves are constructed with pornography conceivably playing a central role in contem-porary constructions of sexuality, we should be careful not to overstate such construction and pornography's role in it. What seems to be leading us astray is the misguided view that we can offer elucidations of complex issues (like women's abilities to self-present) by relying on intuitive and introspective methods. Conceptual clarity and stringent argumentation are surely good things, but for compelling social explanations we need something more.

5.5. DEHUMANIZING OBJECTIFICATION

This chapter has considered what sexual objectification amounts to and the role it supposedly plays in generating pornographic knowledge. In discussing Langton's idea of pornographic knowledge in detail, I argued for two views. First, that some pornographic knowledge may not be maker's knowledge, but a more standard sort of knowledge that mirrors reality; second, that some pornographic maker's knowledge may be nonharmful. These claims hinge on the recognition that who the maker is makes a significant difference to the resultant pornographic knowledge. Furthermore, these differences impact how pornographic works should be ethically assessed—something I will return to in chapter 8.

Before moving on, though, there is one final issue I wish to discuss. As mentioned, MacKinnon equates objectification and dehumanization. She is not alone in doing so. A. Dworkin writes:

> Objectification occurs when a human being, through social means, is made less than human, turned into a thing or commodity, bought and sold. When objectification occurs, a person is depersonalized, so that no individuality or integrity is available ... Objectification is an injury right at the heart of discrimination: those who can be used as if they are not fully human are no longer fully human in social terms; their humanity is hurt by being diminished. (2000, 30–31)

Linda LeMoncheck (1985) too takes objectification to involve dehumanization: sexual objectification constructs women as lesser human beings. The wrong of objectification then is grounded in a failure to treat women as moral equals. However, I am unconvinced that this equation is helpful and fitting and, as I see it, it should be avoided: objectification is one thing, dehumanization another.[12] To see this, consider A. Dworkin's claim above. On the one hand, she claims that persons are *made* into things; on the other hand, persons are treated *as if* they are less than fully human. In the former case, the problem with objectification boils down to a sort of category mistake: human beings are literally and falsely categorized as things, which is morally troubling. However, in the latter case something else is going on: if objectification involves x reducing y's humanity, then x must have attributed humanity to y to begin with. And so, reducing another's humanity and literally treating someone as something are two distinct phenomena, where the former presupposes another's humanity to be reduced while the latter does not. Ann Cahill also agrees: objectification or objectifying images do not represent or portray women as "utterly object-like, as lacking in the traits and abilities usually associated with persons" (2011, 27). This being the case, I contend, reductive objectification accounts like those of MacKinnon and Dworkin are incoherent: one cannot commit a category mistake where one treats *someone* literally as *something* and simultaneously treats them as a lesser person. In the latter case, one treats another as a person to begin with, which shows that one has not committed a category mistake.[13] Or in committing a category mistake, one cannot

12. See David Livingstone Smith (2011) for a similar view. For a detailed account of how I understand dehumanization, see my 2016 book.

13. Another concern about accounts of dehumanizing sexual objectification is that such accounts come close to accepting a highly implausible and dim view about the nature of sex. This view is found in Kant: for him, sexual activity per se seriously damages and debases humanity, although this damage can be morally mitigated if one enters a monogamous marriage relationship (Herman 2002). The view that every act of sex debases humanity, unless

simultaneously reduce the other's humanity or personhood for the simple reason that the other is not viewed as a person to begin with.

Cahill, too, has argued that dehumanizing objectification is problematic in being wedded to a Kantian conception of subjecthood. This is because MacKinnon, A. Dworkin, LeMoncheck, and Nussbaum all accept "autonomy as a hallmark of the person, and objectification as a means of limiting or encroaching upon a person's autonomy" (Cahill 2011, 24). Cahill rejects this picture of personhood because it does not take seriously the embodiment of persons. That is, accounts that take objectification to be autonomy violating, risk defining personhood in atomistic terms, as removed from and prior to relationships, and in an overly individualistic manner. For Cahill, these positions do not sufficiently theorize the body as being contained in the notion of subjectivity, and personhood becomes just about the mind or intellect (2011, 26). As an alternative, Cahill proposes the concept of *derivatization:* "To derivatize is to portray, render, understand, or approach a being solely or primarily as the reflection, projection, or expression of another being's identity, desires, fears" (2011, 32). In the realm of sex, then, this is problematic from a feminist perspective insofar as women are constructed "as reducible to the desires or beings of men"; thus, derivatization "constitutes an act of violence against their ontologically specific being" (2011, 42)—to women's specificity as ontologically self-sufficient individuals.

It is not entirely clear how derivatization differs from Nussbaum's idea that one way to treat another as an object is through denying their subjectivity. Elsewhere Cahill writes:

it takes place within the confines of patriarchal marriage relations, is surely to be rejected. In advancing conceptions of dehumanizing sexual objectification, some antipornography feminists come close to such Kantian-sounding views. This further perpetuates an unhelpful opposition between supposedly sex-negative and sex-positive views.

Derivatization serves to undermine the ethical dynamic of relations by positioning one subject in a determining relation over
the other's identity. That is, the derivatized subject is degraded
not by being mistakenly treated as an object, but by being mistakenly treated as a subject whose subjectivity (actions, speech,
appearance, and so on) can be wholly determined by the subjective needs or desires of another. (2014, 845)

Be that as it may, there is something highly compelling and valuable
about this idea. For a start, it better fits Langton's view discussed
above that one way to objectify another is to affirm their autonomy.
Autonomy affirmation in the service of autonomy denial works
precisely by one agent understanding another as a reflection or
projection of their own wants and desires—in particular, that the
other manifests features characteristic of autonomous subjecthood.
Moreover, derivatization offers a useful critical tool to think about
pornographic depictions. Earlier we saw how difficult it is to assess
that pornography objectifies women or that it involves objectifying
depictions of women. Derivatization enables us to avoid many of
these difficulties. The critical assessment of women's portrayal in pornography won't turn on whether women display signs of subjecthood
but rather on whether the sort of subjecthood they are portrayed as
displaying is defined from a problematically masculinist position.[14]
This allows us to engage with common porn tropes, like money
shots. The problem with such tropes does not hinge on women being
reduced to certain body parts (faces covered in ejaculate), but on
whether this portrayal is a projection or expression of desires other

14. Note that a masculinist perspective is *not* the perspective of all males. It is a perspective
    that takes maleness as "the standard" (MacKinnon 1987, 52). For example, much of our
    language use is conducted from such a perspective, like the convention of using the generic
    masculine pronoun "he" when supposedly speaking gender neutrally. Obviously, not all
    men employ language in this fashion, and many women do too.

than women's. This idea can give us critical tools with which to interrogate pornographic depictions without getting bogged down by unhelpful debates about whether pornography objectifies women and whether it also objectifies men. It can explicate further why reducing male performers to their bodies and cutting off their faces is not obviously morally reproachable: despite this being objectifying following Nussbaum, it is not derivatizing. Male performers' ontological specificity is not under attack in that they are not portrayed as reflections and projections of female desire (at least in heterosexual pornography). The idea of derivatization may have a particularly useful role when thinking about the difference between feminist and mainstream pornography—a topic I will return to in chapter 7.

Chapter 6

The Aesthetics of Pornography

6.1. INTRODUCTION

This book has already considered various debates in feminist philosophy on the topic of pornography. Feminist philosophers have not, however, been alone in considering pornography philosophically: philosophers of art have also notably debated the topic. Nevertheless, these two subdisciplines seldom meet, and there is surprisingly little crossover between them. Feminist debates usually focus on pornography's putative harms to women and what should subsequently be done about pornography in order to advance gender equality, whereas debates in analytic aesthetics have focused on imagination, pornographic fictionality, and media as well as the ethics of represented depictions. One major point of contention dominates discussions in philosophy of art over pornography though: whether something can be both art and pornography.

This chapter aims, on the one hand, to bring debates in feminist philosophy and philosophy of art closer together and, on the other, to discuss central topics of contention in the aesthetics of pornography. I will consider three themes: fictionality of pornography, whether pornography and art are mutually exclusive, and what (if anything) is morally objectionable about digitally generated imagery. In so doing, I will offer support for two broad views. First, that fantasies and pornographic fictions are not beyond moral reproach in virtue of being fantastical and fictitious. Second, to hold that pornography is centrally or necessarily about sexual arousal (as philosophers of art typically do) yields misguided analyses of the phenomenon. This chapter, then, tells us something important not only about issues relevant for philosophy of art debates pertaining to pornography; it also instructs us about the nature and morality of pornography. A note about the subsequent content is in order though. Debates pertaining to the moral status of pornographic fantasies often make use of disturbing examples, such as sexualized violence against women and child sexual abuse. Although I will not describe such examples in detail, I, too, will discuss moral issues pertaining to these examples— something readers should be prepared for.

6.2. PORNOGRAPHY AS FANTASY

Earlier chapters examined the view that pornography *does* something: it systematically subordinates and silences women. It is not uncommon to find resistance to this view in the popular press and teaching settings on the basis that pornography is sheer fantasy. Qua fantasy, the argument goes, pornography is a product of the imagination. Therefore, it cannot do what antipornography feminists claim pornography does: products of imagination cannot shape material social conditions in ways that would enact women's systematic subordination and silencing. There are grounds to be skeptical of this fantasy defense of pornography though. For one thing, social scientific research suggests that although men consume pornography for a number of reasons, like entertainment, escape, or release, they do not consider pornography to be fantasy. Rather, consumers take performers and sex to be real rather than simulated (Ezzell 2014, 17). If consumers (especially younger ones) take pornography to be an authoritative guide to sex "in the real world," they do not receive pornography as fantasy irrespective of how producers intend pornography to be received. This immediately undermines the fantasy defense of pornography.

Assume for argument's sake, nevertheless, that producers intend their products to depict simulated sex with performers rather than real people and that consumers consider pornographic works to be so too. This still might not mitigate pornography's putative harmfulness. For instance, Nussbaum holds that in objectifying performers, pornography

> constructs for the [consumer] a fantasy objectification of a class of real women. Used as a masturbatory aid, it encourages the idea that an easy satisfaction can be had in this uncomplicated way, without the difficulties attendant on recognizing women's subjectivity and autonomy in a more full-blooded way. (1995, 284)

Alison Assiter (1988) also puts forward the idea that the fantasy element of pornography encourages actual sexual objectification of women. She holds that we can condemn "pornographic eroticism" from a feminist perspective, even if it does not in fact increase sexualized violence against women. Even if pornography involves a sheer fantasy, it has

> a causal effect . . . when [a consumer] performs, as internal actor, his fantasy, he is left, as internal audience, in a state that simulates the state he would be in if he had *actually* had a relationship with a woman like the imagined one. (Assiter 1988, 67)

And so, pornographic representations can be condemned because they conceivably reinforce the desire to objectify women (for more, see chapter 5). Although this desire may not be satisfied in one's actual interactions with women, "the man who constantly has such desires is to be condemned, for he is gaining satisfaction from a person whom he has divested of personhood" (Assiter 1988, 68). Despite the lack of conclusive proof that viewing pornography increases sexualized violence, empirical evidence supports the view that viewing pornography has other problematic effects. These include reinforcing the desire to sexually objectify women, becoming more likely to view women as inferior, being more disposed to accept rape myths and engage in victim blaming, and (based on self-reporting) being more likely to commit sexualized violence against women if there were no possibility of being caught (Donnerstein, Linz, and Penrod 1987; see also Williams et al. 2009). And so, pornography consumption—even if pornography is merely fantastical—may enact women's subordination covertly by (re)producing less crude ways in which they are treated dismissively.

There is, however, another way in which the fantasy defense might be untenable and that sidesteps empirical issues. One might argue that even if pornography consumption does not increase women's objectification or sexualized violence against them, if pornography consumption gives rise to prima facie problematic sexual fantasies, it is not beyond moral reproach.[1] John Corvino understands deviant or "naughty" sexual fantasies as "*either imagined or acted out*, involving the eroticization of an activity that is itself morally wrong" (2002, 214). Furthermore, eroticization involves "actively regarding the activity with sexual desire" (2002, 214). If people force their fantasies on others, they can clearly be held morally (and legally) culpable for

---

1. One might doubt whether pornography consumption generates fantasies: Might it not be the case that having certain fantasies encourages consumers to seek out materials that fit their fantasies? This certainly happens. But experimental research shows that "exposing male participants to [inegalitarian] pornography increases rape fantasies, willingness to rape, acceptance of rape myths, and aggression against female targets . . . In other words, pornography affects both fantasies and behaviors" (Williams et al. 2009, 202).

their actions. However, what about cases where such fantasies are brought about by pornography consumption, but they do not result in requisite behavioral manifestations? Some hold that mere sexual fantasies are beyond moral reproach (Kershnar 2005). Nevertheless, one might hold that there is a way to critique such sexual fantasies in and of themselves: entertaining some particularly gruesome fantasies about (say) sexual violence against women is a manifestation of possessing a nonvirtuous moral character (Patridge 2013). After all, fantasizing involves conscious and pleasurable imagining of some scenario. It typically involves imagining that the person fantasizing is doing something in the fantasy. In this sense, prima facie gruesome sexual fantasies involve an agent taking an attitude of pleasure toward something morally vicious, and taking such an attitude toward something vicious is morally reproachable. Furthermore, since fantasizing is typically under our control, taking an attitude of pleasure toward something morally vicious displays a form of voluntarism, which is again an indication of the agent's corrupt moral character. Hence, sexual fantasies are not beyond moral critique. (I will return to this point in section 6.4.)

Above I considered three ways in which a fantasy defense might be undercut: pornography is not fantasy; even if it is fantasy, it can (re)produce subtle discriminatory behaviors; and pornographic fantasies are not beyond moral reproach. The defense has been employed in other ways too. In earlier chapters, we have repeatedly encountered the claim that pornography tells lies about women (e.g., women are sexually submissive, and they enjoy having sex forced on them). A revised version of the fantasy defense then holds that pornography cannot tell lies about women because being fictional it says *nothing* about women: "As fantasy, pornography is a vision of the way things ought to be or could be, regardless of the way things actually happen to be. Pornography cannot [therefore] be charged with falsely and maliciously describing women" (Soble 1985, 73).

As fictional story-telling, pornography does not contain worrisome propositions about women—it asserts nothing at all.

Rae Langton and Caroline West (1999) take issue with this version of the defense. They hold that pornography may say derogatory and false things about women even if it does not do so explicitly and even if pornography is fictional. This is because of the distinction between what is said explicitly and what is presupposed or implied. To illustrate the difference, consider the utterance: "Terry really sucks at basketball." What is explicitly asserted here is obvious: Terry is a very bad basketball player. Now imagine that one utters instead: "Even *Terry* could make that basketball shot." What is being said and/or implied here? At least three things: first, Terry is a bad basketball player; second, the player on whom the speaker is commenting failed to make an easy shot; and third, the speaker is ridiculing or expressing dismay with the player who failed the make the easy shot. The main point here, however, is that one can communicate the view that Terry is a bad basketball player without explicitly saying so: this is presupposed or implied in the utterance "Even *Terry* could make that basketball shot." With this distinction in mind, Langton and West hold that although pornography may not explicitly say (for instance) that sexualized violence against women is acceptable, such propositions may be presupposed or implied by what pornography explicitly says. This is because otherwise consumers cannot easily make sense of what is explicitly going on in pornography.

To sketch this out further, consider the following pornographic example from Langton and West. A story called "Dirty Pool" appeared in *Hustler* magazine in January 1983 and showed a series of pictures of a female waitress being pinched by a male pool player with other players approvingly looking on. A caption read:

Though she pretends to ignore them, these men know when they see an easy lay. She is thrown on the felt table, and one manly hand after another probes her private areas. Completely vulnerable, she feels one after another enter her fiercely. As the three violators explode in a shower of climaxes, she comes to a shuddering orgasm. (Quoted in Langton and West 1999, 311)[2]

This caption and the photo story do not explicitly assert that the waitress really meant *yes* when she said "no" or that women like to be "taken by force." But to make sense of the story, Langton and West hold, it presupposes certain rape myths and implies that when women say "no" they mean *yes*. Consequently, "pornography can say such things, even if it does not explicitly say them" (Langton and West 1999, 312).

Langton and West also consider a further version of the fantasy defense: pornographic sayings are implicit *and* merely fictional. In this case, even if pornography presupposes propositions like "sexual violence is legitimate" or "women enjoy rape," "if they occur within the scope of a fiction operator, pornography—it seems—does not actually *say* such things" (1999, 315). Debunking this variant of the fantasy defense turns on whether we can gain false beliefs from pornography: if we can, fictionality does not prevent pornography from saying things with harmful propositional content. And (the argument goes) even if pornography is fiction, this does not ethically vindicate it. This is because producers may be (1) liars (pornography presents fiction as fact); (2) background liars (pornography lies about particular background propositions supposedly true in fiction and in reality); or (3) background blurrers (pornographic depictions prevent audiences from clearly distinguishing fact from fiction). To illustrate this last point, consider historical fiction. Such

2. Two months after the story had appeared in *Hustler*, a highly publicized gang rape of a waitress at a pool hall in New Bedford, Massachusetts, took place. Four men perpetrated the offense, while other customers watched without intervening. The story was dramatized in the 1988 film *The Accused*.

works involve factual and fictional components, but authors do not typically take much care to distinguish between the two. (In fact, the material may work precisely because the lines between fact and fiction are blurred.) Thus, ill-informed audiences may come to form false beliefs because the distinction between fact and fiction has been muddled. Similar effects may take place with ill-informed audiences of pornography, who cannot distinguish fictional from factual content. This then offers "an alternative mechanism for bringing it about that rape myths purporting to be mere fiction are taken to be true of the world as well" (Langton and West 1999, 317). Consequently, pornography may well say harmful things about women and sexuality, even if it does not do so explicitly and even if it purports to be fictional.

Not everyone agrees that this makes pornography or its producers morally culpable. Cooke appeals to consumers' responsibility and the norm of a responsible "receiver": "don't accept as a belief some proposition expressed or implied by a fictional work, unless the real world provides sufficient evidence for that belief" (2012, 239). If consumers form false beliefs about women from pornography, *the consumers*—not pornography—are to blame by not having adhered to this norm. But appealing to this norm does not let all pornography off the hook because the real world may *not* provide sufficient evidence to the contrary. In substantiating this assertion, one need not appeal to any claims about pornography's power to shape sexual lives or to its power to make us conform to some pornographic vision of what sex should be like. Rather, one can appeal to human psychology. The phenomenon of confirmation bias is ubiquitous (Nickerson 1998): we—human social agents—tend to gather and remember data selectively so that it confirms our beliefs and views. So if one endorses rape myths about women meaning *yes* when they say "no" or if one merely implicitly assents to such myths, the real world may not provide evidence to the contrary because one comes to interpret women's behaviors in ways that fit one's prior views about women's sexual agency (for instance, when women say "no" they mean *yes*). Even though I pretheoretically would welcome adherence to norms like the one Cooke notes, as a matter of fact social agents are not in a good position to do so given human psychology and the general lack of good education about sexuality.

Of course, one might point out that in this case, pornography is still not to blame: again, the fault lies with consumers who are unable to satisfy the norm because of their psychological constitution. But I think that this rebuttal does not succeed: if the existence of confirmation bias makes it substantially harder for consumers to satisfy the norm of responsible receiver, the pornography industry must conceivably take responsibility for what it produces. For instance, imagine that producers of milk products add a chemical to their products, which makes them highly addictive to humans given our biological constitution. I think that we would be hard pressed to say that consumers should simply be more responsible *qua* consumers, subsequently understand the addictive nature of milk products and not consume them, and that the producers bear no responsibility at all in this matter. If consumers form false beliefs from industrial pornography and are unable to satisfy the responsible receiver norm due to confirmation bias, the pornography industry has not been fully absolved: they plausibly should conform to some ethical standards *qua* an industry insofar as they make a profit *because* consumers tend to be ignorant and are not often able to engage in the desired sort of critical reflection about the products they consume.

Taking a more nuanced stance on pornography's fictionality, Liao and Protasi (2013) criticize the opposition that either the fictional character of pornography prevents it from causing any harm or that all pornography is harmful in persuading audiences to treat women in certain ways. They consider how different *kinds* of pornography are likely to impact real-world affairs in divergent ways because distinct pornography genres involve different modes of persuasion. Whether pornography's fictionality morally vindicates it, Liao and Protasi hold, depends on the genre. They start by considering what the fictional character of pornography amounts to. By "fiction" as a technical term in aesthetics, they mean "any *representation* that prompts *imaginings*" (2013, 100). And so, the fictional character of pornography neither implies that all pornographic works are fictive nor that pieces of pornography are causally detached from reality. The authors emphasize that pornography "paradigmatically involves imaginings" (2013, 100), which is connected to a view about sexual desire. Such desire is unlike other mere appetites (like hunger) and instead involves "cognitive wants that interact with other intentional states" (2013, 100–101). It might be possible to perform sexual activities in noncognitive ways or absentmindedly. (In fact, the authors suggest that this is probably what most pornography performers do.) Still, there is a difference between satisfying sexual desire and having sex, where the imaginative component noted above is crucial for the former.

Liao and Protasi go on to discuss how genre makes a difference to our (a) imaginative engagements with and (b) actual responses to fiction. For instance, an identical scene in movies of two different genres elicits different appropriate responses—just think of hitting someone on the head with a frying pan in a period drama versus in a slapstick comedy. Hence: "Genre conventions and expectations partly determine how we are to bring our genuine attitudes to bear on imaginative engagement (*import*) and how we are to bring our imaginative attitudes to bear on reality (*export*)" (2013, 108). In other words, genre is one factor that determines whether some way in which viewers have *imaginatively* been prescribed to respond to a scenario is responsible for how consumers respond to analogous situations involving *actual* persons and situations. If a piece of fiction is from a genre that is response realistic, when we imaginatively sympathize with a fictional character, we are more likely to—and even ought to—do so with an actual person in the same situation. If the work is not from such a genre (e.g., slapstick comedy or satire), we tend not to respond to actual persons in identical circumstances in the same way. This shows there is a difference between the "genuine responses that a fiction cultivates and the imaginative responses that it prescribes," where the difference depends on the work's genre (2013, 110).

With this in mind, we can see that some pornography genres are response realistic *with respect to attitudes towards sexual relationships and practices* while others are not (Liao and Protasi 2013, 110). Fetish pornography genres are typically of the latter kind. For instance, in BDSM pornography that depicts apparent violence, consumers "are prescribed to find imaginatively violent treatments of women to be sexually desirable" (2013, 110). But since fetish pornography "worlds" are usually very different from "ordinary worlds," consumers are not prescribed to respond to actual analogous situations in the same manner. And so, "despite imaginatively finding violent treatment of women to be sexually desirable, the normal consumer would not come to find genuinely violent treatments of women to be sexually desirable" (2013, 111). Mainstream, inegalitarian pornography and pornographic genres are, however, response realistic in being close enough to ordinary reality and can hence persuade consumers to treat women in problematic ways. These consumers are prescribed to find imaginatively violent treatments of women sexy and mainstream, inegalitarian pornographic genres cultivate analogous genuine and problematic responses to women in reality. Once more, this shows that a simple appeal to pornography's fictional character does not morally vindicate it, but it also helpfully makes the case that not all pornographic genres are on a par.

6.3. ART OR PORN?

Philosophers of art have extensively debated the connection between art and pornography: more specifically, whether there can be anything that is both pornography *and* art. This is not a dispute about whether erotic art exists or whether there is art that is somehow pornographic in mimicking pornography or being like it in some respect. The issue is about whether art and pornography are mutually exclusive kinds. There are four prominent ways to draw the distinction (Maes 2011b, 2012). First, in terms of representational content: pornographic representations are sexually explicit, while artistic representation relies on suggestion. Second, pornography is somehow by definition morally flawed, corrupt or immoral, while art is not. Third, pornography lacks any redeeming artistic qualities: pornography is about smut, while art is about beauty. This is because the former is one-dimensional, while the latter is complex and multilayered. Fourth, the two are distinct due to their prescribed responses: pornography makes intellectual contemplation impossible, while art is to be appreciated for its own sake. Or to put the point differently, pornography is antithetical to imaginative activities because it aims sexually to arouse its audiences. As Maes explains the point (without endorsing it):

> [T]he fact that we speak of *consuming* pornography and of *appreciating* art indicates that there is a fundamental difference in how we are meant to engage with both kinds of representation. The term "consumer" suggests that there is less of an intellectually rewarding effort involved. (2012, 22)

All of these ways of demarcating the difference, however, face counterexamples and objections—too numerous to consider here (for overviews, see Maes 2011a, 2011b). I will focus next on points that connect to previous and still forthcoming debates relevant for this book.

First, sexual explicitness can hardly be taken to demarcate a categorical distinction between pornography and art. Some leather fetish pornographic genres are not sexually explicit but rather more suggestive. Furthermore, some fetish pornography genres are not sexually explicit at all in a conventional sense, such as armpit fetishist pornography (pornography directed at people who are sexually aroused by and attracted to armpits). Then again, many art works are sexually explicit rather than merely titillating (just think of Jeff Koons's *Red Butt*; for more examples, see van Brabandt and Prinz 2012). The oft-cited example of explicit anatomy books also clearly shows that sexual explicitness per se cannot establish that as kinds art and pornography are mutually exclusive. With this in mind, Maes suggests that the sexual explicitness requirement should be coupled with another condition: "pornographic representation is (1) made with the intention to arouse its audience sexually, (2) by prescribing attention to its sexually explicit representational context" (2012, 32). This resolves worries raised by anatomy books: they lack the intention to sexually arouse their audiences. I am less convinced that Maes's formulation provides the defining characteristic of pornography though because I find the first condition questionable. (I will say more about this shortly.)

Second, might some putative ethical difference offer a categorical way to differentiate art and pornography? Cooke (2012) argues against this view (see also Kieran 2001). He holds that there are no persuasive grounds for maintaining an ethical distinction between art and pornography as *generic* kinds. Rather, ethical judgments and possible moral condemnation of works ought to depend on the details of *particular* works: some works of art are morally reprehensible, as are some pieces of pornography. Cooke argues against three ways to cash out a categorical moral difference. First, pornography might be morally culpable because it tells lies about women (like women enjoy rape) and thus generates false beliefs in consumers. Cooke rejects the suggestion though: he admits that although we can gain false beliefs through pornography, this does not establish pornography's moral culpability—we can gain false beliefs in parallel fashion from nonpornographic fiction, but we do not *therefore* take authors of fiction to be morally culpable. Second, Cooke considers whether exploitation could distinguish art from pornography (the latter being exploitative, while the former is not). This view is questionable, however, because establishing that some work is exploitative is much trickier than critics of pornography maintain. For one thing, who is exploited by a work of pornography? Plausible candidates include performers, audiences, and third parties (by recommending or causing third-party exploitation). Still, the point is that since establishing the exploitation claim relative to single works of pornography is difficult, establishing that pornography as a whole involves exploitation will be even harder. Furthermore, it is pretheoretically unpersuasive to think that art production utterly avoids all forms of exploitation. Hence, it is implausible to hold that pornography as a kind is and art as a kind isn't exploitative. Finally, Cooke discusses the charge that "life imitates art": pornography has some insidious causal powers, like the power to mold character in undesirable ways or increase the frequency of sexual assaults. However, Cooke argues that empirical evidence does not support this line of argument. Although I think that Cooke is too quick to dismiss the available empirical evidence (see chapter 2), it seems nonetheless right to hold that this suggestion also fails to carve out a meaningful categorical difference between pornography and art.

Third, although it is surely right to say that as things stand pornography typically lacks any redeeming artistic or aesthetic qualities, it is far from obvious that this is necessarily so. To hold that pornography lacks any artistic qualities *by definition* rests on a prejudiced and overly simplified view about pornography. In fact, there are apparent counterexamples. Wakefield Poole's classic 1971 gay pornography film, *Boys in the Sand*, has been hailed as a film that combines aesthetic experience and sexual excitement (Miller 2013). The already-mentioned *Dirty Diaries* is also considered to be a prototypical artistic pornography film (van Brabandt and Prinz 2012; Maes 2011b, 2012). Many self-proclaimed feminist pornographers (to be considered more fully in chapter 7) aim to produce works that are not only ethically commendable but also aesthetically pleasing and engaging. Moreover, the ability to arouse or elicit strong feelings in spectators is generally taken to be "a mark of artistic achievement," but excluding point blank those strong feelings that pornography arouses from the set of relevant or appropriate feelings is simply arbitrary (van Brabandt and Prinz 2012, 165). Although pornography may rely on cheap tricks to elicit certain noncomplex emotional responses, there is nothing about pornography that makes this inevitable. Artful pornography would involve the "kinds of skills that typify art films generally: adding emotional complexity, imposing a distinctive style, and violating genre conventions" (van Brabandt and Prinz 2012, 184).

The three features discussed above fail to establish a categorical difference between pornography and art. However, the fourth difference apparently presents a particularly serious challenge for anyone wishing to avoid the view that art and pornography are mutually exclusive: "It is not the fact that pornography is sexually explicit, but rather the fact that it aims to bring about sexual arousal that is considered to be the big stumbling block for any artistic redemption of pornography" (Maes 2011b, 392). That is, pornography is said to have the function or intention to sexually arouse its audiences, while art does not, where this intended function hinders intellectual contemplation. To put the point somewhat differently: according to Jerrold Levinson, artistic and pornographic interests cannot coexist.

The former is defined as an interest in "the way content is embodied in form, the way medium has been employed to convey content" (2005, 232). This artistic interest produces something that can be contemplated and appreciated for its own sake. But such an interest is and must be lacking in pornography because intellectual contemplation would interfere with pornography's intended function to sexually arouse its audiences. Eliciting sexual arousal need not be the sole intent of pornography; but it is considered to be its *central* or *ultimate* intent. And the view that pornography is "centrally aimed at sexual arousal," which is taken to be a necessary condition of pornography, is something that "almost all theorists" agree on (Maes 2011a, 60). Here are some representative examples. Levinson (who takes pornography and art to be mutually exclusive) claims that pornography has "a paramount aim" of "the sexual satisfaction of the viewer" (2005, 229) and that pornography's "central aim [is] to facilitate sexual arousal in the name of sexual release" (236). Elsewhere, he defines *pornography* as "images whose primary, central, and justifying aim is to produce sexual *arousal*, and in the normal course of events, sexual *release*, in a target audience" (2012, 83). Christy Mag Uidhir, who also endorses an exclusivist view, holds that "a necessary condition for something's being pornography is the purpose of sexual arousal—[sexually arousing its audience is] what pornography does and what it is supposed to do" (2009, 195). Even Matthew Kieran, who critiques Levinson's view, takes pornography as such to elicit arousal "via the explicit representation of sexual behaviour and attributes" (2001, 32). Though pornography may have other aims too (like artistic ones), pornography's *primary* goal is to elicit sexual arousal.

All parties to the debate endorse this assumption about the nature of pornography: it is centrally or ultimately about sexual arousal. My contention is that this assumption is misleading. Pornographers use sexual imagery that can and does arouse. But looking at both historical and contemporary examples calls into question the view that this is (in some sense) the *central* aim of pornography. Determining such a distinctly pornographic aim is actually quite tricky and focusing on pornography's sexual arousal is too simplistic to make sense of a large and multifaceted phenomenon. Let me be clear: obviously pornography has something to do with sexual arousal and eliciting sexual arousal is not somehow an incidental production accident. Still, the standard focus on this sexual aspect of pornography misses something important and hinders the possibility of settling the question about whether some x can be both art and pornography. In fact, I hold that there is no central thing that pornography is about, just as there is no central thing that art is about. There is, then, no prima facie reason to think that it is impossible for some x to be both pornography and art. (I argue for this in more detail in Mikkola 2013.)[3]

---

3. Cain Todd offers a different way to undermine positions like Levinson's (2005) that claim a pornographic work "cannot be appreciated as both art and pornography at one and the same time" (Todd 2012, 96). This is because attending to and appreciating aesthetic features of a work *qua* aesthetic supposedly precludes attending to and appreciating the work's pornographic content *qua* pornographic. Todd distinguishes two kinds of pornography, nonfictional and fictional. The former presents (or is taken to present) real people having real sex while the latter presents (or is taken to present) "fictional narratives, where actors take on chapter roles and where fictional actions and events are represented for us to be imaginatively engaged with" (Todd 2012, 107). Sexual desire is seemingly directed at different objects in these cases: in the former, it is the real people and scenes depicted; in the latter, it "may be a fictional character or fictional state of affairs" (Todd 2012, 107). With these in mind, Levinson's view seemingly applies only to nonfictional pornography. Just showing people having sex usually precludes any aesthetic considerations. Engaging with aesthetic features may even distract us from the pornographic content to the extent that "our sexual arousal will be hindered and the aim of sexual desire [be] potentially thwarted" (Todd 2012, 107). In such a case, we are engaging with the scenes as voyeurs and typically such scenes are used as "masturbation materials," which does not involve imagination. Thinking about fictional pornography though yields different results: "If, however, we begin to imagine ourselves implicated in the scene or using the scene as a 'prop' in some imaginary project ... we have thereby begun to regard the film ... as a piece of fictional pornography" (Todd 2012, 107–108). Such pornography then does allow us to engage with both aesthetic *and* pornographic features *qua* aesthetic and pornographic.

Here are some reasons to accept my (perhaps surprising and controversial) position. Pornography is allegedly produced with the central intention to sexually arouse its audiences. Whether pornographic works can also count as art hinges on some *additional* nonpornographic intentions. But things are much more complicated than this, and producers' intentions are more varied and far less clear-cut. Let me highlight two complications. First, producing sexually arousing materials may be a means to some other end, rather than the central purpose of pornography production per se. Second, the supposed pornographic intention of soliciting sexual arousal may be constitutively intertwined with other intentions in a way that makes it impossible to separate "the" central pornographic intention from additional nonpornographic intentions. To illustrate, consider first a historical example. In her examination of pornography's history, Lynn Hunt claims

> if we take pornography to be the explicit depiction of sexual organs and sexual practices with the aim of arousing sexual feelings, then pornography was almost always an adjunct to something else until the middle or end of the eighteenth century. (1993, 10)

Pornography in this sense was widely used for the purpose of social critique, as was the case during the French Revolution when pornographic imagery of Marie Antoinette was used to attack the French Court. This tells us two things. Arousing sexual imagery was produced for the purpose of social criticism: it was used as a means for an end other than eliciting sexual arousal. Moreover, it is difficult to separate the pornographic sexual intention in this case from the political revolutionary intention. This is because the sexual arousal generated and presumably intended by the images is essentially tied to the *particular figures* depicted (like Marie Antoinette).

Such pornography would not work had it depicted just any person whatsoever—depicting Marie Antoinette for the purposes of social criticism is crucial for such pornography *qua* pornography. To think that we can separate some pornographic sexual intention from other intentions in the manner that is usually presupposed in the art-or-porn debates fails to appreciate how different intentions can be and are constitutively intertwined.

Some contemporary examples are also instructive. Pornography is no fringe industry. Globally its annual revenue is estimated at $97 billion (Maes and Levinson 2012, 1). The industry revenue is reported to surpass those of Microsoft, Google, Amazon, eBay, Yahoo, Apple, and Netflix *combined*, although some question this claim due to the lack of information (Tarrant 2016). Japan's pornography industry is estimated to be worth $4.4 billion in annual sales.[4] Although the exact figures are disputed, the industry revenues in the United States are put somewhere between $5 and $15 billion annually (Tarrant 2016, 42–43). These estimates show that profits play a significant role in pornography production. According to a 2003 CBS report, "Porn in the USA," industry interests were at the time represented in Washington, DC by their very own lobbyist Bill Lyon (the "Free Speech Coalition" currently advocates for the adult entertainment industry). Lyon notes in the report: "[When I started as the lobbyist for the industry] I was rather shocked to find that [those involved] are pretty bright business people who are in it to make a profit. *And that is what it's about*" (Leung 2003; italics mine). When asked about the reactions he receives in Washington for being the pornography industry's lobbyist, Lyon illuminatingly responds:

4. J. McCurry, "Forced into Pornography: Japan Moves to Stop Women Being Coerced into Sex Films," *The Guardian*, May 15, 2017, https://www.theguardian.com/world/2017/may/15/forced-into-porn-japan-moves-to-stop-women-being-coerced-into-sex-films. Accessed August 12, 2018.

Initially, I think there's a degree of shock. But when you explain to [the politicians] the size and the scope of the business, they realize, as all politicians do, that it's votes and money that we're talking about . . . This is an extremely large business and there's a great opportunity for profits in it. (Leung 2003)[5]

This raises serious questions about whether eliciting sexual arousal is the central intention or aim of pornographers. Instead, it is quite conceivable that making money is the central intention and aim of many pornographers, and that the use of arousing sexual imagery is a very effective means to do so. Just consider another large industry like car manufacturing. On the face of it, cars enable us to travel and get to places at our own convenience. But it strikes me as false to claim that *therefore* the automobile industry is about giving people the freedom to travel at their own convenience. Rather, given the profit-making aims of the industry, car manufacturing is about making money *by means of* giving people the freedom to travel, creating certain desires, perhaps even blocking the development of a workable public transport network. It is not inconceivable that the same could be true of the pornography industry—just because pornographic works may and do arouse their viewers, it does not follow that therefore we should analyze such works as being centrally about sexual arousal.

Industrial pornography is not the only game in town. Recall the more independent feminist producers noted in chapter 5 and the film *Dirty Diaries* along with its ten-point manifesto. Only one of the manifesto points specifically pertains to the intention to make sexually arousing films. Common intentions of feminist pornographers include providing alternatives to and subverting the mainstream

5. See also Trinks (2013) who outlines how in medieval Spain sexually explicit images were used for financial gain: churches along pilgrims' routes would display such images to attract pilgrims and thus generate revenue.

industry, and portraying a more realistic picture of sexuality in general and of female sexuality in particular. Now, if we merely focus on the ultimate intention to make a "dirty" sexually arousing movie, we seriously miss the point of the work. And since the entire porn-or-art debate starts from the assumption that the central or ultimate intention of pornographers is to make something sexually arousing, philosophers have potentially based the entire debate on a misguided assumption. To reiterate: that feminist pornography can sexually arouse is not a production accident but clearly intentional. Still, the intentions to subvert mainstream pornography and bring in nonmasculinist perspectives are not just additional to the intention to make something sexually arousing: they are part and parcel *of* that intention in a way that makes it impossible to separate the pornographic and nonpornographic intentions. The upshot of these examples is that pornography cannot be simply analyzed in terms of sexual arousal or the intention to make something sexually arousing. If we accept the view that pornography is centrally about sexual arousal, our analysis of pornography will be impoverished and the art-or-porn debate will be misguided.[6]

In addition to the misplaced focus on sexual arousal, a particular methodological deficiency tends to plague debates over the aesthetics of pornography: philosophers engaged in the

---

6. To drive in the point further, consider Mag Uidhir and Pratt's definition of pornography:

> A work *w* is a work of pornography only if (a) *w* is a depictive work (b) of which the (primary) purpose is sexual arousal of its audience, (c) the primary subject of which is of an explicit sexual nature, and (d) *w* prescribes attention to (c) as the (primary) means of satisfying (b). (2012, 137)

They compare pornographic works so understood with works of fiction that may also be sexually arousing. Nonetheless, in the latter case, "their being sexually arousing is ultimately not an end itself but rather a means of satisfying fiction's entertainment aim" (Mag Uidhir and Pratt 2012, 151). However, given the examples above, it is not clear to me why we could not say the same about pornography: the end is to make money, engage in social critique, or aim to realize liberatory values, where creating something that is sexually arousing is the way to satisfy these ends. Focusing on surface depictions alone may yield the wrong results.

art-or-porn debates tend to rely on very few, if any, examples of pornography. In their discussions, many authors provide ample evidence of artistic works that can be considered pornographic (like Schiele paintings or Mapplethorpe photographs). But the examples of pornography relied on are sparse and unsatisfying. These include Pompeii frescos and other historical examples that modern viewers would hardly recognize as pornographic (let alone as pornography). Recent philosophical discussions of pornography and art contain surprisingly little awareness of actual pornographic works, though there are notable exceptions (see Maes 2012; Mag Uidhir and Pratt 2012; van Brabandt and Prinz 2012). This lack of empirical awareness weakens many philosophical discussions about art and pornography. Philosophical arguments often make claims about pornography a priori without a good grasp of what in fact goes on in the world and works of pornography.

This methodological complaint connects to another related one: a number of authors in the debate fail to consider how different *kinds* of pornography make a difference to their philosophical positions (though above I considered a notable exception to this: Liao and Protasi 2013). This again demonstrates how an awareness of the reality of pornography is lacking. For example, Kathleen Stock (2012) considers the phenomenon of imagining *de se*: imagining something about oneself. She considers the view that enjoying pornography or erotica must involve such imagining, and that erotic/pornographic works invite their recipients to partake in the depicted encounter as participants (erotica) or as voyeurs (pornography). Stock, however, goes on to reject the view that "enjoying erotica or pornography must involve imagining something about oneself" (2012, 116). This hinges on differing sexual psychologies of pornography's consumers (among other things that need not concern us here). For Stock:

To argue that one must imagine, from the inside, perceiving or coming to be aware of situation S in order to be aroused by the thought of S is, effectively, to make all consumers of pornographic fiction satisfy what is, perhaps, the central and defining condition of the voyeur. And this is surely wrong . . . some are turned on by the imaginative thought of various erotic properties . . . *straightforwardly*, whilst others are turned on not just by the thought of such properties, but also by the imaginative representation of those properties *as experienced by oneself*. (2012, 130)

However, one might wonder: Do differing sexual psychologies ultimately settle the matter? What about differences in pornographic genres? Specifically, what about the genre of "point of view" (POV) pornography? Prima facie one might think that POV pornography is precisely an instance of pornography that must involve imagining *de se*. However, Stock does not discuss this genre or consider the difference that genre conventions make. I am not claiming that such pornography would undermine Stock's thesis—my point is that Stock should discuss a paradigm instance of pornography that seemingly involves imagining *de se* in order to make her case that pornography must not involve imagining *de se* because viewers' sexual psychologies differ. For one thing, we might find that pornography must not involve imagining *de se* because of both individual psychologies and genre conventions. Or an engagement with POV pornography might reveal that irrespective of individual psychologies, POV pornography must involve imagining *de se* in order to be interesting and exciting for its consumers. My point is a methodological one: to support many views in aesthetics and philosophy of art, philosophers should demonstrate greater awareness of pornography and engage with it in order to argue for their views convincingly.

6.4. MORALITY OF DIGITALLY GENERATED IMAGERY

In chapter 1 I noted that it is a mistake to call images of children's sexual abuse 'pornography'. Rather, such images are documentations of abuse. In so doing, I reject the label 'child pornography', which implies that such materials are akin to other pornographic genres. My preferred strategy is to call depictions usually so labeled as 'images of children's sexual abuse'. The moral problems with imagery that depicts actual children in sexual contexts and poses against their will or if they are not in a position genuinely to consent I take to be obvious and in need of no further elucidation. But what should we say about pseudo- or virtual depictions of children's sexual abuse? The former is defined as "material that has been digitally manipulated so that images of children are combined with pornography, or are otherwise recontextualized so that they become indecent," while the latter denotes "material that has been entirely constructed from an artist's imagination, for example, in drawings or cartoons such as those in 'lolicon' and 'yaoi' comic books" (Maddison 2010, 43).[7] One might argue that since no actual people were involved in the production of these types of images and no actual children were abused, these pornographic genres are morally and legally unproblematic. In fact, in the United States and Japan pseudo- and virtual "child pornography" do not fall under the legal definition of *child pornography* precisely because their production involves no actual children.[8] Even though

---

7. *Lolicon* is a type of Japanese manga comic where childlike female characters are depicted in an "erotic-cute" manner. *Yaoi* is also a manga genre, but one that focuses on romantic and sexual relations between male characters with homoerotic content. Characters are typically above puberty or adults, although a similar genre that features prepubescent boys in sexually explicit and suggestive ways also exists.

8. The 2002 case *Ashcroft v. Free Speech Coalition* (the lobby group for the US pornography industry) overturned the prohibition of virtual child pornography on the grounds that the prohibition violated the First Amendment of the US Constitution (see chapter 4).

it is extremely difficult legally to regulate these materials, might there still be grounds to morally condemn such digitally generated imagery (DGI for short)? One might advance an argument on instrumental grounds: viewing such materials leads to or increases the likelihood of actual child abuse. Alternatively, one might argue that there is something intrinsically problematic about those images. Let's examine these two in turn.

6.4.1. Instrumental Grounds

Neil Levy (2002) considers putative reasons to find pedophilic DGI harmful. First, viewing it causes consumers to commit actual child abuse. Second, such materials can be used to groom children for abuse. Third, allowing pedophilic DGI renders laws against depictions of actual child sexual abuse unenforceable. Fourth, Internet pedophilic imagery allows isolated and potential perpetrators to contact each other, thus increasing the probability of actual child abuse. Levy rejects all suggestions though on the following grounds.

1. No reliable evidence supports a causal connection between viewing child sexual assaults (actual or virtual) and committing them.
2. There is no strong evidence that depictions of adult-child sex make a difference to perpetrators ability to groom children for abuse, as there are many other effective means to do so.
3. "[T]here is every reason to think that if virtual child pornography is legal, pornographers will abandon production of actual images of children in favor of it. The price of producing virtual pornography is low and falling, so monetary incentives will play a part in encouraging this movement." (Levy 2002, 320)

4. If group polarization is a serious problem, it arises out of Internet discussions among the likeminded, and not out of the viewed images.

How plausible is Levy's view though? I will discuss the first point in more detail shortly—but what about the others? We might accept the second point, but the last two are less compelling. First, one might wonder about whether there would be so many likeminded people were Internet depictions of adult-child sex less prevalent. Second, it is far from obvious that we have *every reason* to think that legalizing pedophilic DGI reduces nondigitally generated imagery. In fact, this is the case in the United States and Japan, but there is no robust evidence to back up Levy's claim (though admittedly finding good information and research on this matter is extremely difficult). Levy's claim also assumes that pedophilic imagery is produced and distributed mainly for profit. Although it certainly generates revenue, it is hard to gain reliable figures on this. What is nevertheless clear is that producing imagery of actual child sexual abuse is cheap, and it requires hardly any technological know-how beyond camera use. Producing comparable digitally generated materials requires much more advanced skills and technological tools, which renders Levy's claim questionable. Furthermore, to assume that users would be satisfied with digitally generated imagery over images of actual abuse is far from obvious. This presupposes that viewers are primarily interested in some sexual aspects of the imagery, which ignores the abusive side of the phenomenon.

What about the causal connection between viewing child sexual assaults (actual or virtual) and committing them? Again, this is extremely difficult to show conclusively, although conviction statistics from the United States are instructive: those convicted of online visual abuse (for possessing indecent images of children) have not generally committed contact abuse, and those convicted of contact abuse are not, generally speaking, users of (what legally would fall under) child pornography. Only a surprisingly small segment of offenders have committed both visual and contact abuse. Instead, contact abusers are much more likely to be heavy consumers of pornography with adult performers (Malamuth and Huppin 2007). This suggests that there is no causal connection between viewing child sexual assaults and committing them. However, this conclusion might be too quick. First, contact abusers tend to be much more opportunistic and abuse children in close proximity to them. Second, virtual abusers might have gone on to commit contact abuse had they not already been caught and convicted: moving from virtual abuse to contact abuse requires overcoming social taboos and restrictions, which may place barriers that merely slow down the causal story. With this in mind, media psychologists Bryant Paul and Daniel Linz empirically tested the assumption that exposure can result in the "sexual abuse or exploitation of minors becoming acceptable to and even preferred by the viewer" (2008, 4). The researchers experimented with the popular genre of barely legal pornography that depicts adults over the age of eighteen portrayed as being younger than eighteen.[9] Paul and Linz hypothesized that the primary conceptual associations barely legal pornography involves pertain to youth and sexual suggestiveness. If exposed individuals develop a network of associations and schemas that couples (1) eroticism and/or sexuality with (2) youth, then viewers should come to associate sexuality with youthful depictions even when the depictions are *not* overtly sexual. That is, if viewing barely legal pornography results in exposed individuals coming to

9. "Teen" is one the most popular search terms for Internet pornography. According to the 2015 survey by Pornhub (one of the biggest online pornography platforms), it was the second-most searched for term worldwide, "lesbian" being the first. Its popularity is also gendered: while it was only the ninth-most searched for term for women, it was the second for men (after "stepmom" and followed by "milf" and "mom"). For more, see: https://www.pornhub.com/insights/pornhub-2015-year-in-review. Accessed August 12 2018.

associate depictions of youth with sexuality even when the depictions are not overtly sexual, viewing barely legal pornography seemingly contributes to conceptual associations between youth and sexuality.

Paul and Linz tested five hypotheses, of which the following two are relevant for the current discussion:

Hypothesis 1: Compared to individuals exposed to control depictions, individuals preexposed to sexually explicit depictions of females who appear to be minors will be faster to recognize sexual words presented directly after sexually neutral images of female minors. (2008, 6)

Hypothesis 5: Male participants exposed to barely legal sexually explicit depictions will be most likely to find the idea of sexually explicit content featuring minors as well as adult sexual interaction with minors more socially acceptable compared to females and those exposed to other forms of sexually explicit content. (2008, 9)

They found support for Hypothesis 1: those exposed to barely legal pornography showed a stronger cognitive association between youth and sexuality than those exposed to materials with older-looking models. However, Paul and Linz found no support for Hypothesis 5: that exposed participants would subsequently find sexually explicit materials featuring actual minors, or sexual interaction between adults and minors, to be more socially acceptable or legitimate than participants pre-exposed to sexually explicit depictions with older-looking performers. And so (one might conclude) although barely legal pornography contributes to forming stronger cognitive associations between youth and sexuality, this is morally troubling only if such cognitive associations causally contribute to the acceptability of actual child abuse. Since no support for the latter hypothesis was found, we should not find pornography that generates such cognitive connections morally problematic.

This might be too fast though. One explanation for why Hypothesis 5 could not be confirmed is that there are strong inhibitors for subsequent sexual behavior. Sexual arousal may not lead to action since agents know the potentially serious social and legal repercussions of acting on their desires. Paul and Linz speculate that we may see disinhibitory effects *if* viewers are emotionally desensitized so that their feelings of anxiety and disgust decrease. After all, there is evidence that "repeated exposure to depictions that juxtaposed violence and sex resulted in diminished affective reactions and the tendency to judge behaviors such as sexual assault and domestic violence as less harmful to women" (2008, 34). And so, it might be too quick to give up the causal thesis. Furthermore, desensitization occurs when, through a process of repeated exposure, one becomes habituated to a particular stimulus that initially evoked strong emotional or behavioral reactions (Gunter 2002). So, although Hypothesis 5 was not confirmed, this may be due to the length of the experiment. As Paul and Linz put it, even though their study says little about the likelihood that exposed individuals will act on cognitive associations formed, it would be inappropriate to reject a causal connection outright (2008, 35–36). This is because

> [t]he first step in any intentional behavior . . . may be a cognitive consideration of performing that behavior. Therefore, exposure to any stimuli that makes the consideration of a particular behavior more likely to occur also seems likely to increase the probability that an individual will participate in that behavior. (2008, 36)

Hence, although there is no conclusive proof of a causal connection between viewing child sexual assaults (actual or digitally generated) and committing them, support found for Hypothesis 1 undermines the claim that viewing pedophilic DGI poses no moral worries at all.

6.4.2. Intrinsic Moral Wrongfulness

Might there be a way to morally critique digitally generated depictions of child sexual abuse, even if their viewing has not been shown to cause child abuse? In other words, might there be ways to morally critique certain images in and of themselves? In chapter 5, I discussed the difficulty of drawing conclusions about apparently objectifying depictions in pornography without considering wider social conditions and backgrounds. Even though I still maintain this view, it is pretheoretically much harder to accept that digitally generated depictions of child sexual abuse should be treated the same. In fact, this discussion requires us to draw a further distinction that I have until now largely ignored: we should distinguish (a) digitally generated imagery that depicts children's sexual abuse and exploitation from (b) imagery that depicts minors in suggestive sexual contexts and poses, where *manga/hentai* cartoon imagery is exemplary of the latter. For now I will focus on the former and ask: How might we make the case that such depictions just are morally problematic? Even if no actual children were sexually exploited in the production of such imagery, and the imagery is entirely digitally generated, many people (myself included) have a strong intuition that it is nonetheless morally wrong. I will consider next how we might ground this intuition.

Consider first Stephanie Patridge's (2011, 2013) social incorrigibility argument. Although she does not develop this relative to pedophilic DGI, Patridge's position can easily be applied to it. On her view, appreciating and taking pleasure in inegalitarian sexual images of women is per se a moral failing because "the images themselves are morally problematic" (2013, 53). For Patridge, a conception of women as being for men's sexual delectation operates as a mechanism to undermine women's autonomy and contributes to their oppression (see chapter 5). Hence, a person who appreciates and enjoys such images is "guilty of a kind of moral obliviousness: he fails to see the obvious social relevance of this imagery and what this [morally] requires of him" (2013, 53–54). What undergirds this is that inegalitarian sexual imagery has incorrigible social meanings. A meaning is incorrigible in that it is "exceedingly difficult to overturn" (Patridge 2011, 308) and one cannot avoid moral condemnation by claiming that one did not intend to reproduce morally problematic meanings. Moreover, a meaning is social in that "it is explained by contingent facts about a particular social reality" (2013, 54). Patridge considers the example of a cartoon depicting Barack Obama eating a watermelon. This cartoon is per se problematic even if it causes no particular harm to Obama and does not encourage further racialized harms. The cartoon is a racist insult and as such has a racist incorrigible social meaning: a meaning that is difficult to overturn, that cannot be defended by claiming that the cartoon was not intended to be a racial insult, and where its being an insult is explained by social and historical facts about US slavery and continued racial injustice. Racially and/or sexually inegalitarian imagery are extensions of racist and sexist social realities. Given their close proximity to our actual social realities, one could not have failed to see the incorrigible social meanings of the imagery, and so taking pleasure in their consumption is illustrative of a morally condemnable character—something has gone wrong with the consumer's attitudinal response to the imagery. Therefore:

> To insist that one's imagination is one's own private affair, detached from one's own actual commitments and similarly detached from the contextual moral facts on the ground, amounts minimally . . . to the thumbing on one's nose at a requirement of

solidarity with the victims of oppression. This is an obvious vice of character . . . [and one is] guilty of being racially and sexually insensitive. (Patridge 2011, 310)

Elsewhere Patridge puts the point slightly differently: "there is something wrong with such individuals [who enjoy morally delectatious imagery], antecedently, otherwise they would be incapable of bracketing" requisite incorrigible social meanings (2013, 55). In short: A morally virtuous agent would not consume such imagery for the sake of pleasure.

This analysis can be used to condemn digitally generated depictions of child sexual abuse. It seemingly involves incorrigible social meanings pertaining to children's sexualization. Sexualization happens when sexuality is inappropriately imposed on someone: for instance, when young girls are "adultified" by inappropriately imposing sexuality on them or when young women are "youthified" through "teeny" dress and appearance codes (Held 2014, 74). It is a kind of inappropriate co-opting of sexuality (Held 2014, 83). Meanings that are sexualizing are exceedingly difficult to overturn, they cannot be defended by claiming that the imagery was not intended to be sexualizing, and inappropriately imposing sexuality on children is explained by background conditions that fix "sexiness" (for more on contemporary constructions of sexiness, see Maes 2017). Given the realities of child sexual abuse and exploitation, it seems highly unlikely that one could have failed to see such incorrigible social meanings of the imagery. And so, the argument goes, taking sexual pleasure in their consumption is illustrative of a morally condemnable character irrespective of whether the consumption leads to any actual contact abuse.

I find the idea that taking sexual pleasure in depictions of child sexual abuse even if digitally generated and even if this leads to no contact abuse pretheoretically compelling. However, I am unconvinced that Patridge succeeds in showing that some images are per se morally problematic (as she aims to). First, the morally problematic nature of some imagery ultimately hinges on the background social and historical conditions. For instance, the above mentioned Obama cartoon would not be problematic were the historical and social facts otherwise. Hence it does not seem that the imagery per se is problematic; instead, background social conditions that give meaning to the imagery are to blame. Second, the social incorrigibility argument ends up morally condemning those who find such imagery enjoyable. Taking pleasure in consuming morally delectatious imagery shows that it is the *consumer* who is morally vicious because they are insensitive to actual oppressive social relations. Once again, this does not substantiate the view that there is something intrinsically condemnable about the imagery per se.

Might there be another way to establish that some imagery just is morally problematic? In order to explore this, consider a parallel between "deviant" fantasies and virtual imagery. If we can establish that there is something problematic about the former in and of itself, we might find a way to show that the same is true of the latter. Recall Corvino's understanding of deviant or "naughty" sexual fantasies as being "*either imagined or acted out*, involving the eroticization of an activity that is itself morally wrong" (2002, 214)—that is, such fantasies involve actively regarding morally vicious activities with sexual desire, which (in a sense) contaminates the fantasies and renders them morally vicious too. Now consider fantasies of children's sexual abuse.[10]

---

10. Psychological research shows that "sexual interest or arousal in children is not confined to a 'sick few'" (Malamuth and Huppin 2007, 793). Significant numbers of male college students have self-reported such interest (around 20 percent) and studies using physiological indices of arousal put the figure as high as 70 percent. That said, Malamuth and Huppin stress that although "a significant portion of the male population demonstrates some pedophilic interests, this does not mean that all men so identified are likely to fit the clinical diagnosis of pedophilia" (2007, 793). This would require "recurrent, intense sexually arousing fantasies, sexual urges, or behaviors involving sexual activity with a

Insofar as pedophilic fantasies involve actively regarding a morally vicious activity with sexual desire, such fantasies would be morally vicious too. By extension, imagery that captures such fantasies could be considered morally condemnable as well. I suspect that many would intuitively assent to this. However, consider now the same line of argument but replace the morally wrongful activity with some other purportedly wrongful activity. For instance, it is not hard to find people who consider BDSM, adultery and nonheteronormative sex to be morally wrongful. Applying the above argument to (say) nonheteronormative sex, however, yields very different results. This tells us two important things: for the argument to work, we must have some principled way to delimit genuinely morally wrongful sexual activities. Otherwise the determination of "deviant" fantasies is too much hostage to individual prejudices and cultural norms—something that we should surely aim to avoid. Moreover, in the case of pedophilic fantasies, the work is done by pretheoretical evaluative judgments about the wrongfulness of child sexual abuse. What might conceivably ground such judgments though? An obvious answer is that such activities take place against the children's will and under conditions where meaningful consent is impossible. In this case, what makes pedophilic fantasies (and, by extension, imagery) morally reproachable is that they involve eroticization of activities that are nonconsensual.

The above argument suggests that pedophilic imagery—even when digitally generated—involves the eroticization of nonconsent in a way that makes it morally reproachable. Thinking about nonconsent further demonstrates a subtle, yet important, point about the content of sexual fantasies. Rape is about nonconsensual sex. Imagining *simulated* scenarios of nonconsensual sex, however, is not the same as

---

prepubescent child or children (generally age 13 years or younger)" over at least a six-month period (2007, 793).

wanting to be subject to *actual* nonconsensual sex. If those who entertain the former do not literally wish to experience the latter, they are not genuinely fantasizing about rape—they are fantasizing about simulations of rape. For instance, "rape play" in BDSM settings is far from nonconsensual and has little to do with nonconsensual sex as a form of sexualized violence (Hopkins 1994). The point is that BDSM activities do not replicate genuinely problematic sexual activities but rather simulate them. To elucidate: "Replication implies that [BD]SM encounters merely reproduce [problematic sexual] activity in a different physical area. Simulation implies that [BD]SM selectively replays surface [problematic] behaviors onto a different contextual field . . . [BD]SM participants do not rape, they do rape scenes" (Hopkins 1994, 123). Importantly, simulation is recognized as such by the participants. It involves (what we might call) consensual nonconsent: consensually engaging in simulated scenarios of nonconsent. But in actual sexualized violence, those attacked are not *participants* in their own violation. The so-called rape fantasies are not fantasies about being raped—in actual cases something is done to the attacked, and they are not active participants in what is done to them.[11]

This distinction between reproduction and simulation (I contend) offers a tool with which to assess the morality of sexual fantasies. If some fantasy involves the simulation of a morally wrongful activity regarded with sexual desire, entertaining the fantasy is not morally condemnable. Entertaining the fantasy may be psychologically puzzling and odd, but doing so would not demonstrate a significant moral failure. Then again, if the fantasy involves a reproduction of the

---

11. Nils-Hennes Stear (2009) challenges Hopkins's analysis of BDSM that relies on the simulation/reproduction distinction and argues that this distinction does not accurately track what goes on in BDSM play. Be that as it may, I am here only interested in the distinction and won't consider further its accuracy with respect to BDSM.

activity, it is morally wrongful per se. To illustrate, let me flesh out the distinction between reproduction and simulation a bit further. This distinction is intended to track a rather intuitive difference that we find in many everyday contexts. Just think of the difference between a talk that aims to document some historical event and a theater play that fictionalizes details of the event without changing the basic historical facts. In the former case, the aim is to reproduce the historical facts of the matter, while the latter aims to simulate them. Of course, it might not always be easy to discern when some fantasy involves simulation rather than reproduction. But the distinction nonetheless allows us to draw principled distinctions between different fantasies and conclusions about digitally generated pedophilic imagery: in a parallel fashion, imagery that involves simulation is not per se morally condemnable, while imagery that involves reproduction is.

With this in mind, return to the distinction noted above between digitally generated imagery depicting children's sexual exploitation and *manga/hentai* cartoon imagery that depicts apparent minors and childlike persons in sexual contexts. Given the typically fantastical and unrealistic nature of the latter, it involves simulation rather than reproduction—the imagery is more akin to a theater play than to a documentary about some historical event.[12] An important clarification is in order though. The fantastical quality of *hentai* should not merely pertain to the background but must (so to speak) suffuse the sexual nature of the imagery too. So, sexually exploitative scenes that look prima facie like reproductions of exploitation but are played against supernatural and fantastical backgrounds does not yet suffice to render the depictions simulative in the sense that I have mind. It is the simulation of the sexual acts that makes a difference, where this depends on (among other things) the background context. The

---

12. I explore this point further with respect to pornographic videogames elsewhere; see Mikkola 2018.

upshot is that simulative *hentai* cartoon imagery is not morally condemnable per se. Of course, if such imagery encourages actual abuse, we have good consequentialist grounds to find it morally reproachable. Nonetheless, if my argument in the section is right, *hentai* materials are not intrinsically morally reprehensible, while digitally generated imagery reproducing children's sexual exploitation is.

6.5. CONCLUDING REMARKS

In this chapter I have considered topics relevant for the aesthetics of pornography. These included fictionality of pornography, whether art and pornography are mutually exclusive, and whether there are reasons to find some depictions morally problematic in and of themselves. These issues are intimately connected with ethical judgments about pornography. They also demonstrate the difficulty of treating pornography as a monolithic phenomenon. However, much of the discussion in this chapter (and the book so far) has involved showing that pornographic fiction, fantasy, or depiction need not be morally reproachable. But might some pornographic works have a claim to being morally *commendable*? Some hold that pornography has emancipatory potential and that it can play a positive role in advancing social justice. I will turn to this topic next.

Chapter 7

Pornography as Liberation

7.1. INTRODUCTION

Issues surrounding sexuality and pornography have tended to polarize the feminist movement, and differences in views led to the so-called sex wars of the 1970s and1980s. The main opposing positions can be denoted with PorNo (short for antipornography positions) and PorYes (denoting pro-pornography and "sex positive" outlooks). PorNo feminist activism has in recent years gained renewed momentum. An international Stop Porn Culture–movement, co-founded by the high-profile antipornography campaigner Claire Dines, is calling for an end to society's "pornification." Concurrently, the production of self-proclaimed feminist pornography has become more prominent. In addition, academic work on pornography that is not premised on a PorNo position has gained impetus with the first-ever peer-reviewed academic journal in such a vein, *Porn Studies,* established in 2014 and published by Routledge. Dines, who likened the journal's editors to climate change deniers relative to pornography, fervently opposed its launch.[1] However, the Stop Porn Culture–movement has been critiqued for being "unwilling

---

1. Carole Cadwalladr, "Porn Wars: The Debate that Is Dividing Academia," *The Observer,* June 16, 2013, https://www.theguardian.com/culture/2013/jun/16/internet-violent-porn-crime-studies. Accessed August 12, 2018.

to acknowledge the counterhegemonic possibilities in feminist and queer porn, unable to consider the possibility of improving rather than eradicating pornography, and [for] reject[ing] the possibility of neutral or even positive uses of sexually explicit materials" (Tarrant 2014, 36). PorNo positions are criticized further for assuming that "sex is inherently oppressive to women—that women are debased when they have sex on camera—[which] ignores and represses the sexuality of women" (Taormino et al. 2013, 15). PorNo feminism is said to amount to a pro-censorship, moralistic, and sex-negative condemnation of pornography. By contrast, pro-pornography positions claim that pornography can be and is empowering. These positions do not have in mind sexually suggestive soft-core materials but rather sexually explicit hardcore depictions that include facets of the Dworkin-MacKinnon definition of *pornography* (see chapter 1). PorYes positions are also tied to pornography being prima facie essentially transgressive in character and therefore positive: for instance, Laura Kipnis famously holds that "pornography obeys certain rules, and its primary rule is transgression. Like your boorish cousin, its greatest pleasure is to locate each and every one of society's taboos, prohibitions, and properties and systematically transgress them, one by one" (1996, 164).

These claims and the PorNo/PorYes opposition are fraught with difficulties. First, it is not entirely clear what exactly is under dispute. There is confusion over whether different sides disagree about how to define the concept of *pornography* or merely about which materials fall under the concept. In the former case, different positions end up talking at cross-purposes, while in the latter case it remains unclear why there is disagreement about which materials properly speaking count as pornography. Moreover, it is far from obvious why and how feminists should oppose pornography (if at all). One might hold that the production of pornography is somehow morally worrisome due to working conditions rather than what is depicted, but this need not raise any specifically feminist worries—one need not be a feminist to oppose the exploitation of workers. Furthermore, the debates are polarized by blatantly misleading and simplistic descriptions of the opposite view(s). To the best of my knowledge, the view that women debase themselves when they have sex on camera is not widely held by antipornography feminist philosophers. It is certainly not a view that one can find in the work of Rae Langton, who is the most well-known contemporary defender of the Dworkin-MacKinnon position. And as discussed in chapter 4, very few (if any) contemporary antipornography positions advocate criminalization and explicit censorship of pornographic materials *contra* prevalent caricatures. Staunch PorNo positions are far less prevalent in academic work on the topic than critics would have one believe. Finally, it looks like a mistake to accept either position in an unqualified sense. As PorYes advocates point out, an unqualified PorNo stance seems blinkered: antipornography critiques miss their target because they treat pornographic materials in too simplistic a manner and because they fail to appreciate differences in sexual tastes and desires. A number of queer theorists have accused antipornography feminism of being heteronormative and heterosexist: that is, treating heterosexuality as the normative standard against which all sexuality is measured. This problematically naturalizes heterosexist sexual practices, where sex between cis-men and cis-women is "normal" while other practices are supposedly deviant. Hence, some queer theorists and philosophers rightly claim that antipornography feminism tends to examine pornography through a strict male-female binary and that antipornography legislation motivated by (white, Anglo-American) feminist concerns would restrict materials that contribute to the emancipation of gay, lesbian, trans*, and queer sexualities. Although these claims have prima facie plausibility, earlier discussions in this book suggest that an unqualified PorYes position is also misguided: such a position ignores that pornography production and consumption are not just harmless private affairs. And to think that the raison d'être of pornography is to transgress societies' bourgeois conventions (as Kipnis does) is surely exaggerated and over-intellectualized.

We can see the makings of new sex wars in popular discourse and culture as well as in academic writings about pornography. Hence this chapter considers two questions. First, is feminist pornography possible, and if so, what would make pornography feminist? Second, might pornography be a force for liberation and emancipation? My answer to both questions is yes, and in this chapter I will consider some features of feminist and/or liberatory pornography. However, it will also become clear that our answers to these questions must be more nuanced and qualified than existing debates typically allow. I will argue that neither an unqualified PorNo nor an unqualified PorYes position is tenable. Furthermore, these positions share many basic commitments; but both sides tend to paint the opposition in an uncharitable light and in a manner that distorts the debate thereby disguising common ground. Before I go on to discuss these points in detail, it is worth noting that very little philosophical literature on issues relevant for this chapter currently exists, especially in analytic philosophy. The discussions in this chapter cannot then draw on a wealth of existing literature and rather aim to motivate further philosophical work on the issues raised.

7.2. WHAT IS FEMINIST PORNOGRAPHY?

Above I noted that this chapter deals with the question of whether feminist pornography is possible. This question is not entirely straightforward, and the answer to it is either self-evident or highly contested. It is self-evident in the sense that there are plenty of producers who self-identify as feminists and who claim to be producing feminist pornography. Then again, such self-proclaimed feminist projects are highly contested by opponents, who claim that self-proclamation is insufficient to make some pornographic materials feminist—producers may declare this to be the case, but this does not guarantee that the materials genuinely embody feminist values. Let's start by looking at how the central features of feminist and mainstream pornography are said to come apart. They are said to differ in (a) what is represented and depicted; and (b) how production is organized. On one prominent characterization, feminist pornography is a genre that

> uses sexually explicit imagery to contest and complicate dominant representations of gender, sexuality, race, ethnicity, class, ability, age, body type, and other identity markers. It explores concepts of desire, agency, power, beauty, and pleasure at their most confounding and difficult, including pleasure within and across inequality, in the face of injustice, and against the limits of gender hierarchy and both heteronormativity and homonormativity ... [It] creates alternative images and develops its own aesthetics and iconography to expand established sexual norms and discourses ... [and] strive[s] to create fair, safe, ethical, consensual work environment and often create imagery through collaboration with their subjects. (Taormino et al. 2013, 9–10)

Tristan Taormino (a well-known pornography producer and sex educator) further specifies this last point by stating that feminist pornography involves a fair and ethical production process that creates "a positive working environment for everyone" (2013, 260). I will say more about production processes in section 7.3. For now, consider what is typically depicted and represented in self-professed feminist pornography. These types of materials typically aim to avoid representations of sexist stereotypes and uses of usual pornography tropes like "money shots" (sex culminating in men ejaculating on women's faces). Anne Eaton further outlines seven positive criteria of feminist pornography. First, women are portrayed in active roles: "as *subjects* of desire and pleasure (rather than merely objects of desire)." Second, "narrative and visuals are not organized around men's orgasms but, rather, centrally feature female pleasure and orgasms." Third, men are also objectified by the female characters in the film as well as by the spectator's gaze. Fourth, feminist pornography includes "erotic representations of male bisexuality." Fifth, men take on submissive roles and women dominant ones. Sixth, "women are represented as powerful and physically strong." And seventh, "realistic female bodies of all ages that do not promote unhealthily thin stereotypes are not only represented but are also eroticized" (Eaton 2017, 254).

With these criteria of putatively feminist pornography in mind, recall the common antipornography critique: what makes pornography problematic is that it *endorses* and *celebrates* women's subordination and degradation—not that it merely depicts women as subordinated (section 1.2.). In endorsing women's subordination, the depicted images are morally problematic because endorsing degradation involves communicating an approval and recommendation of sexual behaviors that devalue women. Degradation is represented as pleasurable for both the male and female performers, and there is "no suggestion that this sort of treatment of others is inappropriate to their status as human beings" (Longino 1980, 43–44). Sex in pornography is degrading in that the desires and experiences of women are usually not regarded as having validity or equal importance (Tong 1982). Celebrating women's degradation makes mainstream pornography sexist. However, many from the PorYes camp *agree* with this assessment of mainstream, industrial pornography. Feminist pornographers typically hold that mainstream pornographic depictions of sexual activities and gender roles are sexist in precisely this manner (Ms. Naughty 2013; Royalle 2000; see also

Rubin 1993). The view that sex depicted in masculinist pornography (that is, pornography produced from a masculinist perspective) ignores and devalues desires and experiences of women is a mainstay of feminist pornography. But, the thought goes, we should not therefore oppose pornography per se; rather, we should oppose exploitative and sexist pornography and aim to undermine its force by depicting sex and sexual agency of women in ways that fit the above characteristics offered by Taormino and Eaton. As Annie Sprinkle famously put it, to solve the problem of bad pornography, women and feminists must make better pornography.

To strengthen this point, consider Catherine Itzin's introduction to a hefty volume on antipornography feminism, where she writes that the book aims to advance a social environment where

> sex might be experienced and presented differently: not in terms of male definition, or of male dominance and female subordination or power and powerlessness, but based on reciprocity, mutuality and equality. [This is being denied by pornography] with its false premises about women, its false promises to men, and its power as a form of sex discrimination to "pornographize" women. (1992a, 19)

This is very close to what self-proclaimed feminist pornographers also aim to advance. These producers typically aim to realize feminist aims by avoiding common pornographic tropes and depictions formed from a masculinist perspective. Candida Royalle—a performer turned director and the "grand dame" of feminist pornography—recounts how she started directing pornographic films in order to undercut sexist depictions of women in mainstream industrial pornography (Royalle 2000). In her work, Royalle refused to use common mainstream tropes like money shots. At the same time, she (in her own words) refused to present herself as pro-porn or "anything goes" director. The point of feminist pornography for her was precisely to say that not everything goes, that some pornography is exploitative, and that some pornographic depictions are sexist—they are based on false premises about women and they offer false promises to viewers. If mainstream masculinist pornography is problematic in endorsing and celebrating women's subordination and degradation and some pornography avoids this due to producers sincerely holding feminist convictions, we have good reasons to think that genuinely feminist pornography is possible.

That said, feminist pornography is sometimes glossed as a "female-friendly" genre, porn for women or porna in order to highlight the break with exploitative, sexist, and male-oriented porno. The term 'porna' arose from the work of female producers, and in 2008 a Dutch Cable-TV channel "Dusk" (https://www.dusk-tv.com) exclusively devoted to porna was launched. (There is now also a worldwide online streaming option for the channel.) Materials shown are partly user-generated: women who subscribe to the channel can take part in a panel that previews films, and decisions about which materials to include take into account ratings and opinions of this panel. Festivals and events on alternative and feminist pornographies are also becoming more prevalent. There are currently two regular awards for feminist pornography: the Toronto-based International Porn Festival Awards (formerly the "Good for Her" Feminist Pornography Awards) and the Berlin-based PorYes Awards.[2] The judging criteria for the former include (in an abridged form):

1. *Quality*: overall production values.
2. *Inclusiveness*: making an effort to explore "sexualities that are often marginalized, fetishized and/or ignored by most porn" including films that contain kink, BDSM, and consensual

---

2. For more on the PorYes Awards, see https://www.poryes.de/.

nonconsent in a fictional context. "We don't include or support films that rely upon sexual stereotypes."

3. *The "it" factor*: "Movies that showcase a unique perspective . . . We are always most impressed when we encounter
something novel, innovative and exciting that causes us to
think about sexuality in a fresh way."

4. *Hotness*: "Bodies are well-lit and framed, desire radiates off the
screen, and all parties involved appear enthusiastic." (http://
www.torontointernationalpornfestival.com/criteria/)

Now, earlier in this book I used the expression 'inegalitarian
pornography' to denote pornography that is objectionable from a
feminist perspective and that is prima facie female unfriendly. This
suggests that feminist pornography is equivalent to egalitarian pornography and that such pornography is always female friendly.
Equating the three (feminist, egalitarian, and female-friendly pornography) is not entirely unproblematic though. Maes takes egalitarian pornography to be "premised on the full equality between
sexual partners" and to be pornography that does not "eroticize any
acts of violence, humiliation, or objectification or any of the gender
stereotypes that help to sustain gender inequality" (2017, 211). He
considers production companies like Puzzy Power and Zentropa to
be creating exemplars of such pornography. However, Maes rightly
notes that a commitment to pro-egalitarian pornography comes with
two provisos. First, and as discussed in chapter 5, films that depict
apparently confident female characters do not ipso facto qualify as
egalitarian pornography. By way of example, Maes discusses Erika
Lust's well-known short film *The Good Girl* (2004). Lust is one of the
best-known producers of putatively female-friendly pornography.
This film depicts Alex, a successful businesswoman, who ends up
having a spontaneous sexual encounter with a tall, handsome pizza
deliveryman that culminates in a money shot. Maes concludes that

the film "continues and even celebrates this most prevalent trope of inegalitarian pornography rather than subverting it. While this may be female-friendly pornography, it is not egalitarian pornography (being friendly toward someone and treating her as an equal are two different things)" (2017, 213). Maes's second proviso holds that even when a work genuinely qualifies as egalitarian pornography, it is not therefore beyond critique. This is so if a film, for instance, makes use of a limited set of performers who all fit some gender stereotypic mold of "sexiness," when "real diversity of bodies" is lacking, if the film is heteronormative or heterosexist, or if the work relies on and reinforces essentialist views about female sexuality (2017, 214). As an alternative to the idea of feminist egalitarian pornography, Maes proposes the idea of radical egalitarian pornography that

> militates against the perpetuation of any harmful stereotype in such a way that exposure to this kind of pornography will no longer have a detrimental impact on our responses of sexual attraction but, on the contrary, might help to bring them in line with our ideas of gender equality. (2017, 215)

In his view, this sort of pornography should be supported and promoted to undercut the pernicious effects of inegalitarian pornography. Calling some pornography feminist or female friendly does not suffice.

In a different vein, Petra van Brabandt also objects to the inegalitarian/egalitarian pornography division. She holds that analyzing "the content and aesthetics of contemporary pornography shows that its meaning is more complex and less stable than the opposition inegalitarian/egalitarian pornography can account for. What at first sight could seem inegalitarian might prove more dynamic and contested" (2017, 221). Van Brabandt also makes the point that looking at surface depictions alone is insufficient because something seemingly inegalitarian may not be so once we appreciate the contested and dynamic nature of what is being depicted. Furthermore, she holds, analytic antipornography feminist philosophers are typically not in a good position to settle the matter because they lack the required training in film theory and aesthetics. That said, van Brabandt is not aiming to defend inegalitarian pornography. As she sees it, although depictions of subordination and violence may be contested, both inegalitarian and egalitarian pornography typically buy into gender stereotypic depictions of male sexual activity and female sexual passivity—and this renders both problematic. As an alternative, van Branbandt champions queer pornography that challenges heterosexual gendered roles, bodies, and scenarios without shunning "the representation and endorsement of sexual power dynamics, including subordination and violence" (2017, 222). Queer pornography can be transgressive without thereby "endorsing a patriarchal sexual gender hierarchy in which men sexually dominate women. Queer pornography therefore has the potential to realize a broader range of pornographic experiences than egalitarian pornography" (2017, 238). (Other oft-drawn distinctions pertain to alternative/independent versus mainstream/industrial pornographies. These are not unproblematic either; I will return to this point in the following section.)

Above I noted that if pornographic depictions do not endorse and celebrate women's sexual subordination, they qualify as feminist. But one might wonder whether the so-called feminist pornography or porna really is pornography. If we are talking about sexually explicit materials that are premised on equality, are we not simply talking about erotica? In this case, the anti- and pro-pornography sides are simply talking past one another and employing different conceptions of *pornography*. If this turns out to be the dispute, it is not a substantive or particularly interesting one. In this case, one side holds that 'pornography' only captures sexually explicit materials that are misogynist while the other side takes the term to pick out a wider range of materials—some of which are misogynistic, while others are egalitarian and even feminist. As I see it, to settle what *pornography* should cover, methodological considerations over who gets to decide become imperative. For a start, recall that antipornography feminists define *erotica* as passionate love; it is about equality and "love making" while pornography is about violence (Steinem 1995). Drawing the distinction in such a way, however, romanticizes sex and ends up connecting sex and love in a way that reflects common gender stereotypes. It reflects a cliché picture of women wanting romance-novel sex and buys into the view that domination, conquest, and submission in a sexual context simply are morally problematic and something that women cannot freely consent to. And importantly, self-proclaimed feminist pornographers are not aiming to depict "love making"; rather, they aim to offer egalitarian *pornographic* alternatives. One could, of course, simply ignore this point and define *pornography* as MacKinnon, A. Dworkin, and Langton do. But this strategy is suspect: it defines *pornography* from the philosopher's armchair and in a way that those involved in pornography's production reject. The problem with this move is that a stipulated antipornography definition ignores and silences an important group of women: those producers and performers who aim to subvert insidious, mainstream depictions and undercut exploitative industry practices. Moreover, philosophers who have little contact with and knowledge of what goes on in the pornography industry are not in a good position to talk authoritatively about it. Our philosophical theories should do justice to the claims of feminist producers and not dismiss them outright. The above discussion, then, should tell us two things: feminist pornography is possible. And if we privilege the perspective of those doing self-professed feminist pornography and accept that they are genuinely involved in pornography production (as opposed to producing erotica), feminist pornography is not only possible—rather, the genre is alive and kicking.

7.3. INDUSTRY PRACTICES

Above I discussed the first part of what might make pornography feminist: what is depicted and represented. However, this is only part of the story, and self-proclaimed feminist pornographers typically pay much attention to ensuring that working conditions are fair and safe. Earlier in this book, I have alluded to a distinction between independent feminist and mainstream industrial pornography, where the latter has been identified with mass-produced inegalitarian depictions of sexuality. This suggests that independent productions that are feminist are somehow by definition good while industrial pornography is always bad. This contrast is quick and dirty, especially when it comes to industry practices. Although "indie" feminist pornography presents an alternative to more mainstream pornography in terms of what is depicted, media theorists hold that the distinction should not be overemphasized. Distinguishing between commercially driven, predictable, dull industrial pornography and new, independent and online-based pornographies that aim to be intellectually and aesthetically challenging, may be

> useful as a way of identifying the variety of features of production, style, and distribution that new pornographies employ. However, an overemphasis on this distinction can work to collapse the variety of online porn into a simple opposition of "old" and "new" and to make invisible the ways that particular forms of style and content may straddle "old" and "new," "online" and "offline," "mainstream" and "alternative" pornographies. (Attwood 2010a, 237)

The highly acclaimed genderqueer performer, Jiz Lee, also rejects the alternative/good versus mainstream/bad distinction.[3] Having worked extensively with different producers in both alternative and mainstream settings, Lee denies that there is a clear and obvious difference between the two. Lee notes that some prima facie alternative sets have been much less open to ethical working conditions and safe-sex practices than many mainstream sets. Ethically oriented, "fair-trade" working conditions that take performers' personal wishes and safe-sex practices seriously are not confined to alternative pornography productions. Again, consider an analogy with food production: not all small independent producers comply with fair-trade requirements (organic farmers can and do exploit undocumented or migrant workers) and not all mass-industrially produced food is *eo ipso* morally condemnable—our moral judgments again depend on various contextual matters and background conditions of production. As Royalle (2000) put it, like with any big industry, the pornography industry too has good people to work with and some "real creeps" that one learns to avoid.

One major difference in industry practices pertains to how performers are paid. An industry standard is to pay different fees for different scenes, with anal and double-penetration scenes usually fetching much higher fees that vaginal penetration or lesbian scenes. This puts pressure on performers to agree to shoots that they might not otherwise have agreed to. By contrast, Shine Louise Houston—a celebrated producer and trailblazer of independent queer pornography—pays the same flat-fee to performers irrespective of the nature of the scene. This ensures that the performers need not feel pressured to do something that they may not wish to do out of monetary considerations (Tarrant 2016). Feona Attwood (one of

---

3. Based on a panel discussion with Jiz Lee, Buck Angel, Laura Méritt and myself during the Berlin PorYes Awards in October 2015.

the editors of *Porn Studies*) describes producers like Houston as the "new porn professionals" for whom

> sex and porn are repositioned as part of a mix of media, life-style, and sexual practices through which the self is expressed and community created, and in which neither is antithetical to commerce . . . "sex work" becomes a stylish and alternative form of self-expression and a way of developing a community. (2010b, 95)

Other facets of this kind of professionalism involve undercutting the idea that commodification of sex is wrongful or that performers (and sex workers more generally) are necessarily exploited and dehumanized by their work. Moreover, new porn professionals like Houston and Lee (among others) aim to show that pornography need not represent a limited range of acceptable and sexually attractive body types. This sort of professionalism is, in the words of a veteran pornography performer, director and avid feminist Nina Hartley, concerned with "responsible hedonism" that focuses on "power relations between producers, how images are produced and distributed, and what kinds of contexts they are consumed in" (quoted in Atwood 2010b, 103).

With the above discussions in mind, it is clear that we cannot neatly equate feminist pornography with alternative, female-friendly, and/or egalitarian pornography. Still, I wish to retain the label 'feminist pornography'. It is conceivable (and likely) that not all self-proclaimed feminist pornography succeeds in being so. However, there are grounds to retain the label in order to denote materials that *genuinely* have been produced under ethical and fair-trade conditions and that celebrate nongender stereotypic bodies, scenarios, and desires. My point is normative and about how we *should* understand feminist pornography: we can fix some conditions of feminist pornographic depictions and production processes; all works that satisfy them will be feminist, irrespective of whether the producers intended their works to fall under the concept *feminist pornography*. Pro-pornography activism should then celebrate and endorse the production of such materials to shape our affective, erotic lives in more gender-just ways. (More on this shortly.) Hence, we can look forward to a day when this sort of material is more prominent at the expense of problematic materials that currently saturate the Internet, even if some self-proclaimed feminist pornography currently falls short of the ideal.

Rebecca Whisnant (2016) critiques Taormino's work in this vein (although Whisnant is much more skeptical than I am about the possibility of there being genuinely feminist pornography). For Whisnant, irrespective of whether pornography can genuinely be feminist, Taormino's much-celebrated brand of putatively feminist pornography does not qualify as genuinely feminist. Some of Whisnant's points certainly have appeal. She critiques Taormino's reluctance to avoid money shots and some other standard pornography tropes. Whisnant also questions simplistic ascriptions of authentic desires to performers given the constraints that pornography production and distribution involve. For Taormino, a choice or desire to perform is authentic when this is "something the person sincerely wants to do or from which she or he derives real (rather than faked) pleasure" (Whisnant 2016, 3). But given the constraints of pornography production, this sort of authenticity is supposedly not available to performers. For instance, one might not sincerely want to have sex at all during the time of filming, but refusing to have sex is (on Whisnant's view) not a viable option on a pornography filming set. Therefore, Whisnant argues that following Taormino's conception of authenticity, a performer who "doesn't feel like it" but still goes along with the shoot, will not sincerely desire to perform in the shoot, and thus the performer partakes in the production inauthentically. This is one way in which Taormino's pornography apparently falls short of genuine feminist commitments. Other ways in which her work allegedly fails to be feminist is in its continued celebration of women's subordination. As Whisnant puts it,

> a tenet basic to the ideology of pro-porn feminism [is]: that it is fine to portray dominance, submission, pain, and hierarchy as sexually exciting, so long as women are shown consenting to them and even enjoying them. (2016, 5)

In short, the worry is that central forms of "misogynist torture and terror" (like choking, slapping, gagging, hair pulling) are presented as sex games, which is inconsistent with feminism.

Now, I agree that relying on standard tropes used in industrial inegalitarian pornography when selling one's product as putatively feminist is disappointing and avoiding common masculinist tropes is something we should expect from feminist pornography. But some of Whisnant's other critiques are unpersuasive. Consider the point about authenticity: performers might be having sex on set absentmindedly, but this is not enough, it seems to me, to render the performance nonfeminist. There are many times when we do not feel like doing our jobs. I am fairly sure that almost every professional philosopher has at some point (and perhaps frequently) felt like not giving a class or a conference talk, and, instead, simply went through the motions. But there is a substantive difference between doing x without a great desire to do x (perhaps because one has a financial incentive or contractual obligation to do x), and doing x against one's will. If the former situation renders one's desire or choice inauthentic, much of what we do ends up being so. Nonetheless, I suspect that few would think an absentmindedly-given philosophy talk should morally concern us. In order for her argument to work, Whisnant would have to say that there is something substantially different about performing in pornography and performing as a professional philosopher, so that when the former is undertaken absentmindedly, there is something morally worrisome about the case. The only way we can plausibly make sense of this is by saying that there is something about sex that renders having sex absentmindedly inauthentic or morally worrisome. This shows that what is ultimately doing the work is Whisnant's view of sex: there is some value to sexual activity that is violated by having sex absentmindedly during pornography production. Once more, we can see that anti- and pro-pornography positions ultimately hinge on different views about when sex is morally good and what the value of sexual activity is—in short, what undergirds the debate are prior evaluative judgments about sex. To clarify: I am not charging Whisnant of being sex negative or prudish; I certainly do not hold that being sex positive and being pro-pornography are equivalent. My point is that many debates about pornography hinge on prior views about what makes sex morally good from a feminist perspective, which are often not made transparent. Without addressing this issue first, many debates about pornography are likely to become intractable.[4]

The above demonstrates that choice and consent play central roles in feminist pornography debates. Consent is often taken to have a "magical" quality (Wertheimer 1996): it turns apparently problematic activities into morally permissible ones. So, if female performers genuinely choose to take part in pornography, this would undermine antipornography positions. However, limits of genuine choice and consent are contested. For instance, Steinem holds that even if "a

4. As a side note, I am not convinced that calling one's opposing view ideological—as Whisnant does—helps debates about pornography. In so doing, she implies that her antipornography position is free from ideological background beliefs and commitments. I have no qualms with philosophical theorizing that is perspectival and even ideologically driven; but we should be frank about our prior evaluative judgments and acknowledge their pull in our philosophical theorizing.

person has chosen or consented to be harmed, abused, or subjected to coercion [this] does not alter the degrading character of such behavior" (1995, 37). It is not uncommon for performers to come from underprivileged socioeconomic backgrounds. MacKinnon is thus skeptical of the idea that women genuinely consent to performing in pornography: "The sex is not chosen for the sex. Money is the medium of force and provides the cover of consent" (MacKinnon 1993, 28). And so, although women were not physically coerced into performing, there is a sense in which the genuineness of their choice is questionable: had these performers had other meaningful economic opportunities, it is far from obvious that they still would have chosen to work in the pornography industry. Antipornography feminists also often claim that since many performers and ex-performers report having been sexually abused as children or groomed into sex work, this renders their apparent choices meaningless (MacKinnon and Dworkin 1997; Russell 1993b). Finally, it is important to bear in mind that even though working conditions in the US pornography industry are highly regulated and seemingly much less exploitative than critics would have one believe, pornography is also produced in other parts of the world where vulnerable individuals are tricked, pressured, and coerced into performing. (At the time of this writing, media reports have highlighted such problems in Japan's lucrative pornography industry—a country that also currently lacks antitrafficking legislation to protect vulnerable individuals.[5])

Settling these issues about consent and choice is complicated. Against negative personal testimonies one can find positive ones. Other performers report having the ability to exert agency and

5. J. McCurry, "Forced into Pornography: Japan Moves to Stop Women Being Coerced into Sex Films," *The Guardian*, May 15, 2017, https://www.theguardian.com/world/2017/may/15/forced-into-porn-japan-moves-to-stop-women-being-coerced-into-sex-films. Accessed August 12, 2018.

control over their work (rather than being exploited); having chosen a career in the industry (rather than having been coerced into it); and that they are proud of their occupation, seeing it as emancipatory rather than oppressive (Arrowsmith 2013; Dylan 2013; Flores 2013; McElroy 1995, chap. 7; Royalle 2000; Strossen 1995, chap. 9). A number of prominent contemporary feminist pornographers have university degrees, and asserting they are simply deluded and brainwashed by patriarchy to partake in the industry would be highly problematic and insulting. Furthermore, the "damaged goods" hypothesis has not been confirmed relative to the US pornography industry. This hypothesis assumes that female performers come from sexually and physically abusive backgrounds, have low self-esteem, suffer from mental health problems, and that substance abuse in the industry is rife. By contrast, empirical evidence comparing performers and "civilians" does not support this perception (Griffith et al. 2013). That said, much of this type of research relies on self-reporting and hence it typically leaves pornography's opponents unpersuaded. There are certainly important and difficult methodological issues to consider when we rely on empirical research. At the same time, available empirical evidence suggests that philosophical intuitions are likely to be ill-suited tools when settling issues pertaining to pornography. A proper assessment of the ethics of pornography must not ignore positive personal stories, but it must also avoid uncritically accepting them. Subsequently, I contend, we cannot draw conclusions about pornography except in a highly contextualized and piecemeal fashion. Analytic philosophers may find this inconvenient and unsatisfying. But when we do philosophical work on such this-worldly topics like pornography, ignoring facts on the ground can be at the expense of plausibility and the persuasiveness of our philosophical theorizing.

7.4. EMANCIPATION OR FETISHISM?

In addition to considering whether feminist pornography is possible, the second central question of this chapter is whether pornography can be a force for liberation and emancipation. Some argue that pornography is indeed highly liberating for women and members of socially and sexually marginalized groups. In fact, one might hold that feminist pornography is also liberating for heterosexual cis-men insofar as such materials go beyond and offer alternatives to the limited sexual scripts found in much of ubiquitous mainstream Internet pornography. Not only are cis-men presented alternative visions of desire; they are also presented a different picture about sexual functioning (one that does not depict men as sexual supermen). In this sense, some pornography may undercut patriarchal depictions of sexuality that harm not only heterosexual cis-women but also cis-men, thus being educationally valuable. This sort of anti-antipornography position, nonetheless, clearly does not equate to a pro-pornography one. Consider Wendy McElroy's (1995) prominent pro-pornography position, which holds that gaining sexual freedom is an integral part of a feminist battle for women's liberation more generally. For her, pornography production and consumption are part of sexual self-determination in being (what McElroy calls) sexual free speech. And so, one's liberty to partake in and/or consume pornography are feminist issues. Furthermore, McElroy holds that pornography benefits women in contributing to their good sexual health, which is essential for good health generally. These benefits (according to her) include women gaining sexual information from pornography, pornographic materials serving as sexual therapy, and pornographic depictions breaking down cultural and political stereotypes about sex (McElroy 1995, chap. 6; see also Palac 1995). In short, pornography offers women new sexual fantasies and ways to explore their sexualities, which traditional gender socialization into "good and bad girls" hampers.

Pornography is said to have especially positive effects on marginalized sexualities. It can function to educate viewers about their sexual identities and to legitimate their desires—in short, it can demonstrate to viewers that they are not sexual deviants or alone with their desires, and help viewers understand sexual feelings that might otherwise be confusing (usually, due to the lack of good sexual and relationship education). Pornographic depictions can also render apparently "disgusting" bodies positively valued objects of desire. In these ways, gay male pornography has allegedly played a significant role in gay liberation and in struggles to gain legitimation for gay sexual lives and desires (Green 2000). The function of gay male pornography is thus said to be quite different from that of industrial pornography aimed at heterosexual cis-men. Furthermore, gay male pornography affords a different way to view sexually explicit materials: because it involves same-sex participants, the spectator can identify with alternative subject positions and is not confined to identifying either as a dominant male or a submissive female (Waugh 1995). This supposedly undermines the view that in gay pornography, subordinating subjects take on a female position—a view that buys into a heterosexist and stereotypical views about supposedly normal sexuality involving dominant males and subordinate females.

Disability advocates and the Fat Acceptance movement have more recently made similar points: those with atypical bodily functionings tend to be viewed as nonsexual, while fat people are often viewed as "disgusting" and "gross."[6] Pornography that portrays atypical and fat bodies as objects of sexual desire challenges these presumptions. For instance, Loree Erickson (a performer with restricted mobility)

---

6. I am using the term 'fat' as a value-neutral descriptive term as it is employed in the field of fat studies and Fat Acceptance communities.

holds that partaking in pornography is one of the most empowering things she has done: "On a political level, it allowed me to make a movie that would not only offer a moment of recognition of how sexy queercrips could be, but also a way to tell others how I wanted to be seen" (2013, 324). Fat Acceptance communities' reactions to BBW pornography (a genre denoting "big beautiful women") vary from "empowerment" to "humiliation and disbelief" (Klumbyte and Smiet 2015). April Flores, a prominent BBW performer, notes that

> the most rewarding part of my work has been the feedback I have received from women, men, and couples who find larger bodies attractive. Other plus-sized women tell me that my work has helped them to view themselves in a more positive light, allowing them to feel just as sexy as women half their size. (2013, 282)

Pornography depicting alternative sorts of bodies, sexualities, and conceptions of sexiness is also positively used in therapy: according to one therapist, it is a good tool "not because it sets out to convince my clients and students that they want to do everything—or anything—they see, but because it helps to build somatic and visual vocabularies from which to make empowered choices" (Lane 2013, 170). This idea is also echoed by Buck Angel, a trailblazing trans* pornography performer and producer (http://buckangel.com/). He describes himself as a "Man with a Pussy" in not having had genital surgery. This self-description importantly points out that one's genital status does not fix gender identity and that one can be a man without a penis. Moreover, pornography can be a powerful vehicle for getting such a message across. In these ways, it can offer us expanded conceptions of bodies, sexiness, and sexualities hence serving liberatory ends.[7]

---

7. Another notable example is http://indiepornrevolution.com/indie-porn/. The site describes itself as "Subversive Smut Made by Ladies, Artists, and Queers" and is owned,

Given these points, antipornography feminism may be particularly detrimental to sexual liberation of marginalized groups: restricting pornography would restrict the free sexual expression of already-repressed identities. This would further perpetuate their oppression and marginalization by rendering sexually explicit depictions of those who do not fit the narrow confines of heteronormative sex and beauty standards morally (and perhaps legally) reprehensible. That said, pornography's emancipatory effects are hard to assess with philosophical tools. Some personal stories attest to the liberating potential of pornography for women (e.g., McElroy 1995), but other claims made by pro-pornography advocates are surely exaggerated. Just think of McElroy's claim that pornography is essential for good health—a satisfying sex life may be essential for good health, but it is surely possible to have one without pornography consumption. Furthermore, there is a real worry that different sides are talking about different things. McElroy, for instance, defines pornography in a "value-neutral manner" as being *the explicit artistic depiction of men and/or women as sexual beings*" (1995, 51). And by "artistic depiction" McElroy has in mind that "pornography is the genre of art or literature which focuses on the sexual nature of human beings" (1995, 51). How this definition is value neutral eludes me: McElroy seems to think that any definition, which is not against pornography, is value neutral. This is clearly false, and taking pornography to be by definition an artistic genre is highly value laden. After all, moral values are not the only sorts of values that can figure in our theorizing, and even if some definition of x is free from obvious moral evaluation, this does not render the definition *eo ipso* value neutral. Moreover, antipornography feminism would not object to materials that fall under this definition. They simply would not attach

---

operated, curated, directed, and edited by Courtney Trouble—another renowned performer and porn professional, who describes herself as a "fat femme queer feminist pornographer."

the label 'pornography' to it and would probably more readily call such materials 'erotica' or 'pornographic art'. Interlocutors easily talk past one another, which frustrates efforts to engage in PorNo/PorYes debates.

Another concern pertains to the risk that emancipatory depictions quickly can become fetishizing. Much of nonfeminist mainstream pornography is said to involve a "male gaze," which denotes

> depiction of the world, and in particular of women, in terms of male or masculine interests, emotions, attitudes, or values. More specifically, "the male gaze" usually refers to the sexually objectifying attitude that a representation takes toward its feminine subject matter, presenting her as a primarily passive object for heterosexual-male erotic gratification. (Eaton 2008, 878)

The currently prevalent "pornographic gaze" is of course not only male: it tends to be heterosexist and heteronormative, racist, ableist, and fattist. One might think that refocusing this gaze would facilitate the emancipation of marginalized identities; but it might worryingly end up focusing our attention to some supposedly deviant aspects in a manner that becomes problematic. For instance, sexualizing disability may problematically fetishize atypically bodied individuals and render them more vulnerable to abuse. And the representation of trans* people in pornography may further fuel and reproduce transphobia (Bettcher 2017). According to Talia Mae Bettcher, transphobia is not necessarily the fear of trans* people, but "any negative attitudes (hatred, loathing, rage, or moral indignation) harbored towards transpeople on the basis of our enactments of gender" (2007, 46). Bettcher (2013) understands trans* discrimination and oppression to be about trans* people opposing mainstream meanings of gender and gendered practices, which results in a conflict between dominant cultural meanings and subcultural trans-meanings. This conflict hinges on what Bettcher takes gender presentation to communicate. In short, "public gender presentation can be seen to euphemistically communicate or symbolically represent genital status" (Bettcher 2013, 58). In her view, we all regularly communicate something about our private genital status in public, which makes asking near-strangers intimate questions about their genitalia a boundary violation, a form of abuse, and harassment. Trans* people, however, opt out of this system: they do not take gender presentation to communicate intimate information about genital status. That is, they reject such dominant cultural practices and ways of generating meanings. As a result, Bettcher holds, trans* people are subject to "reality enforcement": "a mechanism by which acquiescence to the mandate to communicate genital status is enforced" (2013, 58). This sort of enforcement involves invalidation of self-identity claims made by trans* people (like, "you are *really* just a man" directed at trans* women). Reality enforcement further involves thinking about trans* identities as mere appearances (trans* people being told that they are engaging in some form of "gender-deception") (2013, 59). Finally, reality enforcement involves a kind of sexual abuse via attempts to verify trans* people's genital status (such as being asked, "Have you had *the* surgery?"). This sort of questioning "involves the effort to reinforce the cultural mandate to symbolically declare genital status that trans people have effectively opted out of" (2013, 59), which is abusive in being a privacy and intimacy violation. More recently, Bettcher has briefly suggested that depictions of trans* women in pornography may end up eroticizing reality enforcement, for instance when a trans* woman's penis is revealed as a "hidden surprise" (2017, 176). If pornographic materials fetishize and eroticize practices of reality enforcement, they cannot have the desired liberatory force for trans* people.

Feminists of color have also forcefully critiqued oppressive and stereotyping representations of race in mainstream pornography (e.g., Collins 1993, 2000). Jennifer Nash—a professor of African-American studies and gender and sexuality studies—takes there to be common ground in antipornography feminism and black feminism on the following points. First, black women's bodies are "overexposed" insofar as "racialized pornography secures black women's status only as objects to be gazed upon in the ostensibly white spectator's unrelenting search for proof of racialized mythologies" (Nash 2008, 58). Second, interracial voyeurism is pathologized by both, which suggests that "the ostensibly white male viewer's gaze at the black female body is motivated by 'racial fetishism', and thus constitutes a reductive, objectifying form of looking" (2008, 58). Finally, scholars from both traditions maintain that sexualized representations are central to perpetuating white supremacy and racial inequality. With this in mind, the political goal is to "dismantle dominant sexualized representations of black bodies and to encourage black women to launch a 'visual defense' rooted in self-representation" (2008, 58).

In more recent years, strong condemnations of racialized pornography have been challenged: women of color are said to exert agency in pornography in that they contest and manipulate ways in which their racial identities are used for pornographic effects. Performers of color exhibit agency in choosing roles that are on offer, and they engage in acts of resistance in their ways of performing (for instance) hypersexualized racial stereotypes. Robin Zheng's (2017) recent work explores the danger of emancipatory depictions turning fetishizing by looking at racialization in pornography. Drawing on Nash's (2014) work and looking at personal narratives and self-reporting of performers of color, Zheng contends, "we cannot in a principled way regulate or militate against pornography merely on the basis of its racial/ist representations" (2017, 178). However, Zheng is not an apologist for problematic racialized representations in pornography, but carefully discusses the potential dangers that such representations encompass. First, it may be that women of color's resistance won't much improve worrisome representations. Second, although women of color can exercise agency as performers, this is likely to be severely constrained by industry conditions. Black female performers face

> distinct and multiple manifestations of racial discrimination in the industry, from blatant racist remarks and stereotyped and limited roles, to struggling with colorism and the reign of white feminine beauty ideals . . . [They] earn half to three-quarters of what their white counterparts earn. (Cruz 2014, 238)

Third, differences in social positions make a difference to how much and how far one can exercise agency. That is, even if some relatively privileged performers of color can turn down roles they view as perpetuating problematic racialized stereotypes, other performers may not be able to so (for instance) due to economic pressures (Zheng 2017, 180–182).

Producers of color have advanced another line of argument defending racialized representations in pornography, which pertains to the formation of desire and sexuality. Pornography can function as a way to reclaim women of color's sexuality without them having to comply with conservative expectations about respectability. This involves (as Zheng nicely puts it) making the "undesirable desirable." The idea is that pornographic racial representations have a political role to play "in destabilizing narrow, stigmatizing, and otherwise oppressive standards of beauty and attractiveness" (Zheng 2017, 187). Pornography depicting members of sexually marginalized groups as erotically desirable destigmatizes and normalizes their sexuality in ways conducive to social equality (Zheng 2017, 188). This is what the new wave of producers of color like Shine Louise Houston and Nenna Joiner aim to do: they endeavor to transform prevalent depictions and presentations of "black womanhood" in pornography (discussed in Cruz 2014; see also Miller-Young 2013). These producers' work is political and in "challenging normative fictions of black female sexual subjectivity, this work represents a transgressive queering of black female sexuality, and its visual renderings in pornography" (Cruz 2014, 227). Though steadfast and widespread racialized representations persist, where "a ghettoized black female sexuality is often violently objectified by a white and/or black hetero-patriarchal male gaze" (Cruz 2014, 234), producers like Houston aim to offer more pluralistic representations of black female sexuality.[8] In a similar vein, Sinnamon Love (a performer and director of color) writes:

I find that so many black women are afraid of their sexuality . . . the patriarchal image of the hypersexual black female leaves more and more black women on the outside looking in on the sex-positive movement. I want to be a voice for a sex-positive black feminism that is eager to transform pornography into a space where we can have our images and fantasies reflected, too. (2013, 104)

Nevertheless, Zheng counsels against too hasty positive conclusions about racialized representations in pornography. Such representations can result in *fetishization* or *tokenization*. On the one hand, performers of color are "prone to being portrayed in terms of their racial difference," where this difference ends up being a mere deviation from norms and standards of whiteness (Zheng 2017, 189–190). This sort of fetishization of racial difference problematically can promote hypersexualized objectification of women of color.[9] On the

8. In her own words, Houston produces "hardcore indie feminist dyke porn" (quoted in Cruz 2014, 231). Her "Crash Pad Series" https://crashpadseries.com/ is one of the most celebrated, popular, and critically acclaimed queer pornography series currently around.

9. Commenting on BBW pornography, Flores notes likewise: "Some BBW porn is rooted in a celebration of our sexiness from adoration to explicitly fetishizing our size. But too much of it crosses into not so thinly veiled degradation and shame" (2013, 280).

other hand, given that whiteness is valorized and standards of sexual attractiveness employ a "systemic color hierarchy" (where light-skinned performers are preferred over dark-skinned performers, and performers of color are paid worse than white performers), racialized representations may end up tokenizing racial difference: race has "value only insofar as it adds a bit—but not too much—of variety and exoticism to the normative white female body" (Zheng 2017, 191). Racialized representations in pornography can help shape sexuality in more just ways, but as long as social reality is deeply structured by white supremacy, patriarchy, economic exploitation, and ableism (among other oppressive forces), these representations may end up further entrenching oppressive stereotypes (Zheng 2017, 194). And so, Zheng concludes:

> [W]hen it comes to race and pornography, the larger dilemma is that *there is no way to win* . . . My own conclusion is that . . . we cannot in a principled way argue against pornography per se on the grounds of its racism, and that we would do better to focus our criticism on the specific uses of pornographic tokens in specific works. (2017, 192)

Finally, consider the emancipatory potential of gay pornography briefly noted above. Although gay pornography has been hailed as a valuable emancipatory tool in legitimating gay identities, some disagree. John Stoltenberg (1992, 1993, 1995) has repeatedly argued that both heterosexual and gay pornography harm gay men. On this view, sexism and homophobia are *both* integral parts of sexualized male supremacy, which eroticizes male dominance and female submission. All kinds of pornography contribute to maintaining this conception of sex and, in so doing, help maintain and enforce both harmful sexist treatment of women and harmful homophobic treatment of gay men. For one thing, much of gay pornography (according to Stoltenberg) is said to contain derogatory references to women (1993, 71). (Anecdotally, consumers of male gay pornography have refuted this claim. I also could not find empirical research to back up Stoltenberg's view.) And while gay pornography is said to subvert "the patriarchal order by challenging masculinist values, providing a protected space for nonconformist non-reproductive and non-familial sexuality, encouraging many sex-positive values and declaring the dignity of gay people," it exists in a fantasy universe of a gay ghetto: it is produced by, it depicts, and is consumed exclusively by male gays (Waugh 1995, 157).[10] As with all pornography, intersectionality of identities makes a difference. Asian male sexuality (at least in the United States) is deeply racially stereotyped as "asexual" (Dines 2011, 131). Asian male performers are seldom found in heterosexual mainstream pornography and they are much more frequently present in gay pornography than in other genres. This nonetheless constructs another racialized stereotype about Asian males: according to Dines, "the hyperfeminization of Asian women in pop culture and porn leaks down to Asian men, whereby the group as a whole becomes feminized as the sexual object of white masculinity" (2011, 131). In so doing, gay pornography with Asian male performers ends up (re)producing racist stereotypes about effeminate Asian men and "celebrating racist stereotypes of Asian women as hypersexualized" (Dines 2011, 133–134). Whether gay pornography is emancipatory or not, this discussion demonstrates once more a key complication in the debates under examination: we cannot treat pornography as a simple, monolithic entity that we should either censor or celebrate,

---

10. That male gay pornography is exclusive consumed by male gays is no longer the case. In fact, heterosexual cis-women are perhaps surprisingly an avid consumer group of male gay pornography. This may not undermine the point that gay male pornography still exists separated and cut off from a heterosexual society: some have suggested that there exists a peculiar "female gaze" on male gay pornography (Neville 2015), which may still encompass many of the more usual heterosexist ways of viewing such materials.

that either harms or liberates. Whatever stance we take, it will have to be highly contextualized and nuanced.

7.5. THE EDUCATIONAL POTENTIAL OF FEMINIST PORNOGRAPHY

Feminist pornographers and the above-mentioned (so-called) new porn professionals typically hold that pornography can play a valuable educational role. They often agree with antipornography activism that mainstream, industrial pornography offers unhelpful and distorting sex education; still, these producers hold that pornography can be used to correct the situation. Very little has been philosophically said about this possibility. Anne Eaton offers one of the few philosophical elucidations. She discusses the formation of erotic taste, which "should be construed broadly to include a person's sexual taste—for instance, her positive and negative preferences for particular types of sex acts, or orientation toward certain kinds of sex partners" (2017, 245). Eaton holds (and I think rightly so) that "our" collective erotic taste is governed by sexist, cis-gendered, heteronormative, racist, fattist, and ableist norms. Eroticization of masculinity and femininity is a major part of such dominant mode of erotic taste, according to Eaton; and since this is detrimental to social justice, we should seek to alter our erotic tastes (2017, 246). This need not take the form of behavioral conditioning though. Instead, Eaton proposes Aristotelian habituation as a suitable vehicle. On this view, "the disposition to feel properly about some object in the world is inculcated in a subject by repeatedly getting the subject to have that feeling with the right intensity toward the object" (Eaton 2017, 250). This is akin to what advertising is based on: vivid and compelling representations mold our tastes and alter our conceptions of what is desirable, attractive, and praiseworthy. Hence, in order to change the organization of our currently problematic erotic tastes "we must also organize our sentimental lives, and in particular our erotic tastes, around gender equality" (Eaton 2017, 252). Promoting feminist pornography, Eaton holds, is one way in which we can redirect our sentimental, erotic tastes in more gender just ways. This is undergirded by the idea that taste is always somehow conditioned by social and historical circumstances and background conditions. We should thus make sure that our tastes are conditioned in a socially just manner.

I have much sympathy with Eaton's idea. In order to flesh out the story further, recall Ann Cahill's idea of derivatization (see section 5.5). As noted, the "pornographic gaze" is heteronormative, sexist, racist, ableist, and fattist. Eroticizing marginalized identities could subvert this gaze and doing so looks prima facie like a promising strategy to expand our erotic tastes. But (as discussed above) this might ultimately end up reproducing and reinforcing problematic stereotypes. Derivatization may help avoid this. For Cahill, "to derivatize" means "to portray, render, understand, or approach a being solely or primarily as the reflection, projection, or expression of another being's identity, desires, fears" (2011, 32). This can clearly result in problematic portrayals when (for instance) race is fetishized in pornography and racialized conceptions of sexuality come to reflect desires of white, male spectators (such as desiring hypersexualized women of color). In this sense, derivatization is problematic: it constructs black female sexuality in a way that is reducible to the desires of white, cis-men. But in a sense, derivatization need not have this result. As noted above, for Loree Erickson—a performer who uses a wheelchair—partaking in pornography allowed her to demonstrate how "queercrips" can be sexy and "to tell others how I wanted to be seen" (2013, 324). Representations that mirror how we want to be seen can feed into how others come to desire us; and so, representations can become projections of others' desires *without* constructing the one represented as reducible to these desires. In a sense, the projected representation of others' desires is precisely how one wishes to be desired. In connection to this, Zheng's idea that pornography can make the "undesirable desirable" looks fitting and valuable: by retraining our erotic tastes, it may be possible to undercut pernicious derivatization and to make sure that projected representations do not construct the one represented counter to their own wishes and desires. This is admittedly highly tentative and speculative. There is little to no empirical work that shows the impact of alternative, radically egalitarian, feminist pornography on our emotional and cognitive lives. Nevertheless, given how successful advertising is in shaping desire, it is not hugely implausible to hold that by making egalitarian, feminist pornography attractive, it would be possible to shape in beneficial ways what is commonly taken to be desirable.

7.6. SUMMING UP

In this chapter, I have explored whether pornography can be liberatory and what a vision of feminist pornography could look like. In so doing, I further endeavored to demonstrate how complex and nuanced the debate between PorNo and PorYes positions is. Holding that genuinely feminist pornography is possible does not entail accepting that anything goes, that every self-proclaimed feminist pornographic work is therefore feminist, or that works satisfying some basic feminist commitments are beyond critique (they might, for instance, fall short in their representations of race). I also aimed to show that PorNo and PorYes positions actually share many political commitments. These two camps seemingly differ in only two substantive ways: they disagree about pornography's role in correcting the currently pernicious force of mainstream, industrial pornography, and they disagree about the nature and value of sexual activities. Much more philosophical work should be done on the issues that this chapter raises. Be that as it may, in discussing and analyzing the aesthetics (chapter 6) and emancipatory potential of pornography (this chapter), we can see that questions about pornography's status as speech are much less pressing than the earlier chapters suggested. In other words, there are ways to philosophically examine pornography that do not hinge on accepting or rejecting the speech act approach. Subsequently, the next chapter closes the book by reconsidering what pornography is (and should be) with distinctly social ontological accounts in mind—accounts that can be offered as alternatives to the prevalent speech act theoretic accounts, with which this book began.

Chapter 8

What Is Pornography Revisited

8.1. INTRODUCTION

Throughout this book, I have highlighted the (perhaps surprisingly) complicated nature of pornography. Many debates considered pertain to two general issues: What *is* pornography? What does pornography *do* (if anything)? A large bulk of the responses discussed so far advanced from speech act theoretical considerations. This final chapter takes up these pressing and, as of yet, unsettled questions but from a social ontological perspective. The chapter aims to sketch out promising alternative ways to discuss pornography—ways that do not hinge on speech act theory. That said, even this final chapter will leave a number of issues open, and it is not possible here to settle pornography debates in philosophy once and for all. Instead, I hope to motivate alternative ways to think about pornography and to provide an impetus for a continued philosophical examination of the topic. In what follows, I will first consider what pornography apparently does with social ontological tools. Then I will consider some alternative ways to understand what pornography is that diverge from speech act theoretical elucidations. The chapter (and the book) concludes with some final methodological remarks.

8.2. SOCIAL ONTOLOGICAL ANALYSIS OF WHAT PORNOGRAPHY *DOES*

Katharine Jenkins (2017) offers social ontological explications of two central claims that MacKinnon makes: first, pornography subordinates women instead of merely influencing its viewers to treat women in subordinating ways (the subordination claim); second, pornography constructs women's "natures" (the constructionist claim). Jenkins considers these claims specifically relative to what she terms 'misogynistic pornography' or 'm-pornography' for short, which depicts women's abuse or degradation in ways that endorse, condone, or encourage them. In chapter 2, I discussed challenges to making sense of the subordination claim. Relative to the constructionist claim, the challenge is to make good the idea that construction is in some sense successful, but that pornography nevertheless constructs gender in a defective or false manner (see section 3.3). In short, how does women's constructed nature as sex objects square with the idea that pornography tells lies about women in claiming that they are for men's sexual use and abuse? After all, MacKinnon holds:

> If a woman is defined hierarchically so that the male idea of a woman defines womanhood, and if men have power, this idea becomes reality. It is therefore real. It is not just an illusion or a fantasy or a mistake. It becomes *embodied* because it is enforced. (1987, 119)[1]

Nonetheless, if pornography constructs women as sex objects, it no longer tells *lies* about women when women are depicted as sex

---

1. Even more strongly, MacKinnon claims: "Pornography is not imaginary in some relation to a reality elsewhere constructed. It is not a distortion, reflection, projection, expression, fantasy, representation, or symbol either. It is sexual reality" (1987, 172–173).

objects (McGowan 2005; see also Mikkola 2010). In a sense, a socially constructed state of affairs cannot be false because the construction brings that state into being.

In order to expound the subordination and constructionist claims in a novel manner, Jenkins draws on John Searle's (1995) social ontology. For Searle, certain entities are constructed as institutional insofar as they are able to do something—perform some function—only within the context of human institutions. Money is of this kind: some piece of paper functions as a medium of exchange, but this is not because the piece of paper is somehow special given its paper-relevant qualities. Rather, it can buy goods and services because we (human social agents) have imposed something on the piece of paper: we collectively recognize and accept that some pieces of paper have a money function. If there were no relevant human institutions to sustain such collective acceptance, there would be no money. The kind of function that money has (and that constructs institutional entities in general) is called a status function: some pieces of paper fulfill their function as media of exchange in virtue of being recognized and accepted to have the status of being money. In order to capture this, Searle typically employs the following formula: x counts as y in context C (some pieces of paper count as 10 euro notes in the Eurozone).

With such "counts as" formulation in mind, Jenkins suggests a reading of MacKinnon: "*m-pornography determines the status function that defines women as institutional entities*" where "this status function is something like <'females' count as objects for male sexual use [around here]>" (2017, 99).[2] Jenkins then proposes a way to

---

2. Actually, Jenkins notes later on (and rightly so) that in the context of women's oppression the mode of use is not going to be purely sexual (2017, 102–103). However, for my purposes here nothing hinges on whether the use is just sexual or not.

WHAT IS PORNOGRAPHY REVISITED

understand the subordination and constructionist claims with the following argument:

1. Institutional entities are constructed through the collective intentional recognition of status functions.
2. Gendered individuals (e.g., women and men) are institutional entities.
3. The representation of women in m-pornography generates collective intentional recognition of the status function that defines women as institutional entities thus: <"females" count as objects for male use around here>.
4. (From 1–3) M-pornography constructs women as objects for male sexual use. (2017, 99–100)

The above yields, as Jenkins puts it, the core of the argument for the subordination and constructionist claims. The following additional premises are needed to complete the argument for the subordination claim:

5. When a person is constructed as an object for the use of others they are thereby subordinated.
6. (From 4, 5) Subordination claim: M-pornography subordinates women. (2017, 100)

Jenkins takes 6 to explicate how it is that pornography *is* the subordination of women, rather than pornography merely encouraging its viewers to subordinate women: pornography "subordinates women by bringing into being an institutional reality in which they count as objects for male sexual use" (2017, 100). Then again, 4 establishes one element of the constructionist claim (that via the collective intentional imposition of a status function, m-pornography constructs women's natures). Nevertheless, we need something more to make good the idea that this construction is somehow false or defective despite being successful. This (Jenkins holds) can be established in two ways. Drawing on MacKinnon, she notes:

> Faced with an institutional reality that reduces women to objects for the sexual use of men, we simply insist on a *different* institutional reality, one in which women are accorded full personhood . . . On this interpretation of the constructionist claim, describing the dominant misogynistic construction of women as "wrong" or even "false" is simply an expression of our collective refusal to accept it, our insistence on crafting a different social reality. (2017, 101)

Alternatively, we can hold that the status function imposed on women is presented as if it were a brute, natural fact when it is an institutional fact. Women are falsely taken to be naturally subservient to men, rather than this being recognized as a socially instituted and imposed feature of gendered realities. And so: "Correctly recognizing the institutional reality of women's situation for what it is—a social construction maintained through male power—alerts one to this wrongness" (Jenkins 2017, 101).

Jenkins offers interesting and novel ways to make sense of MacKinnon's subordination and constructionist claims with social ontological tools. Given many debates discussed earlier in this book, shifting the debate from speech act theory to social ontology looks prima facie useful. How compelling though is Jenkins's alternative story? Although not in response to Jenkins, Saul (2006a) articulates a possible worry. She objects to Melinda Vadas's (2005) view that to use pornography as a woman is to use it in the role, function, or capacity of a woman, where this hinges on women being for men's sexual gratification (I will discuss Vadas's view in more detail shortly). For Saul, Vadas's analysis is simply mistaken because women do *not* have this function. For the claim "men use pornography to fulfill a function of women" to be true, "some presupposition would need to be met—either that women actually do have a function that gets fulfilled by pornography—for Vadas, providing sexual satisfaction to men—or that men take women to have such a function" (Saul 2006a, 57). But Saul takes this view to be both false and instrumentalizing: "False because women simply do not have the function of producing sexual gratification in men. Instrumentalizing because such a claim attributes this function to all women, regardless of their own needs, desires, or wills" (2006a, 57). Saul's objection, then, seemingly undermines Jenkins's social ontological elucidation of what pornography does and what women are for.

There are, however, different ways to understand the claim "men use pornography to fulfill a function of women," where some formulations are not obviously false, *contra* Saul. This claim can be about how something functions context specifically or about what the function of something is all things considered. This latter sense is better captured in terms of a *purpose* (or an end). To illustrate, some years ago it became popular in artisan coffee-loving circles to use electric popcorn makers to roast coffee beans at home. Now, the purpose of popcorn makers is not to roast coffee beans. Nonetheless, it is perfectly fine to say that they were used to roast coffee beans—electric popcorn makers functioned as coffee bean roasters, even though their purpose is to pop corn. With this in mind, it is not so obvious that women are *not* for men's sexual gratification. They are not so all things considered: it is not the purpose of women as a gendered kind to sexually gratify men. But in certain contexts, this may well be how some women function. This is a deeply troubling and depressing moral state of affairs for sure, but it does not falsify Jenkins's (or Vadas's) functional analysis of gender.

Be that as it may, Jenkins's analysis fails to convince me on different grounds. Jenkins provides perfectly comprehensible reconstructions of MacKinnon's subordination and constructionist claims. But her reliance on Searle's social ontology renders the claims implausible. Recall premises 1 and 2:

1. Institutional entities are constructed through the collective intentional recognition of status functions.
2. Gendered individuals (e.g., women and men) are institutional entities.

The former is a straightforward appropriation of Searle's social ontology. The latter premise draws on MacKinnon's view of gender. Jenkins puts MacKinnon's point as follows: "our existence *as* men and women is not determined by the physical configuration of our bodies, but depends on human activity and attitudes" (2017, 97). As a result, Jenkins concludes that women and men are institutional entities in Searle's sense. Hence, when we apply Searle's social ontology to MacKinnon's conception of gender, it follows that "the existence of women depends on there being collective intentional recognition of some status function that is imposed on some more basic entity" (Jenkins 2017, 97). Now, Searle's notion of collective intentionality plays a crucial role in the story. Collective intentionality is about sharing some intentional state(s). There are many ways to understand this in the literature (for an outline, see Schweikard and Schmid 2013), but for Searle collective intentionality boils down to the following: when a collective acts together, the individual actors share an irreducible we-intention. For instance, when an orchestra plays a symphony together, the musicians do not individually entertain an I-intention to play the symphony that is combined with some further beliefs about the other musicians also entertaining requisite I-intentions. Rather, members of the orchestra share an irreducible we-intention *to play the symphony together.*

Now, insofar as Jenkins's reconstruction is wedded to Searle's account of collective intentionality, is her reconstruction of MacKinnon compelling? I think not. Rewrite Jenkins's premises 1–3 as follows for simplicity:

1–3.* Women *qua* institutional entities are constructed through the collective intentional recognition of the status function <"females" count as objects for male use around here>.

On this view, Searlean collective intentionality figures in gender construction—but how plausible is this view? In some sense, it looks prima facie compelling: in order for such pervasive social structures like the gender system to exist and persist, a number of social agents must seemingly act in concert somehow to reproduce the system. That is, prevalent gendered norms and practices cannot plausibly be reproduced merely accidentally or randomly. But do social agents intentionally and in agreement with another maintain gendered social norms and practices? Is it plausible to think that there is an irreducible we-intention *to define women as institutional entities via the imposition of the status function <"females" count as objects for male use around here>*? I think not. Let me be clear: my qualms are not with how Jenkins formulates the status function. My point is that the construction of women's gendered and sexual "natures" do not seemingly hinge on Searlean we-intentions. Whatever the content of those intentions, for the Searlean story to hold, there would have to be something like a sexist conspiracy that constructs women's natures in some particular manner. After all, there would have to be a *shared collective agreement* to impose particular status functions on groups of people in order to construct them as gendered individuals in some specific way. But this is not compelling because there is no such agreement or a shared irreducible we-intention that defines women as being for men's (sexual or whatever) use. If the subordination and constructionist claims are wedded to the Searlean idea of collective intentionality, I see little reason to accept Jenkins's social ontological reconstruction.[3]

8.3. ARTIFACTUAL ANALYSIS OF WHAT PORNOGRAPHY *IS*

Jenkins provides a way to reconceive what pornography does with social ontological tools. I have recently proposed a social ontological understanding of what pornography *is* (Mikkola 2017b). In short, I offer an elucidation of what makes something a pornographic artifact in a way that that does not hinge on the speech act approach. The term 'pornography' does not pick out an abstract entity but an array of concrete things—something that a proper philosophical understanding of pornography in my view should bear closely in mind. Paradigm examples of pornographic artifacts include films made in San Fernando Valley with sexually explicit content usually sold in specific outlets and accessible via Internet portals like youporn.com; magazines like *Hustler*; pictures we can find in the Internet with ease; and books with sexual scenes not (usually) sold in the "literature"

---

3. One might further take issue with how Jenkins aims to establish that pornography somehow successfully constructs women's nature but in a defective manner. For instance, to say that the construction of women is false just is to express "our" collective refusal of the construction and "our" insistence that we need a different social reality (her first proposed strategy to establish the claim) is surely too weak. I do not see how this in any meaningful sense establishes the *falsity* of the constructed states of affairs. Rather, it turns the dispute into a disagreement akin to (say) liking or not liking pizza: to say that Joe's claim "pizza is delicious" is false just amounts to saying that pizza is not delicious to me. McGowan (2005) explores the idea of false construction from a speech act theoretic perspective. She holds that, strictly speaking, there cannot be false construction—only construction that is somehow defective. And relative to pornography, McGowan concludes that pornography "purports to be tracking an antecedent fact while it also enacts what counts as that very fact" (2005, 45)—this is what pornography's defective construction boils down to.

sections of bookshops. Taking as my starting point such paradigm examples, my view aims to be descriptive though not merely so. As noted in chapter 1, this book aims to elucidate what pornography is and *should be* in a manner that does justice to the pornography industry. Hence, my artifactual analysis aims meaningfully to revise how we should understand what pornography is, but in an empirically informed manner. In this sense, the goal is to strike a balance between normative and descriptive analyses.

This is in contrast to Andrew Kania's (2012) suggestion that we should adopt an ameliorative methodological stance to the definitional question "What is pornography?". Kania draws on Sally Haslanger's work that distinguishes three methodological approaches. First, a conceptual approach would aim to elucidate our everyday manifest concept of *pornography*. Such a project would aim to specify the (necessary and sufficient) conditions under which native speakers commonly think something falls under the concept. Second, a descriptive approach focuses on our terms' extensions and would investigate which empirical kind (if any) everyday uses of the term 'pornography' tracks. Haslanger calls concepts analyzed in this manner everyday operative concepts. Finally, an ameliorative approach aims to "elucidate 'our' legitimate purposes and what concept of *F*-ness (if any) would serve them best" (Haslanger 2012, 376). This method reveals our target concept: the concept we ought to appropriate relative to some legitimate interests. An ameliorative analysis of *pornography* would thus ask: what is pornography, and what do we want it to be relative to feminist emancipatory ends? Given how divergent everyday intuitions about pornography are, Kania holds that when defining *pornography* we should adopt an ameliorative approach. I wish to resist a purely ameliorative analysis, however, because it is likely to hinder conceptual clarity even further. As we have seen in the chapters so far, different people understand *pornography* differently, where this hinges (among other things) on divergent political commitments. My contention is that, rather than further proliferate *pornography* conceptions relative to various political goals (e.g., relative to whether one is antipornography, antiexploitative pornography, or pro-pornography), we should aim to fix some conceptual common ground with an approach that is less ameliorative and more descriptive. In other words, I think that it is a mistake to analyze pornography in either full-blown ameliorative or descriptive ways. Rather, I aim to strike a balance between the two approaches. Subsequently, I have put forward an account of what makes something a pornographic artifact and developed a maker's intentions model of pornography (Mikkola 2017b).[4] My proposal aims to first fix the class of pornographic artifacts, after which we can debate whether some instances are subordinating, liberating, speech in a legal sense or not.

Let me spell out my understanding in more detail. The maker's intentions model draws on Amie Thomasson's (2003) account of what individuates noninstitutional ordinary objects—that is, what makes some ordinary object *that* object. To illustrate, consider what on this view makes an entity a chair. Roughly put, this depends on maker's intentions. The maker must intend that some object x is a chair and they have this intention only if

(a) they have a substantive concept of chairs (they have "some contentful concept that involves (perhaps vague) success criteria" [Thomasson 2003, 598] for creating a chair) and this concept largely matches that held by some prior chair-makers, and

---

4. I originally started thinking about pornography in this way in the hope of bridging the gap between pornography debates in feminist philosophy and philosophy of art, as discussed in chapter 6 (Mikkola 2013).

(b) the maker intends to realize that substantive concept by imposing chair-relevant features on the object (e.g., ensuring that the object has a surface suitable for sitting).

For x to count as a chair, this intention must be largely successful: the maker's creative activities sufficiently succeed in realizing the intention (e.g., the object can be used as a chair, it has some usual chair-like features, is recognized as a chair). Chair-makers may have some other intentions too, like to make money or create design pieces. But these are additional to fixing the artifactual kind: the conditions Thomasson sets out are necessary for something to be a chair—not for it to be an expensive or an aesthetically pleasing chair.

Following Thomasson, I provide the following elucidation of pornography:

Some x (film, book, picture) is of the kind "pornographic artifact" only if it is the product of a largely successful intention to create pornography, where the maker of the artifact intends that the artifact is an instance of pornography only if

(a) they have a substantive concept of the nature of pornography that largely matches the substantive concept held by some group of other prior pornographers, and

(b) the maker intends to realize that concept by imposing pornography-relevant features on the object.

First, what is it to have a substantive concept of the nature of pornography? On this view, something is an artifact only if it is intentionally produced with some identity-conditions fixing description of the object in mind (Thomasson 2003, 592). Hence, pornographic artifacts are intentionally (and not unwittingly or accidentally) produced by human agents under some description that provides criteria for distinguishing such artifacts from others. We may be unable to exhaustively articulate the criteria, but nevertheless people can fairly easily distinguish pornographic artifacts from tables and chairs even in the absence of a clearly articulated concept of *pornography*. In other words, my view presupposes that makers possess some contentful *pornography* conception that is operative in their creative activities. I take everyday paradigm exemplars to support this view, and they tell us something about such a conception. Typically, pornographic artifacts are sexually explicit, contain nudity and scenes of sexual nature; they have the potential to sexually arouse their viewers; and they are often used as "masturbation materials." These are not necessary and sufficient conditions, but rather what is descriptively involved in the concept of *pornography*. Nonetheless, they give us some contentful identity conditions and vague success criteria, which suffices to elucidate a substantive enough of a concept of *pornography*. (For instance, the concept of *red* is nonsubstantive in that it does not individuate objects that are red as being those objects. A red postbox is not individuated as a postbox by virtue of falling under the concept *red*.)

Second, what are the pornography-relevant features that aim at realizing this concept? These are flexible and open to change. Again, paradigm everyday pornographic artifacts suggest that the relevant features include footage, images, and depictions of sexual acts and scenes of a sexual nature (broadly conceived). There need not be collective acceptance of these features across the board—something that the existence of different pornography genres attests to. Still, the features noted strike me as intuitively plausible and not particularly controversial. We can descriptively account for a typical conception of *pornography* and for common ways of realizing this by looking at paradigm pornographic artifacts.

It is more controversial and clearly vague to say that one has created a pornographic artifact only if one has created something that is a product of a *largely successful* intention that *x* is a pornographic artifact. When is an intention largely successful? There are no obvious criteria for fixing this, and there may well be borderline cases because success involves indeterminacy. But, consider cases where the intention is clearly successful or unsuccessful. Examples of the former include sexually explicit materials that Americans spend billions of dollars a year on (chapter 6). An example of the latter would be the following case: imagine that one intends to create a piece of pornography and one has a contentful conception of *pornography* that matches that held by some prior pornographers (e.g., that the artifact be sexually arousing and used as "masturbation material"). But imagine that one intends to realize that concept by imposing no intuitively pornography-relevant features on the object. Rather, imagine that one makes (say) a film of a fully clothed person baking a cake. Despite the intention to create a pornographic artifact, we would be hard pressed to call this 'pornography' precisely because the maker fails to impose any apparently pornography-relevant features on the object—and so, the object created would not count as a pornographic artifact. Or *given the current state of pornography*, it would not. It might in the future though, if footage of fully clothed cake-bakers becomes a way to impose pornography-relevant features on an object. This flags an important aspect of my view: typical pornography-relevant features and ways of realizing them are sensitive to time and place, which enables us to account for pornography's continuity as well as its changing nature.

This social ontological proposal of what pornography amounts to affords four benefits. First, it offers an account of pornographic artifacts that helps fix common ground: we fix the type of pornographic artifacts first, after which we can debate the social meanings of particular tokens (whether they are oppressive or liberatory, and whether they count as speech relevant for legislative purposes). The point of my proposal is precisely to circumvent a situation where the extension of 'pornography' depends on prior idiosyncratic views social agents hold due to which different people end up picking out different objects with the term. Still, one might wonder: why focus on makers' intentions? Ordinary artifactual kinds are typically delimited in one of three ways: by focusing on makers' *intentions*, on artifactual *functions*, or on how consumers and audiences *receive* an artifact. I will say more about audience reception shortly. But let me address a putative counterexample to my view and why we should not define pornographic artifacts in functional terms in order to alleviate initial worries with my focus on makers' intentions.

Consider the following example: a hapless couple engages in spontaneous sex in a car park, which gets recorded by the car park's CCTV system. We have a recording that many would probably judge to be pornographic, and yet there is no maker: the camera simply recorded the event without any intention to produce pornography. Does this not provide a clear counterexample to my view? I think not. There is a qualitative difference between pornographic artifacts and artifacts that contain pornographic aspects (whatever way we fix the latter). If we reject this distinction, we would have to say that the recording is rendered a piece of pornography simply by involving nudity or scenes of sexual nature. However, this would yield the wrong results. There are pornographic genres that do not contain nudity and sex acts in more conventional senses, while many putatively nonpornographic artifacts contain nudity. The so-called giantess point-of-view pornography is an example of the former: voluptuous female performers wearing sexually suggestive clothing squash small toy soldiers without necessarily being nude. This is filmed from a perspective that gives the viewer a point-of-view experience of being smothered or squashed by a giantess. If we focus on nudity, this fetish genre would not qualify as pornography. Conversely, many artifacts contain sexual scenes without thereby being pornography: just think (again) of anatomy books and safe sex guides. So, the CCTV footage should not count as pornography simply by virtue of containing some typical features found in pornographic artifacts—this would render the kind's boundaries too loose.

Imagine however that the car park's security guard finds the footage and posts it on a pornographic Internet portal with the intention to distribute it as pornography. On my view, this would transform the footage into pornography. That is, the maker need not be the direct manufacturer of some material. This is akin to ready-mades in art like Duchamp's *Fountain* and many Warhol pieces, where ordinary artifacts were used to create works of arts. So, even though the footage per se does not count as a pornographic artifact, when the security guard intentionally takes steps to distribute it as pornography, this transforms the footage. With this in mind, we can see why some uses of the term 'pornography' are deeply misguided, like the talk of 'torture porn' and 'death porn'. The former is a horror film subgenre characterized by the *Saw* and *Hostel* series of films (Jones 2013), while the latter involves pictures taken of deceased people. The so-called torture porn films are not sexually explicit, and violence is instead used in a titillating manner. Then again, death porn involves a kind of fascination with boundary and taboo breaking that is seemingly titillating as well. Since these materials were not produced with the intention of making something that is a piece of pornography, calling them 'porn' is misguided following my view. Again, bear in mind that even if something is pornographic, it does not therefore count as pornography. Consider a parallel with Gerhard Richter's photorealist paintings: due to their detailed nature, we can say that some of his paintings are photographic; but this does not render those paintings photographs. Classifying photographic paintings as photographs would be to commit a category mistake. The same is true when we classify something that is pornographic *eo ipso* as pornography.

Now, one might suspect that the above discussion goes against something that I noted in chapter 1: that it is a mistake to describe the phenomenon of revenge porn as porn. What is intuitively doing the work is that the images are sexually explicit and/or suggestive, and pretheoretically pornography is about sexual explicitness. But (in my view) this is not sufficient for something to count as pornography. What makes something a pornographic artifact is the maker's intention to produce pornography. However, the objection goes, when someone posts a sexually explicit image of a former partner online does this not transform the image into a pornographic artifact? The example of the CCTV footage and my earlier comments about revenge porn are seemingly in tension with one another. This tension, however, is merely apparent. Revenge porn is about humiliation and vengeance, where sexually explicit materials are used as the means to achieve these ends. Think back to the discussion in chapter 5 about sexual objectification. There I considered how sexual means can be used to achieve nonsexual ends: for instance, when someone has sex solely for the purpose of reproduction in order to comply with religious teachings. In this case, sex is a means to pursue religious goals. The same is true of revenge porn: sexually explicit imagery is used as a means to pursue nonsexual ends, in this case humiliating the person depicted. This may be a pornographic way to humiliate someone, but it should be distinguished from pornography "proper" as an artifactual kind.

One might nonetheless think that functional analyses of pornographic artifacts would be more fruitful than those that turn on makers' intentions. By contrast, I hold that focusing on functions yields the wrong results. First, take actual functions. Slightly broken chairs might no longer fulfill their function, but it seems wrongheaded to claim that due to this, they are no longer chairs. Similarly, a very bad pornographic film may utterly fail to elicit arousal and so has a deformed actual function. Nonetheless, it would be odd to conclude that this renders the object something other than a pornographic artifact, as we would have to if actual function fixes whether the object is a pornographic artifact or not. Second, consider intended functions: one might claim that even though the bad piece of pornography failed to satisfy its function, it is the intended function to elicit arousal that makes it a piece of pornography. But I am not convinced. Although I think that no pornographic artifacts are made without some function in mind, fixing *the* intended pornographic function is tricky. There is no pornographic function *simpliciter* due to which functional analyses of pornographic artifacts are unsatisfying. This is in line with what I argued in chapter 6 relative to pornographic intentions: we cannot identify such an intention that is somehow clearly distinct from other nonpornographic intentions. Therefore, I argued, we should not take pornography to be centrally or ultimately about sexual arousal. Focusing on some specific intended pornographic function to fix pornographic artifacts fails to appreciate its multifaceted nature and the fact that makers' intentions are much broader than philosophical discussions typically acknowledge. This (I submit) yields the second benefit of my approach: it provides a more nuanced picture of pornography by taking seriously its varied nature, rather than reducing pornography to some allegedly central feature or function. Pornography as a kind is undoubtedly partly about subordination and sexual arousal, but it is about more than that. The historical and contemporary examples that I discussed in earlier chapters suggest that there is no single intended function or purpose of pornography that all producers share.

The third benefit of my view is that it can deal with muddled (ordinary and philosophical) intuitions about some necessary and sufficient conditions that the concept of *pornography* supposedly encodes. Even if we are unable to articulate such conditions, we can fix what makes *x* a pornographic artifact by focusing on its maker's intentions: by looking at the intention to produce a pornographic artifact by imposing typical pornography features on the artifact in a way that largely matches some contentful *pornography* conception of prior makers. We can eschew muddled intuitions about *pornography*'s defining (necessary and sufficient) conditions but are not prevented from fixing the kind of pornographic artifacts.

One might object that this does not deal satisfyingly with ordinary intuitions after all. As Justice Stewart put it, we know pornography when we see it. But different people see different artifacts as pornography. So, perhaps my manner of fixing pornographic artifacts is unhelpful, since I, too, start from paradigm cases that are hostage to our pretheoretical views about pornography. However, there is an important clarification that avoids this worry. The "I know it when I see it" retort fixes the class of pornographic artifacts based on the audience reception—makers' intentions are neither here nor there. My view fixes the class on the basis of makers' intentions to produce pornographic artifacts. Nonetheless, what I am proposing is not insensitive to audience reception. Recall that some *x* is of the kind "pornographic artifact" only if it is the product of a largely successful intention to create pornography. The maker intends that the artifact is an instance of pornography only if (a) their contentful *pornography* conception largely matches that held by some prior makers, and (b) the maker intends to realize that conception by imposing pornography-relevant features on the object. The maker must first and foremost intend to produce a pornographic artifact. Their intention can however go astray; for example, they may fail to impose on the object any features *taken to be* pornography relevant by audiences. (Just think of the earlier "cake-bake pornography.") For something to be a pornographic artifact it does not suffice that one has a mere intention to create a piece of pornography—the intention must be successful. Thus, the maker must produce something that matches the concept of *pornography* held by some prior pornographers and impose some pornography-relevant features on the object in a successful manner. And one way to measure success is in terms of audience reception: the imposed pornography-relevant features are so recognized by viewers. And so, audiences are not irrelevant, although audience reception does not ultimately make some artifact a piece of pornography. Relying on audience reception, which trades on muddled intuitions, would leave fixing the class of pornographic artifacts too much hostage to subjective views. Still, even though ordinary intuitions are rejected as fixing the artifactual kind, I can accommodate these intuitions: they figure in our judgments about whether pornography-relevant features have been imposed on the object and so help adjudicate the successfulness of makers' intentions. The interplay between audience reception and makers' intentions is more refined than with some other extant positions on pornography.[5]

This brings me to the fourth benefit: understanding pornography on the basis of makers' intentions improves Langton's suggestion that pornography produces makers' knowledge (chapter 5). My broad idea is that what fixes the class of pornographic artifacts is the general intention to produce a piece of pornography. What fixes the particular genre of pornographic artifacts hinges on which concept of *pornography* (held by prior makers) producers' intend to match, how producers impose pornography-relevant features on the object, and how successful they are in doing so. For instance, feminist and "mainstream" pornographers

5. Following this, one might hold that Michael Rea's (2001) account of pornography is akin to mine. Rea attempts first to spell out what it is for some person to use or view *x* as pornography, which hinges on that person's desires and beliefs. Rea then takes this prior elucidation of using pornography to account for what makes *x* pornography: this amounts to a reasonable belief that *x* will be used or treated as pornography by most of the audiences for which it was produced (2001, 134). This may seem close to what I say, but I disagree. My account opposes the first move and rejects the idea that we can view or use whatever as pornography willy-nilly depending on our desires/beliefs. Moreover, Rea's second move isn't akin to mine. It is unclear whether the "reasonable belief" should be had by makers, nonpornography-consuming bystanders, pornography's consumers, or all of the above for *x* to count as pornography. If it were the first only (makers' beliefs), this would make Rea's view closer to mine. However, if Rea has in mind audience and bystander reception, his position departs substantially from mine.

are both in the business of producing pornographic artifacts. But given their particular and more fine-grained intentions, the resultant artifacts come to diverge considerably from one another. Thus, these artifacts do not generate uniform pornographic knowledge. Given the more fine-grained intentions producers have, in addition to the intention to produce pornographic artifacts, the resultant knowledge may not be maker's knowledge or it may be morally innocuous maker's knowledge. This is because (as I already discussed extensively in chapter 5) who the maker is makes a difference. Feminist pornographers intend to create pornography in a particular way. They have a substantive (contentful) conception of *pornography* in mind, which comes apart from prototypical mainstream conceptions but that largely matches the one held by other prior feminist pornographers. This conception includes (among other things): the aim to depict a less distorted picture of female sexuality, and the view that promoting—ethically and aesthetically—better pornography can play a valuable educational role by correcting false, mainstream depictions of sexuality. Furthermore, feminist pornographers intend to realize this substantive conception by imposing particular pornography-relevant features on the object (e.g., by avoiding money shots and lengthy "gynecological" footage of genitalia). Bearing in mind these makers' intentions relative to other makers alerts us to how pornography can create a wider range of pornographic knowledge, *contra* Langton. Just consider how differently feminist and nonfeminist pornographers view the nature of pornography, which groups of prior pornographers they have in mind, and how they intend to realize "their" conceptions of pornography (which pornography-relevant features they impose on pornographic artifacts). Given their divergent intentions, mainstream pornographic knowledge may well be and probably is harmful in Langton's sense, but feminist pornographic knowledge conceivably is not. Nonetheless, both types of producers are in the business of producing pornography insofar as they both aim to realize (in different ways) the intention to produce pornographic artifacts.

8.4. PERSONIFICATION OF PORNOGRAPHY

Above I proposed a way to understand pornography as an artifactual kind. There is another—rather puzzling—way to conceive of pornography's nature in a social ontological spirit proposed by some antipornography feminists: that men's use of pornography as a woman personifies pornography due to which pornographic artifacts end up being ontologically on a par with flesh-and-blood women. I will consider and argue against this view next.

For MacKinnon, pornography involves "sex between people and things, human beings and pieces of paper, real men and unreal women" (1993, 109). That pornography is used as a sexual partner is said to be "uncontroversial" (Langton 1995, 180). This claim has been developed most notably by Vadas, who defines pornography as "any object, whether in appearance male, female, child or transsexual . . . that has been manufactured to satisfy sexual desire through its sexual use or consumption as a woman" (2005, 187). "To use pornography as a woman" means to use it "in the role, function, or capacity of" a woman (Vadas 2005, 178). And this function (for radical feminists like Vadas and MacKinnon) is to satisfy men's sexual desires and needs. Saul (2006a) coins the term "personification" to capture the general idea of treating things as people. Putting all of this together yields: someone personifies pornography when they treat pornography as a woman—in the function of a woman—in using pornography to satisfy their sexual desires.

Following pornography's personification both MacKinnon and Vadas hold that when men view (say) pornographic magazines, they literally have sex with pieces of paper.[6] The consumption of pornography is said to be an appetitive act that moves "from sexual arousal to sexual satisfaction or orgasm"; in so doing, it is a real sex act (rather than an imaginary or simulated one) because "no other sort of act begins with sexual arousal and ends with orgasm and ejaculation" (Vadas 2005, 179). Vadas draws an analogy with sexual satisfaction and satisfaction of hunger to make her case. Viewing representations of food cannot satisfy hunger (representations of food are clearly not food). Representations of sexual objects should likewise not be able to satisfy sexual desire; however, pornography use suggests otherwise. And so: "If his [*sic*] body is in fact and in reality sexually satisfied through the consumption of the presented object, then that object must itself be a sex object and not a mere representation of a sex object" (Vadas 2005, 182).

Why should we think that personification is morally problematic from a feminist perspective (and not just philosophically puzzling)? It is allegedly linked to objectification: when men personify pornography they objectify women (MacKinnon 1993). We can understand this causally or constitutively, and gloss the causal connection between the personification of pornography and the objectification of women in terms of sexual socialization. Langton maintains that men who use violent and misogynistic pornography tend subsequently to treat women as sex objects. In fact, she thinks that this happens as a matter of human psychology (Langton 1995, 178). Roughly put: in personifying pornography, men learn to view women as objects to be used for sexual gratification. Consider the constitutive sense. In personifying pornographic artifacts, Vadas claims, the objects in

6. MacKinnon and Vadas are not alone in advancing this sort of view. Recall Schauer's view from chapter 4: pornography does not count legally as speech because it is really a "sexual surrogate" that merely takes pictorial or linguistic form (1979, 922). Pornography use is akin to sex and therefore not covered by the First Amendment of the US constitution—having sex is not a free speech issue.

question are placed in the same ontological category as women. This is problematic because

> a new category of reality is simultaneously created and populated by pornography's manufacture-for-use; it is the category of those individuals who are both women and non-persons. This category is filled with all the sexual objects of pornography's manufacture, objects which are formally of the same sex class as flesh-and-blood women. (Vadas 2005, 189)

Hence, in personifying pornography its users end up committing a category mistake that places sexual objects and real women in the very same ontological category. This depersonalizes flesh-and-blood women and constructs their sexual identity as "rapeable" (Vadas 2005, 188). Women's consent thus becomes irrelevant:

> Some men might prefer to have sex with women who consent just as some men might prefer to drive cars that are red, but neither the consent of the woman nor the redness of the car has anything conceptually to do with the subsequent sex as sex, or of the subsequent driving as driving ... having sex with a consenting or a non-consenting woman is equally sex. (Vadas 2005, 190)

Since giving consent is a distinctly person-related ability, in personifying pornography that makes consent sexually irrelevant for flesh-and-blood women, consumers end up objectifying women in the sense of dehumanizing them (see chapter 5).

How plausible is the connection between personification and objectification though? Papadaki argues against the causal connection. She questions the idea that men personify pornography: "It is hard to see how male consumers of pornography treat pornography *as a person* in treating it as a mere sexual tool" (Papadaki 2017, 149).

I agree, and I am skeptical of Langton's claims that consumers treat pornography as a sexual partner. When one is a partnered with another relative to some activity, the two presumably have some intentional mental states toward the activity, and the partners share some common knowledge about what they are doing. Imagine that Billy is my tennis partner in a video game and Sally is my flesh-and-blood tennis partner. Are Billy and Sally exactly alike as my tennis partners? Unless I am seriously deluded about Billy, the answer is no. In fact, given that Billy has no intentional mental states, Billy is merely my pseudo-partner. Consider then pornography and flesh-and-blood women as sexual "partners." It strikes me as implausible to say that pornography is used as a sexual partner in the proper sense of *being a partner* precisely because pornographic materials lack mental states and our interactions with them are not reciprocal. Or this is at least the case with more standard spectator-type pornography, like magazines and films. Newer interactive forms like virtual reality pornography are developing, though, which might alter things. I cannot say much about this type of pornography here though since it is only just developing and its precise nature and consequences are still largely unknown. At any rate, MacKinnon, Langton, and Vadas have in mind the more standard, inert kind of pornography. But to think that having sex with such pornographic materials is equivalent to having sex with a person displays an alarmingly impoverished view about what it is to have sex (see also van Brabandt 2017). Moreover, I am not convinced that this is as prevalent as antipornography feminists assume.

Now, it might be that men who consume violent and misogynistic pornography end up treating women as mere objects for sexual (ab) use because such pornography depicts abusive treatment as permissible. But accepting this, Papadaki holds, does not establish a causal connection between men's personification of pornography and women's objectification. In order to establish both the constitutive and the causal claims, we would need robust psychological evidence that supports the connection along with Langton's claim that personification causes objectification as a matter of human psychology. Langton provides no such evidence and, in its absence, Papadaki concludes that it is more plausible to hold that "it is the actual *content* of pornography, the ideas and messages in pornography, that can influence some men to treat real women as objects" (2017, 152).

Vadas's constitutive connection between personification and objectification is suspect, too, given her conception of *pornography*. More specifically, the analogy between hunger and sexual desire meant to establish that pornography consumption *is equivalent to* having sex is flawed. This analogy takes food and pornography consumption to be on a par *qua* means of desire-satisfaction. For Vadas, this hangs on the idea that they both involve appetitive consumption: they involve certain kinds of desires that can only be satisfied by consuming the object of desire. But there is an obvious sense in which hunger and sexual desire come apart: if the former goes unfulfilled, a person dies. If the latter goes unfulfilled, one's life may be miserable but not threatened. This suggests that sexual desire is akin to a more specialized desire, like the desire to consume French cheese. Satisfying this desire is highly pleasurable (at least for some), but not being able to consume French cheese is clearly not life threatening. If we accept that this is a more fitting parallel, what is it to satisfy one's desire for sex or for French cheese? Although there are many ways to do the former, it typically hinges on engaging in some types of sexual activities; eating French cheese, then again, typically satisfies the desire for such cheese. But can my desire for French cheese be satisfied by representations of French cheese as well? To an extent, yes. Imagine that my hometown has no French cheese purveyor. Given my appetitive desire, I subscribe to a gourmet magazine that contains ample representations and depictions of French cheese. Viewing these representations clearly isn't the same as eating the cheese. But it is akin to a sort of "dry use"—when recovering addicts exchange stories about consuming drugs or alcohol in ways that amount to reliving the consumption. Viewing images of French cheese is like "dry using." It amounts to a sort of pseudo-consumption that does not quell the appetite but satisfies it to a degree. If it is more appropriate to think about sexual desire being parallel to the desire for French cheese (as opposed to the desire to eat for survival), we can avoid the conclusion that consuming pornography is equivalent to sex. Masturbating to achieve an orgasm while viewing pornography is like eating French cheese while reading a magazine about it; but we can also engage in the latter activities on their own, which satisfies our respective desires to a degree, if not fully. If pornography consumption is not equivalent to having sex, there is no category mistake that places women and pornographic artifacts ontologically on a par and thus dehumanizes the former.

In a footnote, Vadas seemingly replies to this line of objection: "I am not claiming that sexual desire is in *all* ways like hunger, only that it is like hunger in that the object that satisfies it cannot be representational" (2005, 181; fn. 12). But (I contend) sexual desire is precisely *unlike* hunger in this respect. Our disagreement seemingly turns on how to understand desire-satisfaction. According to Vadas:

> The satisfaction-producing object cannot, *qua* satisfaction-producing object, be a mere representation because . . . the ontological grammar of appetitive consumption decisively disqualifies representations from playing such a satisfaction-producing role. (2005, 182)

But this conception of satisfying an appetitive desire appears to assume a cathartic conception of desire-satisfaction. My point is that this is not the only way to satisfy an appetitive desire: we can and do satisfy appetitive desires less absolutely and to a degree all the time.

In other words, there is a difference between quelling a desire and satisfying a desire, where the latter can come in degrees. And so, there seems to be no difficulty in saying that representations of x can satisfy my desire for x without quelling it. Consequently, pornographic representations can play the satisfaction-producing role, and this shows that consuming pornography is not equivalent to having sex. Having rejected the parallel, then, undermines the puzzling constructionist claim that in using pornography, men personify it: that men's use of pornography supposedly renders pieces of paper ontologically on a par with flesh-and-blood women.

8.5. THE PHILOSOPHY OF PORNOGRAPHY: FINAL METHODOLOGICAL REMARKS

The above discussions aimed to offer examples of philosophical examinations of pornography that are not wedded to a speech act approach. This move is motivated by methodological considerations: there are still many avenues open to us to debate the topic of pornography philosophically and to advance our knowledge of the subject. Throughout this book I have made a further methodological plea: philosophical investigations should be more empirically engaged and informed when they deal with applied topic like pornography. Of course, philosophy is not an empirical science. But our philosophizing should endeavor to avoid being empirically inadequate. How should one then proceed when doing philosophical work on pornography? For one thing, I have highlighted the importance of fitting examples. Pornography cannot be analyzed from the philosopher's armchair a priori, and speaking authoritatively about issues relevant to pornography requires knowing something about those issues. In other words, philosophical theorizing about pornography requires having knowledge about the empirical realities of pornography as a cultural phenomenon and as an industry–otherwise one is not in a good position to advance empirically adequate analyses of pornography. (Just compare this to doing philosophy of biology while knowing practically nothing about the natural world or its workings.) What this requires in turn is open-mindedness and willingness to engage empirically with pornography. Of course, given how emotive a topic it is, this may be psychologically challenging.

One might wonder whether my view entails that philosophers *should* view pornography if they wish to write about it in a manner that is empirically adequate. In a parallel fashion, one might hold that philosophers of art not only produce better philosophy if they view works of art; actually, given their subject matter, they should view works of art. If the same is true of those engaged in philosophical pornography debates, I am asking philosophers to do something highly demanding and potentially harmful, which seems an unreasonably tall order. As I see it, though, empirical familiarity with pornographic materials need not involve viewing pornography. Or rather, much depends on what debates one is engaged in. In order to discuss a number of topics I have considered in this book, one need not view pornography but can rely on research from other disciplines, like media theory and cultural studies. Writing about the aesthetics of pornography is conceivably a different matter. Perhaps precisely because the aesthetic side of these debates requires familiarity with pornographic works and because philosophical pornography debates have been predominantly conducted from antipornography positions, there has been so little crossover between feminist philosophical and philosophy of art debates. Whatever the explanation, the take-home message is the following. Good philosophical work on pornography requires familiarity with and knowledge of the topic. Still, one can gain this without necessarily needing to view pornographic materials. In this sense, there is no requirement to view pornography, provided that one can gain the requisite knowledge through interdisciplinary research.

I should add though that one difficulty with doing empirically engaged philosophy of pornography is the lack of decisive empirical research on the topic. Much of the relevant psychological and social scientific literature is inconclusive, and all sides to the debate will probably find some support for their views. In an attempt to fulfill my preferred methodological desiderata, I have tried to engage with empirical literature as much as possible while writing this book. Unfortunately, some of the literature that initially appeared highly promising ultimately turned out to be disappointing. For instance, Shira Tarrant's 2016 book *The Pornography Industry* initially looks like a hugely valuable source of information. Although it provides good information for people who are utterly oblivious to the workings of the pornography industry in California, it is in other ways methodologically lacking. For one thing, Tarrant aims to provide a neutral account of the facts without being judgmental about the pornography industry. The tone of the work is nevertheless clearly on the side of the industry and against antipornography feminism. In a striking and recurrent move, Tarrant documents empirical evidence and research against pornography, but when she goes on to debunk this research with empirical evidence to the contrary, Tarrant fails to reference her sources. In just one paragraph (Tarrant 2016, 104), she notes three studies supporting the view that pornography has a positive effect on young people's and young women's lives without providing any reference information or the names of the researchers who apparently conducted the research. The studies were merely noted as being from Sweden and Canada. Those who may find such research suspect, then, have no way of verifying their suspicions since the readers are not told where the research is to be found. Here is another example. Although not a book in philosophy, Tarrant mentions two philosophers: Lori Watson and Nancy Bauer. Watson's antipornography statement was indirectly referenced, but Bauer's nonjudgmental take on pornography was in no way referenced (which does not mean that Bauer was making a pro-pornography statement). In a peculiar manner, Tarrant defends the pornography industry but fails to substantiate her defense.

In short, it is hard to find empirical research that takes a genuinely dispassionate look at pornography's harms and benefits, and what pornography conceivably does. This being the case, doing empirically engaged philosophy of pornography is an endeavor fraught with difficulties—but this is something that we ought to be frank about. When it comes to empirical issues about what pornography does, one will probably find conflicting evidence and research that shows pornography to be either deeply detrimental to individuals and societies, or that it has no influence on human psychology and social relations whatsoever. It seems warranted to say that both of these extreme views are highly likely to be false. This does not justify philosophical theorizing that is woefully out of sync with reality, and philosophical work should acknowledge the massive differences that exist within the phenomenon of pornography. Nonetheless, I am issuing a plea that philosophical work on pornography should wear its normative commitments on its sleeve and recognize the massive differences that exist within the pornography industry. This will not only make our philosophical accounts better, but it will also ensure that we gain knowledge about a concrete topic using philosophical tools and that we can apply our philosophical theorizing to deal with important and pressing real-life matters.

BIBLIOGRAPHY

Adams, Don. 2000. "Can Pornography Cause Rape?" *Journal of Social Philosophy* 31 (1): 1–43.

Albury, Kath. 2014. "Porn and Sex Education, Porn as Sex Education." *Porn Studies* 1 (1–2): 172–181. doi: 10.1080/23268743.2013.863654.

Antony, Louise. 2011. "Against Langton's Illocutionary Treatment of Pornography." *Jurisprudence* 2: 387–401.

———. 2014. "Pornography and the Philosophy of Language." In *The Philosophy of Pornography: Contemporary Perspectives*, edited by Lindsay Coleman and Jacob M. Held, 147–176. Lanham: Rowman and Littlefield.

———. 2017. "Be What I Say: Authority Versus Power in Pornography." In *Beyond Speech: Pornography and Analytic Feminist Philosophy*, edited by Mari Mikkola, 59–90. New York: Oxford University Press.

Archard, D. 1999. "The Mens Rea of Rape." In *A Most Detestable Crime*, edited by Keith Burgess-Jackson, 213–229. New York: Oxford University Press.

Arrowsmith, Anna. 2013. "My Pornographic Development." In *Pornographic Art and the Aesthetics of Pornography*, edited by Hans Maes, 287–297. Basingstoke: Palgrave-MacMillan.

Assiter, Alison. 1988. "Autonomy and Pornography." In *Feminist Perspectives in Philosophy*, edited by Morwenna Griffiths and Margaret Whitford, 58–71. Bloomington: Indiana University Press.

Attwood, Feona. 2010a. "Toward the Study of Online Porn Cultures and Practices." In her (ed.) *Porn.Com: Making Sense of Online Pornography*, 236–244. New York: Peter Lang Publishing, Inc.

————. 2010b. "'Younger, Paler, Decidedly Less Straight': The New Porn Professionals." In her (ed.) *Porn.Com: Making Sense of Online Pornography*, 88–106. New York: Peter Lang.

Austin, J. L. 1962. *How to Do Things with Words*. Oxford: Clarendon.

Bachy, Victor. 1976. "Danish 'Permissiveness' Revisited." *Journal of Communication* 26 (1): 40–43.

Baird, Robert, and Stuart Rosenbaum, eds. 1991. *Pornography: Private Right or Public Menace?* Buffalo: Prometheus.

Baker, Peter. 1992. "Maintaining Male Power: Why Heterosexual Men Use Pornography." In *Pornography: Women, Violence and Civil Liberties*, edited by Catherine Itzin, 124–144. Oxford: Oxford University Press.

Baron, Marcia. 2001. "I Thought She Consented." *Philosophical Issues* 11: 1–32.

Bart, Pauline, and Margaret Jozsa. 1980. "Dirty Books, Dirty Films, and Dirty Data." In *Take Back the Night*, edited by Laura Lederer, 204–217. New York: William Morrow.

Bauer, N. 2015. *How to Do Things with Pornography*. Cambridge, MA: Harvard University Press.

Berger, Fred R. 1977. "Pornography, Sex, and Censorship." *Social Theory and Practice* 4 (2): 183–209.

Bettcher, Talia Mae. 2007. "Evil Deceivers and Make-Believers: On Transphobic Violence and the Politics of Illusion." *Hypatia* 22 (3): 43–65.

————. 2009. "Feminist Perspectives on Trans Issues." *The Stanford Encyclopedia of Philosophy* (Winter 2009 edition), edited by Edward N. Zalta. http://plato.stanford.edu/archives/win2009/entries/feminism-trans.

————. 2013. "Trans Women and 'Interpretive Intimacy': Some Initial Reflections." In *The Essential Handbook of Women's Sexuality*, vol. 2, edited by Donna Marie Castañeda, 51–68. Santa Barbara: Praeger.

————. 2017. "Getting 'Naked' in the Colonial/Modern Gender System: A Preliminary Trans Feminist Analysis of Pornography." In *Beyond Speech: Pornography and Analytic Feminist Philosophy*, edited by Mari Mikkola, 157–176. New York: Oxford University Press.

Bianchi, Claudia. 2008. "Indexicals, Speech Acts and Pornography." *Analysis* 68: 310–316.

Bignell, P. 2013. "Playboy Is Art, Not Porn, Says Hefner Heir." *The Independent*, January 6. https://www.independent.co.uk/news/people/news/playboy-is-art-not-porn-says-hefner-heir-8439849.html.

Bird, Alexander. 2002. "Illocutionary Silencing." *Pacific Philosophical Quarterly* 83: 1–15.

Brison, Susan. 2014. "'The Price We Pay'? Pornography and Harm." In *The Philosophy of Pornography: Contemporary Perspectives*, edited by Lindsay Coleman and Jacob M. Held, 89–104. Lanham: Rowman and Littlefield.

Brod, Harry. 1988. "Pornography and the Alienation of Male Sexuality." *Social Theory and Practice* 14 (3): 265–284.

Bronstein, C. 2011. *Battling Pornography: The American Feminist Anti-Pornography Movement, 1976–1986*. Cambridge: Cambridge University Press.

Brownmiller, S. 1975. *Against Our Will: Men, Women and Rape*. New York: Simon and Schuster.

Brownstein, Michael, and Jennifer Saul, eds. 2016. *Implicit Bias and Philosophy*. Vol. 1: *Metaphysics and Epistemology*. Oxford: Oxford University Press.

Burgess, Alexis, and David Plunkett. 2013. "Conceptual Ethics I." *Philosophy Compass* 8 (12): 1091–1101.

Burns, C. 2005. *Sexual Violence and the Law in Japan*. New York: Routledge.

Butler, J. 1997. *Excitable Speech: A Politics of the Performative*. New York and London: Routledge.

Cadwalladr, Carole. 2013. "Porn Wars: The Debate that Is Dividing Academia." *The Observer*, June 16. https://www.theguardian.com/culture/2013/jun/16/internet-violent-porn-crime-studies.

Cahill, Ann. J. 2011. *Overcoming Objectification: A Carnal Ethics*. New York: Routledge.

———. 2014. "The Difference Sameness Makes: Objectification, Sex Work, and Queerness." *Hypatia* 29 (4): 840–856.

Califia, P. 1994. *Public Sex*. Pittsburgh, PA: Cleis.

Cameron, Deborah, and Elizabeth Frazer. 1992. "On the Question of Pornography and Sexual Violence: Moving Beyond Cause and Effect." In *Pornography: Women, Violence and Civil Liberties*, edited by Catherine Itzin, 240–253. Oxford: Oxford University Press.

Carse, Alisa L. 1995. "Pornography: An Uncivil Liberty?" *Hypatia* 10: 155–182.

Chester, Gail, and Julienne Dickey, eds. 1988. *Feminism and Censorship*. London: Prism Press.

Cocks, J. 1989. *The Oppositional Imagination*. London: Routledge.

Collins, Patricia H. 1993. "Pornography and Black Women's Bodies." In *Making Violence Sexy: Feminist Views on Pornography*, edited by Diana Russell, 97–104. Buckingham: Open University Press.

———. 2000. *Black Feminist Thought: Knowledge, Consciousness, and the Politics of Empowerment*. 2nd ed. New York: Routledge.

Cooke, Brandon. 2012. "On the Ethical Distinction between Art and Pornography." In *Art and Pornography*, edited by Hans Maes and Jerrold Levinson, 229–253. Oxford: Oxford University Press.

Cornell, Drucilla, ed. 2000a. *Feminism and Pornography*. New York: Oxford University Press.

———. 2000b. "Pornography's Temptation." In her (ed.) *Feminism and Pornography*, 551–568. New York: Oxford University Press.

Corvino, John. 2002. "Naughty Fantasies." *Southwest Philosophy Review* 18 (1): 213–220.

Coward, R. 1984. *Female Desire*. London: Paladin.

Coy, Maddy, Liz Kelly, Fiona Elvines, Maria Garner, and Ava Kanyeredzi. 2013. "'Sex without Consent, I Suppose That Is Rape': How Young People in England Understand Sexual Consent." London: Office of the Children's Commissioner. Accessed August 1, 2015. http://www.childrenscommissioner.gov.uk/publications/sex-without-consent-i-suppose-rape-how-young-people-england-understand-sexual-consent.

Cruz, Ariane. 2014. "Sisters Are Doin' It for Themselves: Black Women and the New Pornography." In *The Philosophy of Pornography*, edited by Lindsay Coleman and Jacob M. Held, 225–248. Lanham: Rowman and Littlefield.

Davies, Alex. 2016. "How to Silence Content with Porn, Context and Loaded Questions." *European Journal of Philosophy* 24 (2): 498–522. doi:10.1111/ejop.12075.

De Gaynesford, Maximilian. 2009. "Illocutionary Acts, Subordination and Silencing." *Analysis* 69: 488–490.

Dines, G. 2011. *Pornland: How Porn has Hijacked our Sexuality*. Boston: Beacon Press.

Donnerstein, Edward I., Daniel G. Linz, and Steven Penrod, eds. 1987. *The Question of Pornography: Research Findings and Policy Implications*. New York: Free Press; London: Collier Macmillan.

Dority, Barbara. 1991. "Feminist Moralism, 'Pornography,' and Censorship." In *Pornography: Private Right or Public Menace?* edited by Robert Baird and Stuart Rosenbaum, 111–116. Buffalo: Prometheus.

Drabek, Matt L. 2016. "Pornographic Subordination, Power, and Feminist Alternatives." *Feminist Philosophy Quarterly* 2 (1): 2.

Dworkin, A. 1981. *Pornography: Men Possessing Women*. London: The Women's Press.

———. 2000. "Against the Male Flood: Censorship, Pornography, and Equality." In *Feminism and Pornography*, edited by Drucilla Cornell, 19–38. New York: Oxford University Press.

Dworkin, R. 1978. *Taking Rights Seriously*. Cambridge, MA: Harvard University Press.

———. 1981. "Is There a Right to Pornography?" *Oxford Journal of Legal Studies* 1 (2): 177–212.

———. 1991. "Liberty and Pornography." *New York Review of Books* 38 (14): 12–15.

———. 1993. "Women and Pornography." *New York Review of Books* 40 (17): 36–42.

Dwyer, Susan, ed. 1995. *The Problem of Pornography*. Belmont, CA: Wadsworth.

Dyzenhaus, David. 1992. "John Stuart Mill and the Harm of Pornography." *Ethics* 102: 534–551.

Easton, S. 1994. *The Problem of Pornography: Regulation and the Right to Free Speech*. London: Routledge.

Eaton, Anne W. 2007. "A Sensible Antiporn Feminism." *Ethics* 117: 674–715.

———. 2008. "Feminist Philosophy of Art." *Philosophy Compass* 3 (5): 873–893.

―――. 2012. "What's Wrong with the (Female) Nude? A Feminist Perspective on Art and Pornography." In *Art and Pornography*, edited by Hans Maes and Jerrold Levinson, 277–308. Oxford: Oxford University Press.

―――. 2017. "Feminist Pornography." In *Beyond Speech: Pornography and Analytic Feminist Philosophy*, edited by Mari Mikkola, 243–257. New York: Oxford University Press.

Einsiedel, Edna. 1992. "The Experimental Research Evidence: Effects of Pornography on the 'Average Individual.'" In *Pornography: Women, Violence and Civil Liberties*, edited by Catherine Itzin, 248–283. Oxford: Oxford University Press.

Erickson, Loree. 2013. "Out of Line: The Sexy Femmegimp Politics of Flaunting It!" In *The Feminist Porn Book: The Politics of Producing Pleasure*, edited by Tristan Taormino, Celine Parreñas Shimizu, Constance Penley, and Mireille Miller-Young, 320–328. New York: The Feminist Press at CUNY.

Ezzell, Matthew B. 2014. "Pornography Makes a Man: The Impact of Pornography as a Component of Gender and Sexual Socialization." In *The Philosophy of Pornography: Contemporary Perspectives*, edited by Lindsay Coleman and Jacob M. Held, 17–34. Lanham: Rowman and Littlefield.

Feinberg, J. 1985. *Offense to Others: The Moral Limits of the Criminal Law*. Oxford: Oxford University Press.

Finlayson, Lorna. 2014. "How to Screw Things with Words." *Hypatia* 29 (4): 774–789.

Fish, S. 1993. *There's No Such Thing as Free Speech: And It's a Good Thing, Too*. New York: Oxford University Press.

Flores, April. 2013. "Being Fatty D: Size, Beauty, and Embodiment in the Adult Industry." In *The Feminist Porn Book: The Politics of Producing Pleasure*, edited by Tristan Taormino, Celine Parreñas Shimizu, Constance Penley, and Mireille Miller-Young, 279–283. New York: The Feminist Press at CUNY.

Forna, Aminatta. 1992. "Pornography and Racism: Sexualizing Oppression and Inciting Hatred." In *Pornography: Women, Violence and Civil Liberties*, edited by Catherine Itzin, 102–112. Oxford: Oxford University Press.

Frug, Mary J. 2000. "The Politics of Postmodern Feminism: Lessons from the Anti-Pornography Campaign." In *Feminism and Pornography*, edited by Drucilla Cornell, 254–263. New York: Oxford University Press.

Garry, Ann. 1978. "Pornography and Respect for Women." *Social Theory and Practice* 4 (4): 395–421.

Green, Leslie. 1998. "Pornographizing, Subordinating, and Silencing." In *Censorship and Silencing: Practices of Cultural Regulation*, edited by Robert Post, 285–311. Los Angeles: Getty Research Institute for the History of Art and the Humanities.

―――. 2000. "Pornographies." *Journal of Political Philosophy* 8: 27–52.

Griffith, James D., Sharon Mitchell, Christian L. Hart, Lea T. Adams, and Lucy L. Gu. 2013. "Pornography Actresses: An Assessment of the Damaged Goods Hypothesis." *Journal of Sex Research* 50 (7), 621–632.

Griffiths, Mark. 2001. "Sex on the Internet: Observations and Implications for Internet Sex Addiction." *Journal of Sex Research* 38 (4): 333–342.

Gruen, Lori, and George Panichas, eds. 1997. *Sex, Morality, and the Law.* New York: Routledge.

Grünberg, Angela. 2014. "Saying and Doing: Speech Actions, Speech Acts and Related Events." *European Journal of Philosophy* 22 (2): 173–199.

Gunter, B. 2002. *Media Sex: What Are the Issues?* Mahwah, NJ: Lawrence Erlbaum.

Hald, Gert, Neil Malamuth, and Carlin Yuen. 2010. "Pornography and Attitudes Supporting Violence against Women: Revisiting the Relationship in Nonexperimental Studies." *Aggressive Behavior* 36: 14–20.

Harel, Alon. 2011. "Is Pornography a Speech or an Act and Does it Matter?" *Jerusalem Review of Legal Studies* 3: 5–14.

Haslanger, Sally. 1993. "On Being Objective and Being Objectified." In *A Mind of One's Own: Feminist Essays on Reason and Objectivity,* edited by Louise M. Antony and Charlotte Witt, 209–253. Boulder, San Francisco, Oxford: Westview Press.

———. 2000. "Gender and Race: (What) Are They? (What) Do We Want Them to Be?" *Noûs* 34: 31–55.

———. 2012. *Resisting Reality.* New York: Oxford University Press.

Held, Jacob M. 2014. "The Problem with the Problem of Pornography: Subordination, Sexualization, and Speech." In *The Philosophy of Pornography: Contemporary Perspectives,* edited by Lindsay Coleman and Jacob M. Held, 129–146. Lanham: Rowman and Littlefield.

Herman, Barbara. 2002. "Could It Be Worth Thinking about Kant on Sex and Marriage?" In *A Mind of One's Own,* edited by Louise M. Antony and Charlotte Witt, 53–72. Boulder: Westview Press.

Hill, Judith M. 1987. "Pornography and Degradation." *Hypatia* 2 (2): 39–54.

Hopkins, Patrick D. 1994. "Rethinking Sadomasochism: Feminism, Interpretation, and Simulation." *Hypatia* 9 (1): 116–141.

Hornsby, Jennifer. 1995a. "Disempowered Speech." *Philosophical Topics* 23 (2): 127–147.

———. 1995b. "Speech Acts and Pornography." In *The Problem of Pornography,* edited by Susan Dwyer, 220–232. Belmont, CA: Wadsworth.

———. 2014. "Pornography and 'Speech.'" In *The Philosophy of Pornography: Contemporary Perspectives,* edited by Lindsay Coleman and Jacob M. Held, 129–146. Lanham: Rowman and Littlefield.

Hornsby, Jennifer, and Rae Langton. 1998. "Free Speech and Illocution." *Legal Theory* 4: 21–37.

Hunt, Lynn. 1993. "Introduction." In her (ed.) *The Invention of Pornography, 1500–1800,* 9–45. New York: Zone Books.

Hunter, Nan D., and Sylvia A. Law. 1997. "Brief Amici Curiae of Feminist Anti-Censorship Taskforce, et al., in American Booksellers Association v. Hudnut."

In *Sex, Morality, and the Law*, edited by Lori Gruen and George E. Panichas, 199–222. New York: Routledge.

Itzin, Catherine. 1992a. "Introduction: Fact, Fiction and Faction." In her (ed.) *Pornography: Women, Violence and Civil Liberties*, 1–24. Oxford: Oxford University Press.

―――. 1992b. "Legislating Against Pornography without Censorship." In her (ed.) *Pornography: Women, Violence and Civil Liberties*, 401–434. Oxford: Oxford University Press.

―――. 1992c. "Pornography and Civil Liberties: Freedom, Harm and Human Rights." In her (ed.) *Pornography: Women, Violence and Civil Liberties*, 553–586. Oxford: Oxford University Press.

―――, ed. 1992d. *Pornography: Women, Violence and Civil Liberties*. Oxford: Oxford University Press.

Itzin, Catherine, and Corinne Sweet. 1992. "Women's Experience of Pornography: UK Magazine Survey Evidence." In *Pornography: Women, Violence and Civil Liberties*, edited by Catherine Itzin, 222–235. Oxford: Oxford University Press.

Jacobson, Daniel. 1995. "Freedom of Speech Acts? A Response to Langton." *Philosophy and Public Affairs* 24: 64–79.

―――. 2001. "Speech and Action." *Legal Theory* 7 (2): 179–201.

Jenkins, Katharine. 2017. "What Are Women For: Pornography and Social Ontology." In *Beyond Speech: Pornography and Analytic Feminist Philosophy*, edited by Mari Mikkola, 91–112. New York: Oxford University Press.

Jones, Steve. 2013. "The Lexicon of Offense: The Meanings of Torture, Porn, and 'Torture Porn.'" In *Controversial Images*, edited by Feona Attwood, Vincent Campbell, I. Q. Hunter and Sharon Lockyer, 186–200. London: Palgrave-Macmillan.

Jütten, Timo. 2016. "Sexual Objectification." *Ethics* 127 (1): 27–49.

Kania, Andrew. 2012. "Aesthetics, Feminism, and Methodology." In *Art and Pornography*, edited by Hans Maes and Jerrold Levinson, 255–274. Oxford: Oxford University Press.

Kershnar, Stephen. 2004. "Is Violation Pornography Bad for Your Soul?" *Journal of Social Philosophy* 35: 349–366.

―――. 2005. "The Moral Status of Sexual Fantasies." *Public Affairs Quarterly* 19 (4): 301–315.

Kieran, Matthew. 2001. "Pornographic Art." *Philosophy and Literature* 25: 31–45.

Kipnis, L. 1996. *Bound and Gagged: Pornography and the Politics of Fantasy*. New York: Grove Press.

Klaassen, Marleen J. E., and Jochen Peter. 2015. "Gender (In)equality in Internet Pornography: A Content Analysis of Popular Pornographic Internet Videos." *Journal of Sex Research* 52 (7): 721–735.

Klumbyte, Goda, and Katrine Smiet. 2015. "Bodies Like Our Own? The Dynamics of Distance and Closeness in Online Fat Porn." In *Fat Sex: New Directions in*

Theory and Activism, edited by Helen Hester and Carolin Walters, 133–151. Farnham: Ashgate.

Kohut, Taylor, Jodie. L. Baer, and Brendan Watts. 2016. "Is Pornography Really about 'Making Hate to Women'? Pornography Users Hold More Gender Egalitarian Attitudes Than Nonusers in a Representative American Sample." *Journal of Sex Research* 53 (1): 1–11.

Kristol, Irving. 1997. "Pornography, Obscenity, and the Case for Censorship." In *Sex, Morality, and the Law*, edited by Lori Gruen and George Panichas, 174–180. New York: Routledge.

Kutchinsky, Berl. 1970. "Pornography in Denmark." In *Technical Reports of the Commission on Obscenity and Pornography*, vol. 6. Washington, DC: US Government Printing Office.

Lane, Keiko. 2013. "Imag(in)ing Possibilities: The Psychotherapeutic Potential of Queer Pornography." In *The Feminist Porn Book: The Politics of Producing Pleasure*, edited by Tristan Taormino, Celine Parreñas Shimizu, Constance Penley, and Mireille Miller-Young, 164–176. New York: The Feminist Press at CUNY.

Langton, Rae. 1990. "Whose Right? Ronald Dworkin, Women, and Pornographers." *Philosophy & Public Affairs* 19 (4): 311–359.

———. 1993. "Speech Acts and Unspeakable Acts." *Philosophy and Public Affairs* 22: 293–330.

———. 1995. "Sexual Solipsism." *Philosophical Topics* 23 (2): 181–219.

———. 1998. "Subordination, Silence and Pornography's Authority." In *Censorship and Silencing: Practices of Cultural Regulation*, edited by Robert Post, 261–283. Los Angeles: Getty Research Institute.

———. 2000. "Feminism in Epistemology: Exclusion and Objectification." In *Cambridge Companion to Feminism in Philosophy*, edited by Miranda Fricker and Jennifer Hornsby, 127–145. Cambridge: Cambridge University Press.

———. 2009a. "Autonomy-Denial and Objectification." In her *Sexual Solipsism: Philosophical Essays on Pornography and Objectification*, 223–240. Oxford: Oxford University Press.

———. 2009b. "Pornography's Divine Command? Response to Judith Butler." In her *Sexual Solipsism: Philosophical Essays on Pornography and Objectification*, 103–116. Oxford: Oxford University Press.

———. 2009c. "Speaker's Freedom and Maker's Knowledge." In her *Sexual Solipsism: Philosophical Essays on Pornography and Objectification*, 289–310. Oxford: Oxford University Press.

———. 2012. "Beyond Belief: Pragmatics in Hate Speech and Pornography." In *Speech and Harm: Controversies over Free Speech*, edited by Ishani Maitra and Mary Kate McGowan, 72–93. Oxford: Oxford University Press.

———. 2017. "Is Pornography Like the Law?" In *Beyond Speech: Pornography and Analytic Feminist Philosophy*, edited by Mari Mikkola, 23–38. New York: Oxford University Press.

Langton, Rae, and Caroline West. 1999. "Scorekeeping in a Pornographic Language Game." *Australasian Journal of Philosophy* 77 (3): 303–319.

LeMoncheck, L. 1985. *Dehumanizing Women: Treating Persons as Sex Objects.* Lanham: Rowman and Littlefield.

———. 1997. *Loose Women, Lecherous Men: A Feminist Philosophy of Sex.* Oxford: Oxford University Press.

Leung, Rebecca. 2003. "Porn in the U.S.A." *CBS 60 Minutes,* November 21. http://www.cbsnews.com/stories/2003/11/21/60minutes/main585049.shtml. Accessed January 17, 2011.

Levinson, Jerrold. 2005. "Erotic Art and Pornographic Pictures." *Philosophy and Literature* 29: 228–240.

———. 2012. "Is Pornographic Art Comparable to Religious Art? Reply to Davies." In *Art and Pornography,* edited by Hans Maes and Jerrold Levinson, 83–94. Oxford: Oxford University Press.

Levy, Neil. 2002. "Virtual Child Pornography: The Eroticization of Inequality." *Ethics and Information Technology* 4 (4): 319–323.

Liao, Shen-yi, and Sara Protasi. 2013. "The Fictional Character of Pornography." In *Pornographic Art and the Aesthetics of Pornography,* edited by Hans Maes, 100–118. Basingstoke: Palgrave-Macmillan.

Longino, Helen. 1980. "Pornography, Oppression, and Freedom: A Closer Look." In *Take Back the Night,* edited by Laura Lederer, 40–54. New York: William Morrow.

Loots, Lliane. 2000. "Looking for Women's Rights in the Rainbow: Pornography, Censorship, and the 'New' South Africa." In *Feminism and Pornography,* edited by Drucilla Cornell, 423–437. New York: Oxford University Press.

Love, Sinnamon. 2013. "A Question of Feminism." In *The Feminist Porn Book: The Politics of Producing Pleasure,* edited by Tristan Taormino, Celine Parreñas Shimizu, Constance Penley, and Mireille Miller-Young, 97–104. New York: Feminist Press at CUNY.

MacKinnon, Catharine A. 1987. *Feminism Unmodified.* Cambridge, MA: Harvard University Press.

———. 1989a. "Sexuality, Pornography, and Method: Pleasure under Patriarchy." *Ethics* 99 (2): 314–346.

———. 1989b. *Toward a Feminist Theory of the State.* Cambridge, MA: Harvard University Press.

———. 1993. *Only Words.* Cambridge, MA: Harvard University Press.

———. 2000. "The Roar on the Other Side of Silence." In *Feminism and Pornography,* edited by Drucilla Cornell, 130–153. New York: Oxford University Press.

MacKinnon, Catharine A., and Andrea Dworkin, eds. 1997. *In Harm's Way: The Pornography Civil Rights Hearings.* Cambridge, MA: Harvard University Press.

Maddison, Stephen. 2010. "Online Obscenity and Myths of Freedom: Dangerous Images, Child Porn, and Neoliberalism." In *Porn.Com: Making Sense of Online Pornography,* edited by Feona Attwood, 17–33. New York: Peter Lang.

Maes, Hans. 2011a. "Art or Porn: Clear Division or False Dilemma?" *Philosophy and Literature* 35: 51–64.

———. 2011b. "Drawing the Line: Art versus Pornography." *Philosophy Compass* 6: 385–397.

———. 2012. "Who Says Pornography Can't Be Art?" In *Art and Pornography*, edited by Hans Maes and Jerrold Levinson, 17–47. Oxford: Oxford University Press.

———. 2017. "Falling in Lust: Sexiness, Feminism, and Pornography." In *Beyond Speech: Pornography and Analytic Feminist Philosophy*, edited by Mari Mikkola, 199–220. New York: Oxford University Press.

Maes, Hans, and Jerrold Levinson, eds. 2012. *Art and Pornography*. Oxford: Oxford University Press.

Mag Uidhir, Christy. 2009. "Why Pornography Can't Be Art." *Philosophy and Literature* 33: 193–203.

Mag Uidhir, Christy, and Henry Pratt. 2012. "Depiction, Fiction, and Sexual Predilection." In *Art and Pornography*, edited by Hans Maes and Jerrold Levinson, 137–160. Oxford: Oxford University Press.

Maitra, Ishani. 2004. "Silence and Responsibility." *Philosophical Perspectives* 18 (1): 189–208.

———. 2009. "Silencing Speech." *Canadian Journal of Philosophy* 39 (2): 309–338.

Maitra, Ishani, and Mary Kate McGowan. 2007. "The Limits of Free Speech: Pornography and the Question of Coverage." *Legal Theory* 13 (1): 41.

———. 2010. "On Silencing, Rape and Responsibility." *Australasian Journal of Philosophy* 88 (1): 167–172.

Malamuth, Neil M., Tamara Addison, and Mary Koss. 2000. "Pornography and Sexual Aggression: Are There Reliable Effects and Can We Understand Them?" *Annual Review of Sex Research* 11: 26–91.

Malamuth, Neil, and Mark Huppin. 2007. "Drawing the Line on Virtual Child Pornography: Bringing the Law in Line with the Research Evidence." *NYU Review of Law and Social Change* 31 (4): 773–827.

Marino, Patricia. 2008. "The Ethics of Sexual Objectification: Autonomy and Consent." *Inquiry* 51 (4): 345–364. doi: 10.1080/00201740802166643.

May, L. 1998. *Masculinity & Morality*. Ithaca, NY: Cornell University Press.

Mayall, Alice, and Diana E. H. Russell. 1993. "Racism in Pornography." In *Making Violence Sexy: Feminist Views on Pornography*, edited by Diana E. H. Russell, 167–178. Buckingham: Open University Press.

McCurry, J. 2017. "Forced into Pornography: Japan Moves to Stop Women Being Coerced into Sex Films." *The Guardian*, May 15. https://www.theguardian.com/world/2017/may/15/forced-into-porn-japan-moves-to-stop-women-being-coerced-into-sex-films.

McElroy, W. 1995. *XXX: A Women's Right to Pornography*. New York: St. Martin's Press.

McGowan, Mary Kate. 2003. "Conversational Exercitives and the Force of Pornography." *Philosophy and Public Affairs* 31 (2): 155–189.

———. 2005. "On Pornography: MacKinnon, Speech Acts, and 'False' Construction." *Hypatia* 20: 23–49.

———. 2009a. "On Silencing and Sexual Refusal." *Journal of Political Philosophy* 17 (4): 487–494.

———. 2009b. "Oppressive Speech." *Australasian Journal of Philosophy* 87: 389–407.

———. 2014. "Sincerity Silencing." *Hypatia* 29: 458–473.

———. 2017. "On Multiple Types of Silencing." In *Beyond Speech: Pornography and Analytic Feminist Philosophy*, edited by Mari Mikkola, 39–58. New York: Oxford University Press.

McGowan, Mary Kate, Sara Helmers, Jacqueline Stolzenberg, and Alexandra Adelman. 2011. "A Partial Defense of Illocutionary Silencing." *Hypatia* 26 (1): 132–149.

McGowan, Mary Kate, Ilana Walder-Biesanz, Morvareed Rezaian, and Chloe Emerson. 2016. "On Silencing and Systematicity: The Challenge of the Drowning Case." *Hypatia* 31 (1): 74–90.

McLeod, Carolyn. 2002. "Mere and Partial Means: The Full Range of the Objectification of Women." *Canadian Journal of Philosophy* 32 (sup1): 219–244.

Mercer, Kobena. 2000. "Just Looking for Trouble: Robert Mapplethorpe and Fantasies of Race." In *Feminism and Pornography*, edited by Drucilla Cornell, 460–476. New York: Oxford University Press.

Metz, Cade. 2008. "Pr0n Baron Challenges Google and Yahoo! to Build Better Child Locks." *The Register*, February 15. http://www.theregister.co.uk/2008/02/15/vivid_slaps_google_yahoo/.

Mikkola, Mari. 2008. "Contexts and Pornography." *Analysis* 68: 316–320.

———. 2010. "Is Everything Relative? Anti-Realism, Truth and Feminism." In *New Waves in Metaphysics*, edited by Allan Hazlett, 179–198. Basingstoke: Palgrave-Macmillan.

———. 2011. "Illocution, Silencing and the Act of Refusal." *Pacific Philosophical Quarterly* 92: 415–435.

———. 2013. "Pornography, Art and Porno-Art." In *Pornographic Art and the Aesthetics of Pornography*, edited by Hans Maes, 27–42. Basingstoke: Palgrave-MacMillan.

———. 2016. *The Wrong of Injustice: Dehumanization and Its Role in Feminist Philosophy*. New York: Oxford University Press.

———. 2017a. "Feminist Perspectives on Sex and Gender." *The Stanford Encyclopedia of Philosophy* (Summer 2017 edition), edited by Edward N. Zalta. https://plato.stanford.edu/archives/sum2017/entries/feminism-gender.

———. 2017b. "Pornographic Artifacts: Maker's Intentions-Model." In her (ed.) *Beyond Speech: Pornography and Analytic Feminist Philosophy*, 113–134. New York: Oxford University Press.

———. 2018. "Pornographic Videogames: A Feminist Examination." In *The Aesthetics of Video Games*, edited by Jon Robson and Grant Tavinor, 212–227. New York: Routledge.

Mill, J. S. (1869) 1974. *On Liberty*. Reprint. London: Penguin Books.

Miller, Edward D. 2013. "Clear Feet and Dirty Dancing: The Erotic Pas de Deux and Boys in the Sand." In *Pornographic Art and the Aesthetics of Pornography*, edited by Hans Maes, 205–220. Basingstoke: Palgrave-Macmillan.

Miller-Young, Mireille. 2013. "Interventions: The Deviant and Defiant Art of Black Women Porn Directors." In *The Feminist Porn Book: The Politics of Producing Pleasure*, edited by Tristan Taormino, Constance Penley, Celine Parrenas Shimizu, and Mireille Miller-Young, 105–120. New York: The Feminist Press at CUNY.

Morgan, Robin. 1980. "Theory and Practice: Pornography and Rape." In *Take Back the Night*, edited by Laura Lederer, 134–140. New York: William Morrow.

Ms. Naughty. 2013. "My Decadent Decade: Ten Years of Making and Debating Porn for Women." In *The Feminist Porn Book: The Politics of Producing Pleasure*, edited by Tristan Taormino, Constance Penley, Celine Parrenas Shimizu, and Mireille Miller-Young, 71–78. New York: The Feminist Press at CUNY.

Nash, Jennifer. 2008. "Strange Bedfellows: Black Feminism and Antipornography Feminism." *Social Text* 97 (26): 51–76.

———. 2014. *The Black Body in Ecstasy: Reading Race, Reading Pornography*. Durham, NC: Duke University Press.

Neville, Lucy. 2015. "Male Gays in the Female Gaze: Women Who Watch M/M Pornography." *Porn Studies* 2 (2–3): 192–207.

Nickerson, Raymond S. 1998. "Confirmation Bias: A Ubiquitous Phenomenon in Many Guises." *Review of General Psychology* 2: 175–220.

Nielson, S. 1988. "Books Bad for Women: A Feminist Looks at Censorship." In *Feminism and Censorship: The Current Debate*, edited by Gail Chester and Julienne Dickey, 17–25. London: Prism Press.

Nussbaum, Martha. 1995. "Objectification." *Philosophy and Public Affairs* 24: 249–291.

Osman, Sona. 1988. "Should It Be Unlawful to Incite Sexual Violence?" In *Feminism and Censorship*, edited by Gail Chester and Julienne Dickey, 151–160. London: Prism Press.

Palac, Lisa. 1995. "How Dirty Pictures Changed My Life." In *Debating Sexual Correctness*, edited by Adele M. Stan, 236–252. New York: Dell.

Pally, M. 1994. *Sex & Sensibility: Reflections on Forbidden Mirrors and the Will to Censor*. New York: Ecco Press.

Papadaki, Lina. 2007. "Sexual Objectification: From Kant to Contemporary Feminism." *Contemporary Political Theory* 6 (3): 330–348.

———. 2010. "What Is Objectification?" *Journal of Moral Philosophy* 7 (1): 16–36.

————. 2015a. "Feminist Perspectives on Objectification." *The Stanford Encyclopedia of Philosophy* (Winter 2015 edition), edited by Edward N. Zalta. http://plato.stanford.edu/archives/win2015/entries/feminism-objectification.

————. 2015b. "What Is Wrong about Objectification?" In *Current Controversies in Political Philosophy*, edited by Thom Brooks, 87–99. London: Routledge.

Parent, William. 1990. "A Second Look at Pornography and the Subordination of Women." *Journal of Philosophy* 87: 205–211.

Parmar, Pratibha. 1988. "Rage and Desire: Confronting Pornography." In *Feminism and Censorship*, edited by Gail Chester and Julienne Dickey, 119–132. London: Prism Press.

Patridge, Stephanie. 2011. "The Incorrigible Social Meaning of Video Game Imagery." *Ethics and Information Technology* 13: 303–312.

————. 2013. "Exclusivism and Evaluation: Art, Erotica and Pornography." In *Pornographic Art and the Aesthetics of Pornography*, edited by Hans Maes, 43–57. Basingstoke: Palgrave-MacMillan.

Paul, Bryant, and Daniel G. Linz. 2008. "The Effects of Exposure to Virtual Child Pornography on Viewer Cognitions and Attitudes toward Deviant Sexual Behavior." *Communication Research* 35 (1): 3–38.

Paul, P. 2005. *Pornified: How Pornography Is Damaging Our Lives, Our Relationships, and Our Families.* New York: Times Books/Henry Holt.

Posner, R. A. 1994. *Sex and Reason.* Cambridge, MA: Harvard University Press.

Rea, Michael. 2001. "What Is Pornography?" *Noûs* 35: 118–145.

Ross, Becki L. 2000. "'It's Merely Designed for Sexual Arousal': Interrogating the Indefensibility of Lesbian Smut." In *Feminism and Pornography*, edited by Drucilla Cornell, 264–317. New York: Oxford University Press.

Royalle, Candida. 2000. "Porn in the USA." In *Feminism and Pornography*, edited by Drucilla Cornell, 540–550. New York: Oxford University Press.

Rubin, Gayle. 1993. "Misguided, Dangerous, and Wrong: An Analysis of Antipornography Politics." In *Bad Girls and Dirty Pictures: The Challenge to Reclaim Feminism*, edited by Alison Assiter and Avedon Carol, 18–40. London: Pluto Press.

Russell, Diana. 1993a. "Introduction." In her (ed.) *Making Violence Sexy: Feminist Views on Pornography*, 1–20. Buckingham: Open University Press.

————, ed. 1993b. *Making Violence Sexy: Feminist Views on Pornography.* Buckingham: Open University Press.

————. 2000. "Pornography and Rape: A Causal Model." In *Feminism and Pornography*, edited by Drucilla Cornell, 48–93. New York: Oxford University Press.

Ryan, Dylan. 2013. "Fucking Feminism." In *The Feminist Porn Book: The Politics of Producing Pleasure*, edited by Tristan Taormino, Celine Parreñas Shimizu, Constance Penley, and Mireille Miller-Young, 121–129. New York: The Feminist Press at CUNY.

Saul, Jennifer. 2006a. "On Treating Things as People: Objectification, Pornography, and the History of the Vibrator." *Hypatia* 21 (2): 45–61.

———. 2006b. "Pornography, Speech Acts and Context." *Proceedings of the Aristotelian Society* 106: 229–248.

Scanlon, Thomas. 1972. "A Theory of Freedom of Expression." *Philosophy & Public Affairs* 1: 204–226.

———. 1978–9. "Freedom of Expression and Categories of Expression." *University of Pittsburgh Law Review* 40: 519–527.

Schauer, Frederick. 1979. "Speech and 'Speech'—Obscenity and 'Obscenity': An Exercise in the Interpretation of Constitutional Language." *Georgetown Law Journal* 67: 899–933.

Schwartzman, Lisa. 2002. "Hate Speech, Illocution, and Social Context: A Critique of Judith Butler." *Journal of Social Philosophy* 33: 421–41.

Schweikard, David P., and Hans Bernhard Schmid. 2013. "Collective Intentionality." *The Stanford Encyclopedia of Philosophy* (Summer 2013 edition), edited by Edward N. Zalta. https://plato.stanford.edu/archives/sum2013/entries/collective-intentionality/.

Scoccia, Danny. 1996. "Can Liberals Support a Ban on Violent Pornography?" *Ethics* 106 (4): 776–799.

Searle, J. 1995. *The Construction of Social Reality*. London: Penguin Books.

Segal, Lynne. 1990. "Pornography and Violence: What the 'Experts' Really Say." *Feminist Review* 36: 29–41.

Shrage, Laurie. 2004. "Feminist Perspectives on Sex Markets." *The Stanford Encyclopedia of Philosophy* (Fall 2016 edition), edited by Edward N. Zalta. https://plato.stanford.edu/archives/fall2016/entries/feminist-sex-markets.

———. 2005. "Exposing the Fallacies of Anti-Porn Feminism." *Feminist Theory* 6 (1): 45–65.

Simmons Bradley, Joy. 2014. "In the Arms of the Angel: Playfulness, Creativity, and Porn's Possibilities." In *The Philosophy of Pornography: Contemporary Perspectives*, edited by Lindsay Coleman and Jacob M. Held, 261–275. Lanham: Rowman and Littlefield.

Skipper, Robert. 1993. "Mill and Pornography." *Ethics* 103: 726–730.

Smith, D. L. 2011. *Less than Human: Why We Demean, Enslave, and Exterminate Others*. London: Macmillan.

Soble, Alan. 1985. "Pornography: Defamation and the Endorsement of Degradation." *Social Theory and Practice* 11 (1): 61–87.

———. 2002. *Pornography, Sex, and Feminism*. Amherst: Prometheus Books.

Stark, Cynthia A. 1997. "Is Pornography an Action? The Causal vs. the Conceptual View of Pornography's Harm." *Social Theory and Practice* 23: 277–306.

Stear, Nils-Hennes. 2009. "Sadomasochism as *Make-Believe*." *Hypatia* 24 (2): 21–38.

Steinem, Gloria. 1995. "Erotica and Pornography: A Clear and Present Difference." In *The Problem of Pornography*, edited by Susan Dwyer, 29–33. Belmont, CA: Wadsworth.

Stock, Kathleen. 2012. "Pornography and Imagining about Oneself." In *Art and Pornography*, edited by Hans Maes and Jerrold Levinson, 116–136. Oxford: Oxford University Press.

———. 2015. "Sexual Objectification." *Analysis* 75 (2): 191–195.

Stoltenberg, John. 1992. "Pornography, Homophobia and Male Supremacy." In *Pornography: Women, Violence and Civil Liberties*, edited by Catherine Itzin, 145–165. Oxford: Oxford University Press.

———. 1993. "Pornography and Freedom." In *Making Violence Sexy: Feminist Views on Pornography*, edited by Diana Russell, 65–77. Buckingham: Open University Press.

———. 1995. "Gays and the Pro-Pornography Movement: Having the Hots for Sex Discrimination." In *The Problem of Pornography*, edited by Susan Dwyer, 162–169. Belmont, CA: Wadsworth.

Strossen, Nadine. 1995. *Defending Pornography: Free Speech, Sex, and the Fight for Women's Rights*. New York: Anchor Books.

Sunstein, Cass R. 1986. "Pornography and the First Amendment." *Duke Law Journal* 1986: 589–627.

Sweet, Corinne. 1992. "Pornography and Addiction: A Political Issue." In *Pornography: Women, Violence and Civil Liberties*, edited by Catherine Itzin, 179–200. Oxford: Oxford University Press.

Taormino, Tristan. 2013. "Calling the Shots: Feminist Porn in Theory and Practice." In *The Feminist Porn Book: The Politics of Producing Pleasure*, edited by Tristan Taormino, Constance Penley, Celine Parrenas Shimizu, and Mireille Miller-Young, 255–264. New York: The Feminist Press at CUNY.

Taormino, Tristan, Celine Parreñas Shimizu, Constance Penley, and Mireille Miller-Young, eds. 2013. *The Feminist Porn Book: The Politics of Producing Pleasure*. New York: The Feminist Press at CUNY.

Tarrant, Shira. 2014. "Truth Claims about Porn: When Dogma and Data Collide." In *The Philosophy of Pornography: Contemporary Perspectives*, edited by Lindsay Coleman and Jacob M. Held, 35–54. Lanham: Rowman and Littlefield.

———. 2016. *The Pornography Industry: What Everyone Needs to Know*. New York: Oxford University Press.

Thomasson, Amie. 2003. "Realism and Human Kinds." *Philosophy and Phenomenological Research* 67: 580–609.

Tibbals, Chauntelle A. 2014. "Gonzo, Trans, and Teens—Current Trends in US Adult Content Production, Distribution, and Consumption." *Porn Studies* 1 (1–2): 127–135.

Tirrell, Lynne. 1999. "Pornographic Subordination: How Pornography Silences Women." In *On Feminist Ethics and Politics*, edited by Claudia Card, 226–243. Lawrence: University of Kansas Press.

Todd, Cain. 2012. "Imagination, Fantasy, and Sexual Desire." In *Art and Pornography*, edited by Hans Maes and Jerrold Levinson, 95–115. Oxford: Oxford University Press.

Tong, Rosemarie. 1982. "Feminism, Pornography and Censorship." *Social Theory and Practice* 8 (1): 1–17.

Trinks, Stefan. 2013. "Sheela-na-gig Again: The Birth of a New Style from the Spirit of Pornography." In *Pornographic Art and the Aesthetics of Pornography*, edited by Hans Maes, 162–182. Basingstoke: Palgrave Macmillan.

Vadas, Melinda. 2005. "The Manufacture-for-Use of Pornography and Women's Inequality." *Journal of Political Philosophy* 13: 174–193.

Valverde, Mariana. 1995. "Beyond Gender Dangers and Private Pleasures: Theory and Ethics in Sex Debates." In *The Problem of Pornography*, edited by Susan Dwyer, 177–191. Belmont, CA: Wadsworth.

Van Brabandt, Petra. 2017. "In/Egalitarian Pornography: A Simplistic View of Pornography." In *Beyond Speech: Pornography and Analytic Feminist Philosophy*, edited by Mari Mikkola, 221–241. New York: Oxford University Press.

Van Brabandt, Petra, and Jesse Prinz. 2012. "Why Do Porn Films Suck?" In *Art and Pornography*, edited by Hans Maes and Jerrold Levinson, 161–190. Oxford: Oxford University Press.

Vance, Carole S. 1992. "More Pleasure, More Danger: A Decade after the Barnard Sexuality Conference." In her (ed.) *Pleasure and Danger: Exploring Female Sexuality*, 1–28. London: Pandora.

Vernon, Richard. 1996. "John Stuart Mill and Pornography: Beyond the Harm Principle." *Ethics* 106: 621–632.

Waldron, J. 2012. *The Harm in Hate Speech*. Cambridge, MA: Harvard University Press.

Watson, L. 2010. "Pornography." *Philosophy Compass* 5: 535–550. doi:10.1111/j.1747-9991.2010.00292.x.

Waugh, Thomas. 1995. "Men's Pornography: Gay vs. Straight." In *The Problem of Pornography*, edited by Susan Dwyer, 142–161. Belmont, CA: Wadsworth.

Weaver, James. 1992. "The Social Science and Psychological Research Evidence: Perceptual and Behavioural Consequences of Exposure to Pornography." In *Pornography: Women, Violence and Civil Liberties*, edited by Catherine Itzin, 284–309. Oxford: Oxford University Press.

Wertheimer, Alan. 1996. "The Moral Magic of Consent." *Legal Theory* 2 (2): 121–146.

West, Caroline. 2003. "The Free Speech Argument against Pornography." *Canadian Journal of Philosophy* 33: 391–422.

———. 2013. "Pornography and Censorship." *The Stanford Encyclopedia of Philosophy* (Fall 2013 edition), edited by Edward N. Zalta. http://plato.stanford.edu/archives/fall2013/entries/pornography-censorship/.

Whisnant, Rebecca. 2016. "'But What about Feminist Porn?' Examining the Work of Tristan Taormino." *Sexualization, Media, and Society* 2 (2): 1–12. doi: 10.1177/2374623816631727.

Wieland, Nellie. 2007. "Linguistic Authority and Convention in a Speech Act Analysis of Pornography." *Australasian Journal of Philosophy* 85 (3): 435–456.

Williams, Bernard, ed. 1981. *Obscenity and Film Censorship: An Abridgement of the Williams Report*. New York: Cambridge University Press.

Williams, Kevin. M., Barry S. Cooper, Teresa M. Howell, John C. Yuille, and Delroy L. Paulhus. 2009. "Inferring Sexually Deviant Behavior from Corresponding Fantasies: The Role of Personality and Pornography Consumption." *Criminal Justice and Behavior* 36 (2): 198–222.

Willis, Ellen. 1995. "Feminism, Moralism, and Pornography." In *The Problem of Pornography*, edited by Susan Dwyer, 170–176. Belmont, CA: Wadsworth.

Wyre, Ray. 1992. "Pornography and Sexual Violence: Working with Sex Offenders." In *Pornography: Women, Violence and Civil Liberties*, edited by Catherine Itzin, 236–247. Oxford: Oxford University Press.

Zheng, R. 2017. "Race and Pornography." In *Beyond Speech: Pornography and Analytic Feminist Philosophy*, edited by Mari Mikkola, 177–189. Oxford: Oxford University Press.

Zillmann, Dolf, and James B. Weaver. 1989. "Pornography and Men's Sexual Callousness toward Women." In *Pornography: Research Advances and Policy Considerations*, edited by Dolf Zillmann and Jennings Bryant, 95–125. Hillsdale, NJ: Lawrence Erlbaum Associates, Inc.

INDEX